Children's
Solution Work

A Norton Professional Book

Children's
Solution Work

Insoo Kim Berg   Therese Steiner

W. W. Norton & Company
New York • London

Note to Readers: Standards of clinical practice and protocol change over time, and no technique or recommendation is guaranteed to be safe or effective in all circumstances. This volume is intended as a general information resource for professionals practicing in the field of psychotherapy and mental health; it is not a substitute for appropriate training, peer review, and/or clinical supervision. Neither the publisher nor the author(s) can guarantee the complete accuracy, efficacy, or appropriateness of any particular recommendation in every respect.

Composition and book design by Bytheway Publishing Services.
Manufacturing by LSC Harrisonburg.

Library of Congress Cataloging-in-Publication Data

Berg, Insoo Kim.
    Children's solution work/Insoo Kim Berg and Therese Steiner.
        p.   cm.
    "A Norton professional book."
    ISBN 0-393-70387-8
        1. Child Psychotherapy.   2. Solution-focused brief therapy.
    I. Steiner, Therese.   II. Title.
    RJ504.3 .B47 2002
    618.92'8914—dc21   2002029570

W. W. Norton & Company, Inc., 500 Fifth Avenue, New York, N.Y. 10110
www.wwnorton.com

W. W. Norton & Company Ltd., 15 Carlisle Street, London W1D 3BS

10 11 12 13 14 15

Dedication

To my husband and best friend, Andreas, whose patience, wonderful sense of humor, and generous support made this book possible. To my children, Ursula and Christian, who took me by their hands and introduced me to the world of children. Last but not least, to all my young clients, who over the years taught me to be creative through their own creativity.

Therese Steiner

To Andreas, a good friend and a technical wizard.

To Steve, who supported me, as usual, during the many months I was preoccupied with this book.

Insoo Kim Berg

Contents

Preface

WE WROTE THIS BOOK FOR THOSE READERS WHO ARE ALREADY FAMILIAR with Solution-Focused Brief Therapy (SFBT) as well as for those of you who lack the confidence to implement it in your daily work with children. Many parents, child care workers, therapists, counselors in a variety of settings, teachers, and recreation and day care workers who come in contact with children would also benefit from this book. Any consultants, program designers, managers, and supervisors involved with children and their parents would benefit from this book because of its clear and practical applications of very respectful ways to interact with children and their parents.

Those readers who are not familiar with SFBT would also find this approach useful, not only for the many tools that one can adapt to many settings and environments, but because of its application of the philosophy of accepting and embracing children's views and unique ways to work with their own creative ideas for solutions.

For those readers without extensive experience working with children, especially young children, we hope to encourage you to do so, and we will show you how to talk to them, what to say, how to engage a reluctant child, and how to tap into children's unique resources and generate solutions. We will give you some step-by-step suggestions to help you become comfortable working with them. Readers are required to bring a sense of curiosity and courage to learn from a child and willingness to discover their own creativity.

We want to emphasize that "working with children" is a somewhat artificial field whose boundary we drew. It is a different path to arrive at the same place—the place where both parents and children are satisfied with their lives and are getting along the best way they know how, where they both grow closer, care about and help one another in times of need, and where they also know that they have a safe relationship to return to every day. We want to describe some ways of assisting parents and children to make good choices for themselves.

We somewhat artificially define "young child" as those from day care age to around age 7; "child" as those between ages 7 and 12; "teenagers" as those between 13 or 14 to 18. We find that some of the techniques that work with a child may be used successfully with adults as well. We warn you, however, that the question of what technique will fit with what child or parent is your clinical decision to make, based on your clinical intuition. By and large, this intuition and wisdom come from years of experience working with hundreds and hundreds of children.

This book is divided into nine chapters. In the first three chapters you will learn why we believe that SFBT is not only appropriate but a good fit in working with children and their parents. We present some underlying assumptions about children and parents and how these assumptions are utilized to engage with children and parents. We describe general step-by-step methods by walking you through many cases. The differences and similarities in using similar techniques with adults are described throughout the book. Chapter 3 describes the basic tools of SFBT that are essential to working with most clinical populations. We believe that those readers who are familiar with the SFBT approach and are quite adept at its application to a variety of situations can easily skip this chapter. However, for those who are familiar with the concept but have not had extensive experience working with this model, it might be beneficial to review the model once more.

Chapters 4 and 5 explain how to prepare yourself to meet the child and how to think about the initial assessment of the child and the family, with particular emphasis on goal negotiation. Because SFBT is a goal-directed approach, we describe many different ways to achieve goal negotiation. Chapter 6 describes all the useful tools available for working with children, such as how to utilize children's natural tendency to play, imagine, and be creative, as well as to serve their needs to please and get along with adults.

Chapter 7 includes our responses to numerous questions we hear from clinicians on how to adapt SFBT to working with children and parents with uncommon needs and who are considered "difficult" to work with. After consulting our colleagues and agonizing over whether to include a chapter on working with adolescents, we decided to include a short chapter (8) to address the special trials and tribulations of the adolescent phase which can be stormy and delightful at the same time, for parents as well as for professionals.

Chapter 9 describes what to do when you, the clinician, feel like a failure in spite of your best efforts and when you feel that you have "hit a brick wall"—an impasse in treatment that is worrisome and discouraging to many. We also present a course of treatment for a single case, from beginning to end.

Throughout the book we describe numerous case examples in various settings, special as well as common situations, so that you, too, will discover the extraordinary ability children and their parents and caretakers possess to overcome their difficulties with a little help from professionals.

Most of all, we hope you come to share our enthusiasm for playing with small and older children and their parents.

Introduction

PERHAPS MORE THAN MANY THERAPEUTIC MODELS, SOLUTION-FOCUSED Brief Therapy (SFBT) emphasizes the precise use of language as an important tool. Language is used throughout: from negotiating the treatment goal in the beginning of the contact, to measuring progress toward a more desirable state of life, to finding out what successful steps clients have taken to achieve their own goals.

When I (TS) first learned about the model, I immediately became fascinated by its deep respect for clients' wishes for a more desirable state of life, and its assumptions about the clients' ability to shape their lives. Being a medical doctor, I was trained to think in categories and classifications of human problems, tragedies, and sorrows. Most of all, the medical training I received focused on all the things that didn't function well enough, or not at all, for some people. So, my first and immediate reaction to this introduction to SFBT was relief: Rather than feeling burdened by the problems and deficits that my patients brought to me all day long, I began to focus on resources and the parts in human relationships that worked well. I was convinced that I finally found the form of therapy I had been seeking for a long time. It fit with my reason for entering psychiatry and my view of how I wanted to make a difference with my patients.

When I was first trained in Milwaukee, it was quite clear to me that I was going to apply SFBT only with adults. It seemed almost impossible to adapt the model to working with children who did not have the necessary language skills or the ability to use abstract concepts to translate complex ideas into words so that their needs and desires could be understood.

Two things in my personal life prompted me to think about a possible way to adapt this approach to working with children. The first is my recognition that I had been a difficult child. I often lost my temper, and the demands from adults to keep order, to be organized, and to behave and follow directions, were all extremely difficult for me.

I attended first grade with thirty-nine girls and boys. The teacher, Mrs. Mueller, had many years of experience teaching children. She demanded discipline and obedience from her students. She had definite ideas on how to behave. I, along with other children in the class, learned to read, write, and count. My predominant memory of first grade was how bored I was. I still remember the different ways I tried to make time pass more quickly: I looked out the window; I started to chat with the kid next to me; and I sometimes got up and walked around. The solutions I came up with to deal with my boredom were all forbidden and didn't help me one bit because I got into so much trouble with Mrs. Mueller.

One summer I discovered something that did not get me into trouble and was actually fun for me: I started to draw little pictures on my clothing. Sometimes these pictures appeared on my skirt, sometimes on my pants, socks, and even on my shoes. It helped! I came up with a solution only a child can think of! It made it easier for me to go to school and, importantly, the difficult discussions with my mother every morning were gone! This memory from my childhood stayed with me for many more years and it kept me thinking: Is this not proof that children can come up with very personal and "childlike" solutions that make a difference for them?

The second important memory I have is also related to school. I never liked to write compositions. One day we had a new teacher in German language class, Mrs. Schmid, and the first topic she asked us to write about was a sentence out of a poem by Hermann Hesse: "in every new start lives a miracle that protects you and helps you to manage life" (und jedem Anfang liegt ein Zauber inne, der uns beschuetzt und der uns hilft zu leben). I liked that text, and from then on, I enjoyed writing compositions.

What had happened? Surely this discovery did not help me to develop overnight any ability to write my thoughts in a clear and orderly manner. Instead, it gave me the idea of a new way to think about how to use this miracle that lived in every new beginning. I gradually discovered that I was able to write good compositions and that my ability had been hidden under many, many layers of bad grades. The new teacher, Mrs. Schmid, and the magical sentence changed my point of view, and I was able to come up with a new way of seeing myself.

I am sure that I was not the only child to have such experiences, and for this reason, I believe it would almost be a pity not to work in a solution-focused way with children. Why not try to help them be aware of moments when things are working, to find this kind of dialogue about their small successes, strengths, and resources within each child to solve even big problems!

After all, the solution-focused approach fits very well with the way children think and view the world. I have never met a child who liked to talk about problems. When you observe small children, how they solve little everyday problems goes along the predictable pattern of trial and error. They always look ahead, and they almost never sit down and analyze the difficulties in order to come up with a solution. The longer I thought about these characteristics, the more it became clear to me that SFBT paralleled a child's way of being in the world.

The next step was to find out what had to be adapted in order to apply SFBT to working with even young children. With the SFBT model in the back of my head, I began to realize what was the most important point: Children are very direct in the way they solve many problems. I had only to observe them and give them the opportunity to teach me.

I remember Thomas, an eight-year-old boy, who was sitting in his chair trying to answer some questions. But it was quite obvious to me that he would have much preferred to move around. He picked up a ball and started to throw it toward the ceiling. Then I made a gesture inviting him to throw the ball to me. And there we went. Whenever he threw the ball to me, he asked me a question and I had to answer it. Then it was my turn to ask a question, and before he threw the ball back, he had to answer my question. Pretty soon we were having a wonderful conversation. (He caught the ball more often than I did.)

For a long period of time I observed children and learned how they showed me what their needs were. This reminded me of my own two children's behavior when they were babies, unable to "tell" me what they needed or wanted. I don't think babies can be frustrated about their inability because they do not think in such an abstract manner. It meant I had to be open and sensitive to little signals through sounds and gestures. I had to use a sort of "floating" attention to figure out what they needed and wanted.

It was easy to be open in this manner with very young children. It was much more difficult when children reached kindergarten age or older. I realized I had quite fixed ideas on how they should behave or how they should use language they were learning. I had never realized how strongly I demanded that children behave and talk in a certain manner. I believe all adults do this with good intentions, wanting what is best for the children. But in order to meet the children in the solution-focused approach, it was obvious that I first had to change this way of viewing children. I realized that my expectations of what to hear and see, and my intentions as to what to do and how to do it, were in fact getting in the way. I had to trust each of the children as they presented themselves, being aware that I was being shown the most valuable information. Only then would my interaction with them be useful to them.

I know that many of you are shaking your heads and thinking, "But there have to be some rules and limits for the children, otherwise how can they learn?" I absolutely agree that there must be rules and limits. We aren't helpful to children if we offer them complete freedom. We don't do them any favors by raising them without rules and expectations. What I mean is that we adults must tune in to each child so that we may find an "entrance ticket" to the child's world that will put us in touch with his or her vast resources.

I refer to the very special way to connect with the child quickly and in a manner that is respectful of each child's unique needs. This is similar to working with adult clients who are mandated to come to therapy by the court or some official. We take their views seriously and accept their belief that coming to therapy is useless, unnecessary, or even harmful to them in some manner (Berg & Kelly, 2000). We first meet them "where they are at" without criticism and without trying to educate or convince them to see things differently. We will discuss in detail how to do the same with children who essentially come to us involuntarily, sent by the adults who care about them.

When working with young children, this initial process of connecting with them in a very personal way is accomplished not by talking to them but by playing, touching, and moving around. By doing so, we, as therapists, will meet the strength of each child, enabling us to find out how to phrase solution-focused questions in order to be understood. Some children live in a fantasy world where stories and their heroes are important. Others have to transform everything into actions because they like to move and experience a lot through the sensations they feel in their bodies. Still other children like to draw and have to give everything a color. When we are very open to learning their ways, children will teach us how and where to meet them.

Some people think you have to be very creative in order to work with children. I don't agree: The creativity is within the child. Just as solution-focused therapists meet and work with what adult clients bring with them, we need to do the same with children. The children are the experts and will teach us what they need when we listen and observe carefully, and take what they say and do very seriously. We will describe this in much more detail later in this book.

—Therese Steiner

Although I was the one primarily responsible for looking after my three younger siblings, and my only daughter turned out to be a delightful source of joy, I don't believe my parenting ability to be very considerable—I was just lucky to have had a fairly healthy and well-functioning child and siblings. I have never considered myself to be very good with children, nor did they particularly fascinate me. I primarily dedicated my career to working with adults, with and without children in the sessions, who have gotten themselves into lots of difficulties, either with their lives or with their children. Even though I have had my share of successes with children and teenagers, my main interest was in working with the entire family as a problem-solving resource and figuring out how to make rapid changes with adults and their children because doing so seems to get things done faster. In addition, I was always interested in working with larger units of people, such as groups, extended families, businesses, various sizes of organizations, and programs.

A little girl named Brenda changed my view. Brenda was a bubbly, bright-eyed, cute-as-a-button, eight-year-old girl whose social worker brought her to see me because she did not have an adult in her life who was able to care for her enough to bring her to the first meeting in my office. Brenda lived with her very tired and worn-out grandmother, who had numerous physical problems of her own, and demanded that the social worker place Brenda in a foster home. The social worker explained that the grandmother was adamant; she claimed that since Brenda began wetting the bed some time ago, this problem caused the grandmother an extra burden that she could no longer manage.

Brenda's mother disappeared some years ago and was never heard from again. Brenda came to live with her grandmother and an uncle and his two children. Of course, Brenda did not "want to go to no foster home" and insisted that she wanted to stay with her grandmother and her cousins because she liked to play with her cousins the most. I tried to contact an adult family member—grandmother, uncle, an aunt—who might be interested in working with me to help solve her bed-wetting problem so that Brenda could continue to live with her grandmother and her cousins. The grandmother declined, even when offered free transportation to and from the office. So did the uncle. Nobody was interested except the social worker, who was willing to bring Brenda to the session each time, wait for her, and then take her home. It was the first glimpse I had that sometimes I needed to work with children alone because there are many children in Brenda's situation who do not have adults to take care of them. This heartbreaking situation made me realize that my good intentions and good efforts to build family strengths and cohesiveness were not always fruitful. Sometimes, not forcing my views on the family was also the most respectful stance I could take.

Eventually Brenda got her problems solved all on her own, and she was only eight years old! She got what she wanted: to stay with her grandmother and cousins. This case helped me realize that some children have to take care of their problems on their own and sometimes raise themselves. It was my first clue that I must learn how to work with young children like Brenda. Unfortunately, since then I have met many more children whose situation was worse than Brenda's.

—Insoo Kim Berg

ABOUT THIS BOOK

This book is a coming together of two professionals careers: Therese Steiner is a successful child psychiatrist practicing in Switzerland, while Insoo Kim Berg is a codeveloper of the Solution-Focused Brief Therapy (referred to as SFBT from now on) whose passion is to write about different applications of SFBT to various settings and clinical populations. Therese studied medicine in Switzerland and Austria and earned a doctorate in child psychiatry at the University of Berne. She studied systemic family therapy and hypnosis before coming across the SFBT approach. She speaks several languages, which gives her the opportunity to treat children and their families from different cultural backgrounds, as well as in different countries. Born and raised in Korea, Insoo immigrated to United States as a student and has built her career as a therapist, teacher, consultant, and writer.

What binds the two of us (from very different cultural backgrounds, languages, upbringing, and career paths) is our common belief in learning and teaching successful applications of SFBT approaches in a variety of settings and what we have learned from our work with clients from a very collaborative stance.

Our respect for the clients' ability and innate desire to be helpful in discovering their strengths is what binds us as well. We have seen that dramatic changes can occur within a short time. We also bring unbounded curiosity and interest to learn from our clients, and we are connected in our desire to make small, positive differences in people's lives. We share an enthusiasm and excitement for our work and delight in the smallest successes that our clients accomplish.

Chapter 1

What is Solution-Focused Brief Therapy?

SOLUTION-FOCUSED BRIEF THERAPY IS CHARACTERIZED BY A PARTICULAR career of development as well as by a number of keypoints of therapeutic practice. Beginning as a quiet revolt against the prevailing view of what is helpful to people with problems of living, Solution-Focused Brief Therapy (SFBT) took many twists and turns, successes and some mistakes to arrive where it is today. The current state of the model took more than 25 years of trial and error to evolve, long before the word "managed care" was coined. Even though it began in an outpatient clinical setting, the SFBT model was quickly adapted to work in a variety of settings and populations. Currently the approach is applied to work in schools, alternative schools, prisons, courts, hospitals, pain clinics, social service programs, shelters, day care centers, residential treatment homes, and in businesses and many other settings. Members of the clinical population that benefit from adaptation and modification of this approach include: substance abusers, domestic violence offenders, people experiencing marital and family problems, chronic mentally ill patients, people in crisis, trauma survivors, troubled children, people with supervision and management problems, and people who are having difficulty navigating their lives as well as getting along with those who are important to them.

THE BASICS OF SFBT

Team Approach

As is the case with most innovations, SFBT evolved because of many contributions of team members, especially in the beginning phase of its development. Over the years, the team's membership changed, but what distinguished the team was the diversity of professional backgrounds of its members, ranging from medicine, education, social action (in the 1970s), to engineering, biology, linguistics, psychiatry, psychology, social work, and sociology. Even though the model development began in Milwaukee, led by Steve de Shazer and Insoo Kim Berg, its continuing evolution is taking place in many settings around the globe. The original team members dispersed over the years for different reasons; however, de Shazer and Berg continued to write about their work and both remained in Milwaukee. They cultivated a culture of openness to learn new ways to discover clients' ability to solve their own problems and professionals' openness to learn from clients with infinite respect for their integrity and professional curiosity, tempered with "a not-knowing" posture (Anderson & Goolishan, 1992). This culture of open inquiry continues in mental health clinics, academia, and even in some unlikely places such as prisons and courts, fostered by innovative people who want to provide efficient and effective services and relieve suffering as quickly as possible.

Exceptions to the Problem

We cannot ignore the timing and place of the SFBT model's inception. The team drew on many resources: the 1960s and 1970s culture of questioning traditional approaches to everything done from the classical Western, scientific views; the work of the Palo Alto group (Watzlawick, Weakland, & Fisch, 1974) who challenged the traditional view of mental illness; and the innovative work of Milton Erickson (1954), Erickson and Rossi (1979), and Haley (1973). The team was energized to improve the state of mental health services and how they were delivered.

In late 1970s and in early 1980s, a startling discovery was made that almost every problem contains an element of solutions. Called exceptions to problems, it directed the team's attention to this ignored element of solutions that every problem contained. An exception, as defined by SFBT clinicians, includes the times when even the most depressed person experiences a little bit of relief from oppressive depression. By studying these small pieces of relief in detail—such as when, where, and how it occurred, and who was involved, and other details—the motivated client was able to extend this small segment of solutions to bigger and wider areas. When the team looked carefully at this exception, they discovered that almost all problems contain exceptions if only we pay close enough attention.

Arising from the belief that problems and solutions are socially constructed and negotiated, SFBT (Berg, 1994; Berg & DeJong, 1996; Berg & Dolan, 2001; Berg & Kelly, 2000; Berg & Miller, 1992; Berg & Reuss, 1997; Davis & Osborn, 2000; DeJong & Berg, 2001a; DeJong & Berg, 2001b; de Shazer, 1985, 1988, 1991, 1994; Lee, Sebold & Uken, 2002; Miller & de Shazer, 2000) emphasizes that the problem is not a fixed entity but a changeable, negotiable item that is dependent on social contexts. Therefore, it is easy to see that some children exhibit problematic behaviors only in school but not at home, while others experience difficulties only with friends but not with adults, and still others have problems everywhere they go. However, because even the most difficult problems have exceptions (times when the problem could have happened but did not), we have to believe that there is no causal relationship between problems and solutions. If a problem is contextually decided, then so can the solutions be contextually determined. With adults, changing the meaning of problematic behaviors can be negotiated and determined through language. With children, we can do the same but with pictures, games, stories, and whatever the child is comfortable with—hence the title of "Solution-Focused," meaning it is the focusing on the solution that leads to potential dissolution of problems.

Along the way, the team discovered and improvised other important tools to make the therapeutic conversation useful and productive to clients. More detailed explanations of the tools used and the philosophy behind their use will be described in Chapter 3

Does it Work?

The original team members recognized the need for validation that what they were doing was working, and as soon as the clinic opened its doors officially in 1978, the team began collecting client feedback, mostly in client follow-up conducted in telephone surveys by interns and students. An independent, small, outpatient clinic operating on a shoestring budget, the Center, did not have the resources to launch a "scientific" study that compared the pre- and posttreatment data. In addition, as an inductive approach to the model development conducted in a clinical setting, the team believed that the most important evaluation must come from the consumers of their services. The initial studies were comparable to most other such studies of various approaches to evaluation of effectiveness, that is, approximately between 80–85% of the clients reported that they met their goal for coming to therapy. What was amazing, however, was that those reported were the result of less than 6–8 sessions. More recent studies indicate this number has been reduced even further, to an average of 4 sessions.

Universities became attracted to SFBT's postmodern view of human problems, combined with the influence of social constructionist views of problems and solutions to them, and so they began to teach SFBT in increasing numbers. Academic rigors began to be applied to studying the outcome data using pre- and posttreatment data comparisons outside of Milwaukee, not by the original developers but by those students who had no personal connections to the original team members. This trend is continuing and increasing numbers of published and unpublished research data indicate that this approach warrants attention and further study (Gingerich & Eisengart, 2000). These studies covered a wide variety of populations, including domestic violence offenders who are mandated and coerced into treatment, rehabilitation of workers to return to their jobs, people serving time in prison, as well as children in schools. There is no currently known study outcome conducted on children's problems, but a number of programs are planning or conducting comparison studies that involve children's problems.

The question "Does it [SFBT] work?" is difficult to answer because we need to know what is meant by "work." The same is true of the question, "Is it successful?" Does this mean a child with many problems will never have problems again? Does it mean a change in personality of the child or the parent? Obviously we are not attempting to change or reconstruct anyone's personality because it is neither possible by any means, nor is it desirable. Furthermore, we don't believe it is respectful.

So, we define "success" as having achieved the client's stated goal. This sounds rather simple but it is actually complex, because children's caregivers have multitudes of ideas regarding what would be in each child's best interest. Nevertheless, we must begin somewhere and end somewhere. Recognizing this limit, in Chapter 4 we will continue our discussion of conflicting and multiple goals.

SFBT VERSUS TRADITIONAL PLAY THERAPY

There are some fundamental differences in the beliefs, procedures, and emphasis between traditional play therapy and SFBT, which will become clear as you read Chapters 2, 3, and 4. Traditional play therapy is based on the assumption that it is helpful to act out feelings of anger, frustration, aggression, insecurity, and uncertainty in a safe environment with a therapist. A long-term relationship with an accepting therapist is thought to be a healing or corrective experience for a child. At times children are encouraged to regress emotionally so that they can start rebuilding different behavioral patterns and develop new skills. By and large, play is used as a diagnostic tool to determine the child's deficits and the remedial steps to be taken in a long-term, profoundly intimate relationship between the child and the therapist. The parent's role is marginal. Parents are not involved in therapeutic activities and play only a supportive role in this mysterious process that takes place between their child and another adult behind closed doors.

Even though it makes perfect sense to think that we need to know what caused a child's problem in order to solve it, we are frequently surprised at how little connection there seems to be between what the problem is and what the solution to it might be. The emphasis on uncovering the "root causes" of a child's problem can take many sessions but can also have the unintended result of placing "blame" for what or who caused the problem in the first place. It is very common for parents to feel blamed for "messing up" the child's life—if not directly stated, then certainly by inferences and suggestions. Many parents are reluctant or even refuse to show up at schools, day care, or other settings where professionals are involved in their child's life. We also met many professionals who indeed place the blame squarely on the parent; they claim that the parent is "sabotaging" the child's treatment by refusing to bring the child to the therapist or by minimizing the importance of therapist to the child.

The SFBT approach to working with children is very similar to that with adults: the therapeutic work is very much focused on the client's real life outside of the therapy room, how the individual functions with friends, teachers, family members, and so on, in normal daily activities. We believe the real change occurs by changing the way a child interacts with others, for example, when playing with friends, learning to get along with other children and adults, and fighting and loving. We also believe that children have all the resources they need to learn to do these things. By paying attention to the skills and abilities they already have, the therapist can uncover and build on them, rather than try to make up for the child's deficits. The therapist's role is to make the child's strengths, competencies, and abilities more evident to the child and to involved adults.

Working with children in this way takes less time than traditional approaches, which can take years of weekly sessions. The quality of our relationship with the children is different as well. We do not assume that engaging them is difficult to do, and we do not try to replace the most important people in their life, that is, their parents or caretakers. We view our relationship with the children as short-term and transitional, fully acknowledging that their relationship with their parents was there long before we came into their lives and will remain long after we are out of their lives.

PROBLEM-SOLVING ASSUMPTIONS AND PROCEDURES

The most commonly used and accepted way of solving problems—whether the problem is chronic tardiness at school or fixing a broken down car—can be thought of as a scientific or "cause and effect" approach. DeJong and Berg (2001b) call it a "problem-solving" approach. As DeJong and Berg wrote, the traditional problem-solving practice begins with assessing the problem to determine its cause. An assumption exists of a direct relationship between a problem and its cause; thus, problem-solving involves finding and fixing the cause. Many problems are solved this way, and this method works reasonably well when the problems are simple, mechanical, and routine. Logic requires us to find out what went wrong, what caused the problem. And, by determining the root cause of why the car does not start on a bitterly cold morning, we are able to fix the problem and therefore get the child to school on time. Figuring out why a student is habitually tardy for school is a little more complicated than learning the root cause of a stalled car or a toaster that burns the toast every single time. When such mechanical problems are beyond the limits of our abilities or schedules, we find an expert, the best mechanic in the neighborhood. This option is perfectly acceptable and considered normal within our society. However, when no direct causal relationship can be pinpointed, a situation is often considered mysterious, and consequently no one is sure what to do about it.

The major difficulty in applying the problem-solving approach to life's everyday problems is that a relatively simple problem such as being tardy for school in the morning involves human factors that differ from child to child, household to household, parent to parent, and school to school. There can be numerous reasons why a child is chronically tardy, and they may depend on who is involved in making sure that the child gets to school on time—the child, the parent, teachers, school principal, guidance counselor, or even a best friend. Therefore, the method of fixing the problem is also very different. For example, explanations for Bob being late for school could range from a simple one of a battery running out in his parents' digital clock, to a very complex one such as how Bob's parents do not value his getting a good education, or that Bob is lazy, or that he has problems with his peers, or that he fears failure in whatever he undertakes, just as his mother has done. Therefore, a simple solution offered by the teacher to "get an alarm clock" not only may not work but also may be insulting to Bob and his parents. In addition, Bob may be tardy only to school but not to other events such as the movies, church, or soccer practices.

More complicated problems, such as why Bob is underachieving in spite of his very high IQ scores, may require more involved solutions. The usual first step in treatment may require a lengthy investigation of the problems by learning the detailed history of the onset of symptoms, any possible family history with similar problems, and a detailed description of the problematic symptoms. The second step is to speculate on the root causes of the problem, thus making sense of where the problem may have originated, and what might be the immediate and long-term causal factors. Many professional training activities place a great deal of emphasis on these two steps. Only after these two steps are accomplished can the third step of finding a proper solution to the problem can be taken. Then, in the fourth step, the professionals prescribe what the solutions to the client's problems might be. Clearly this procedure should be familiar to most of you, since most training and education programs are based on this medical or scientific model. It is not difficult to imagine that the problem of "noncompliance" or "resistance" would come to play a significant role in the problem-solving model because possible solutions are generated by the professionals, and not the client.

THINKING OUT OF THE BOX

Also described as the solution-building approach, SFBT is quite different from this traditional view. Some even describe SFBT as "leading from one-step behind" (Cantwell & Holmes, 1994), and view it as nonmedical or even nonscientific in the traditional sense. SFBT begins with an assessment of possible solutions, that is, the outcome that the client expects and desires. During this assessment phase, the therapist can learn a great deal about the client's talents and skills and how the individual came to develop them. From this the therapist learns how to use those abilities to arrive at solutions. Then the therapist begins learning how to assist the client in repeating past and present successes until the desired level of satisfaction is reached. Since the focus is on enhancing and increasing the level of existing resources either in the client or in the environment, and the goal is to achieve what the client wishes, it is fairly easy to see why the treatment is short-term and that the working relationship remains collaborative. Clients become more hopeful about themselves, and thus, their motivation for making the desired changes is high since the solution ideas are theirs and they know what is needed to achieve their goal.

In this book we show that children and SFBT are a good match because both operate in a similar manner. SFBT was developed inductively, that is, finding out what works in clinical practice and then selecting those elements that work and discarding those that do not. The result is a very pragmatic and common-sense approach that can be easily learned and procedures that require observation and listening. We need to emphasize that even though the basic premise is easy and simple, the actual practice requires considerable discipline and an ability to keep it simple.

CULTURAL COMPETENCE

We are working with clients from increasingly diverse cultural, ethnic, and national backgrounds, and this will become even more so in coming years. These diversities not only can stand between people from different racial, national, and cultural backgrounds, but often within the same families. Young children, by and large, follow their parents' lead in learning their cultural and spiritual heritage, and readily accept what parents teach them about various foods, habits, customs, rituals, values, and so on. The conflict around differences in preferences for doing things in certain ways manifests itself strongly when the children become teenagers. Like all adolescents in all families, regardless of background, they have their own ideas and preferences and are able to assert their wishes to their parents.

Parents and adolescents from ethnic families are faced with a wider gap than those of mainstream families. In a rather short span of time and life experiences, teenagers from ethnic families, especially those who were born and educated in the mainstream cultures, want to assimilate and adapt to the mainstream adolescent culture. This is certainly understandable, given the adolescents' pressure to conform and be like each other while being different from their parents. Yet, their adolescent task to separate and differentiate from their parents is the same as the children whose parents are native born and educated.

When the topic of cultural diversity is introduced among professionals, whether in university classes, seminars, conferences, or in supervision, it usually means emphasizing what differentiates and separates one ethnic culture from that of the mainstream. Therefore, many discourses unwittingly emphasize how Hispanic families are different, how African-American families are unique, how Asian families are different from Hispanic, and so on. Such studies of each cultural group and their unique attributes were initiated with good intentions, hoping to educate mainstream people and future professionals about the unique aspects of each ethnic group. We worry that such emphasis on differences may inadvertently result in a negative outcome and may even become a disservice to the families themselves, and to the practitioners who must serve these families. We think such an approach is not only divisive but also tends to focus on a narrow view of ethnicity, thereby unintentionally stereotyping and categorizing families of different ethnic backgrounds.

We are often asked to describe how the solution-building approach can be adapted and applied in a wide variety of cultures, settings, and problem configurations in the face of such diversities in belief, customs, values, lifestyles, religion, and so on. As we show throughout this book, rather than viewing ourselves as experts on different cultures, we view and respect clients as experts on their own ways of doing things and conducting their lives, according to their own values, preferences, and traditions. In addition, rather than focus on differences between the therapist and client, we focus on the similarities. We think that focusing on differences can be divisive, while focusing on what we have in common contributes to a sense of unity and brings people together. Therefore, rather than believing that only Spanish-speaking therapists can and must serve Spanish-speaking clients, only Asians can service Asians, and so on, our experience tells us otherwise.

Except for the convenience of speaking the same language, we find that some ethnic families are reluctant to meet with same ethnic background therapists, fearing that their problem can become known to their entire community, which is often very closely knit. Of course, if we lived in an ideal world, ethnic families would be more open to seeking therapeutic help from a long list of choices that would be available. Unfortunately the reality is that such options and choices are much more limited, and clients cannot wait until such professionals from the same ethnic groups are trained in sufficient numbers, because they need help now.

Fundamentally, we believe that regardless of cultural and ethnic differences or similarities between the therapists and clients, all people want to be treated with respect, want to be valued and accepted, loved, and cherished, and made to feel they are making important contributions to society and that their wishes and desires are heard and respected. Our assumptions about parents and children that will be described in Chapter 2 hold true in most cultures.

Not-Knowing Postures

SFBT generally embraces the posture of viewing clients as experts of their own situations and solutions to their difficulties, and a willingness to learn from clients is even more crucial when working with ethnic families. Such willingness is expressed by asking what the client's view of solutions might be as well as ways to implement the procedures. For example, a Hispanic mother, who had recently lost her husband, brought her 14-year-old son Enrico, who was becoming involved with a neighborhood gang. His mother was rightly concerned because not only did Enrico refuse to go to school, but he also would stay away from home for hours without letting his mother know where he was. When "interrogated," as Enrico described it, he absolutely refused to answer any questions his mother asked. Even though generally pleasant, he also decided not to answer any of my questions, although I tried not to "interrogate" him.

I felt unsure of how I might help Enrico, so I asked the mother how she would have handled the situation had she still lived in Puerto Rico. Without hesitation, the mother replied that she would send Enrico to live with his uncle, his father's older brother, because that's what they would do had she lived with the extended family nearby. When I asked how such a solution would be helpful to Enrico, she mentioned that his uncle would certainly be glad to take him into his family, and that he would know what to do to help Enrico go straight. In fact, his uncle was already familiar with her problems with Enrico and had suggested the solution himself, but she thought she could handle him on her own. However this had become more difficult since her husband's death. She added that a 14-year-old boy was almost a man, and he needed a man's influence that she could not provide. The mother called later to cancel our second appointment, saying that Enrico had already left for Puerto Rico and she was relieved.

This "not-knowing" posture permeates everything we do when working with children and parents from different cultures and customs, and our willingness to learn from them is the cornerstone of our clinical work.

Ways to Work with Parent and Teenagers in Ethnic Families

It has been our experience that when parents' hopes and dreams for their children's successful future are located in the new environment (that is, in the country they now call home), it is easier to negotiate goals to narrow the gap between generations. This gap in aspirations and values between generations seems to widen even more for those parents who see themselves returning to their country of origin than those parents who want to see their children become successful in the new environment. For parents of the latter group, the parents and adolescents share the same dreams and future aspirations. For the parents who aspire to return to their "homeland," we can assist them and their children to negotiate interim solutions until they can return "home."

It makes sense that it would be difficult for ethnic parents who hardly speak the mainstream language to adopt the culture of the mainstream, while the adolescents who have been raised in the mainstream culture have practically no memory or experience of "life back home." For these children it is difficult to comprehend or entertain the same dreams as their parents because life in the new world is all they know.

Brief Contacts

Most ethnic families are interested in concrete services that will benefit them immediately, not in weeks or months. Often described as "not psychologically minded" by Western standards, most ethnic clients can describe their goals and assessments of the benefits in immediate, measurable terms. For example, such parents may firmly believe that "our son will listen, come home every day without stopping anywhere on the way, and achieve only As and Bs." Thus, they are perfect candidates for brief therapy. When they do not see results quickly, they are not likely to be curious about what might be contributing to this lack of progress. Rather, they will quickly conclude that the professionals are not useful to them and they stop coming. In addition, many immigrant parents work long hours, well into the late evening, and the supervision of children is impossible while they are focused on earning enough to live. Therefore, children are often left to their own devices, thus making it easier for them to get caught up in troublesome behaviors. Some practical solutions to these unavoidable situations can make a great deal of difference for the child.

Therefore, when meeting with ethnic or immigrant parents, just as you would with any other parents, finding out their indicators for successful treatment outcome is important. Working with ethnic clients and families often means working with a much more traditional and hierarchical family relationship; therefore, paying special deference to the parents is important and it is much more beneficial to consider parents as consultants to their adolescent rather than clients who are seeking help for themselves.

It is fairly easy to become caught in the middle or, at times, take the side of the adolescent. This is because they are fairly successful at articulating and communicating with professionals, usually with aspirations and dreams similar to most mainstream teenagers. Frequently parents need the help of a translator just to conduct an interview. We find this fact has unanticipated beneficial side effects: The pace of the sessions must be slowed down somewhat while both the parents and the therapist wait for the translation of the comments. The positive result it that since the session is slowed somewhat, it is easier for the therapist to be very focused on getting key tasks accomplished such as negotiating for good goals.

Chapter 2

Solution-Focused Brief Therapy and Children: A Natural Fit

WE ARE FREQUENTLY ASKED IF SOLUTION-BUILDING THINKING APPLIES TO working with children and, if so, how. The doubt behind these questions is understandable because most practitioners rightly believe that working with children requires approaches and techniques that are less dependent on the use of language than what is needed when working with adults. Some practitioners also believe that children are more fragile, and therefore more vulnerable to damages that can be unwittingly inflicted by misunderstanding them. Working with children is often viewed as a mysterious process that is more difficult to comprehend because children have a limited vocabulary and less ability to express themselves to adults. We hope to demystify this process, to make it more transparent and more doable.

LEARNING CHILDREN'S WAYS

We believe, you, as practitioners, can learn a great deal about children from observing and listening to them respectfully and attentively. Many parents have done so successfully over the years, not with training, but with love and appreciation for how unique each child is in temperament, traits, and preferences. Your intuitive sense matters a great deal, and we want to help you learn to be comfortable with this process, which will lead to having fun and enjoying working with children. When you have fun with children, they will learn that they are fun to be around, which will contribute to their sense of well-being as unique individuals. We will describe some important and practical points to remember when working with children. However, before we do so, we must lay the foundation for how we think and the assumptions we make about children and their parents.

We recognize that since children do not have fully developed language skills, they communicate with body movements, looks, imagination, fantasy, and many other creative ways that adults knew once but have forgotten. Therefore, working with children requires different ways of observing and listening. The underlying principle is to listen to them to learn how unique each child is and how each one makes sense of the world in a unique way. The more respectful we are of these characteristics, the more we will empower children to discover their own unique personalities and to thrive as individuals.

We believe there is good harmony between solution-focused brief therapy and children because there are so many similarities between how children think and make sense of the world around them and the assumptions and procedures of SFBT.

For example, children rarely need to know what caused the problem that they are facing. They certainly do not think deductively or search for explanations of what caused the problem. Close observation of children shows that they experiment with a variety of approaches and solve problems through trial and error. This is all similar to the way solution-focused brief therapy developed: in an inductive manner by finding out what works and what doesn't. Children by and large think "out of the box," and are just interested in what will work.

Children as Involuntary Clients

In our combined careers, we have never had an occasion where a child called us up and said, "Hello doctor, I have a behavioral problem and I need help." At times, the children might indirectly ask for help from their teachers, parents, or other people close to them, but they rarely have enough know-how to call for help directly. All children's problems are defined by adults, and the decision that they need extraordinary help is usually made by those caring parents, teachers, medical doctors, judges, social workers, police officers, priests, probation officers, and other adults who are obviously concerned about the child. Most children have a somewhat blurred concept of what a doctor, counselor, therapist, or psychologist does. Many believe that they may get poked with needles, be given pills, be asked to undress and check their breathing, and be made to talk about strange things that they don't know how to respond to. They have no idea of what a counselor or a therapist does, for that matter, and yet they are told that this person has the ability to make them behave better, or even be a better person who does not lie, steal, or fight with other children.

Children essentially have no control over what happens to them regarding minor as well as more major events that affect them. Decisions such as where they will live and with whom, and when, why, and how these changes, big and small, will alter their life circumstances are made by the adults in their lives. It is reassuring, on one hand, since these important decisions are made by those who care about them deeply. At the same time, it may be difficult for children to understand fully what all of this means, even if it is explained to them repeatedly. Therefore, before a child begins therapy, it is important to explain what will happen every step of the way, from the first step into your office to termination. At times you may need to repeat the explanations because, like most adults, when children are tense and anxious, they cannot absorb all the new information at the same time.

We cannot emphasize enough the importance of gently easing the child into a strange and perhaps even frightening situation by allowing time to integrate the new situation in his or her own way. One of the quickest ways to establish a connection with a child is not to be overly intrusive in the beginning, especially when we have no idea what the child was told by the referring person, teacher, doctor, parent, nurse, or social worker. Some children are told that they are going to see a doctor, a dentist, or a nice lady, a lady who is going to tell the child what he did wrong and might send him to a "foster home." One child was even told that he was going to a McDonald's! Was he angry when he realized that he was told a fib!

Laying the Groundwork

Clearly there are differences between working with adults and children, as we mentioned before, and we want to list some basic points you will need to know about children that will help you assess them.

- Children are still learning language skills; therefore, adults who work with them must have knowledge in communicating with children in ways that are not dependent on linguistic skills only.
- It is essential to have knowledge of a "normal" or "average" child's developmental milestones.
- Always work with parents and caregivers since this is the most important person in the child's life. It means you will always work with two clients simultaneously.

- Since children are dependent on adults, you will need to know how to work with the network of adults in the child's life, such as teachers, health care professionals, and, at times, other adults in the child's social network.
- Working with children means you may need to be a translator on behalf of the child to help bridge the gap between the child and the responsible adult(s).
- Working with children sometimes requires us to take on a leadership role, and we may need to make decisions that will affect the child.
- Different responsibility is required when working with children: not only finding out what might be a useful process to reach the solution, but, at times, helping to implement the solutions as well.
- Working with children often requires that we travel to other settings for meetings, e.g., schools, day care centers, classroom visits, hospitals, detention centers for adolescents, and at times, to prison.
- Working with children requires us to be flexible and willing to spend more hours on the phone, in meetings, and on visits; thus, the length of overall treatment may become more extended than with adults and demand more varied skills, such as networking with many professionals.

ASSUMPTIONS WE HOLD
IN WORKING WITH CHILDREN
AND PARENTS

It is important that we lay out some of the basic assumptions and beliefs that guide our clinical activities. The Milwaukee team did not know what their assumptions were when they set out to develop the SFBT model (Berg, 1994; Berg & Miller, 1992; de Shazer, 1984, 1985, 1994), but they did realize that they had some basic assumptions and beliefs about their clients. Some of the basic assumptions about the change process are presented elsewhere in detail (Berg, 1994; Berg & Miller, 1992; DeJong & Berg, 2001a; Miller & de Shazer, 2000), so we will list them here only briefly. However, if you are new to the SFBT approach, we strongly suggest that you consult these resources. Even though we were trained in traditional therapeutic models, after years of observation and repeated trial and error, we evolved in favor of SFBT, which we believe is a practical and efficient approach that produces an effective outcome. We see ourselves on a continuing path of learning from our clients and always in the process of revising our thoughts and techniques; therefore, these assumptions are not written in stone and we expect them to evolve.

The Role of the Parent in SFBT

We strongly believe that parents should play an important role in the treatment of the child, regardless of the setting or the nature of the program. The importance of a parent in a child's life cannot be measured, nor should it be undermined. All parent-child relationships, even damaged ones, can and should be mended if at all possible. If the relationship cannot be restored immediately, and even if both sides express a desire to sever the relationship, we must at least leave open the possibility of mending it at some future time when they are ready. Our task is to honor this inherent bond, restore it, and help build the bridge between the parent and the child whenever possible. It means parents are included in every step of the child's treatment and informed and consulted as the true experts on their own child. Therefore, from the beginning to the end of the contact, the parent should be included and informed about the progress the child is making, and should also become a part of the treatment process, as we will describe in greater detail later in this chapter.

Assumptions About Parents

Until proven otherwise, we believe that all parents want to:

- be proud of their child
- have a positive impact on their child
- hear good news about their child and learn at what their child is good
- give their child a good education and a good chance at success
- see that their child's future is better than their's
- have a good relationship with their child
- be hopeful about their child.

Even the most frustrated, angry parents, when they calm down, want to feel pride in their offspring, regardless of the child's age. This is ingrained in the fabric of our culture and also holds true across cultures. It is our task to give hope to this desire and restore parents' pride in their own children. We also believe that all parents have good will toward their child (of course we have come across some exceptions) and want their child's life to be better than what they currently have or what they had in their own childhood. Even those parents who abused, neglected, or abandoned their child, or gave up their child for adoption, say they want what is best for their child. Believing in these premises helps us professionals to continue to have hope for the people we work with. When we have hope for them, we convey these beliefs in many subtle and not so subtle ways so that they, too, can have hope for a different future for themselves and their children. As you will see in the following pages, like all models of treatment, our clinical practices flow from these assumptions. These beliefs in the people we work with guide us at every turn, even when we face situations for which we have no answers. Thus, it is helpful to have the parent imagine a clear picture of the situation when they have a positive impact on the child; find out in as much detail as possible what kind of relationship the parent wants to have with the child; and work out the most effective ways to achieve these objectives.

The next step in applying these assumptions is to interact with parents in such a way that they clearly understand the goals of treatment and can do what is necessary to help achieve those goals.

Assumptions about Children

It is also helpful to have a clear understanding of what you believe about what children want and need. Since children are not always able to articulate their needs easily, our summary is derived from observing their behaviors and listening to them. We believe that all children want to:

- have their parents be proud of them
- please their parents and other adults
- be accepted and be part of the social group in which they live
- learn new things
- be active and be involved in activities with others
- be surprised and surprise others
- voice their opinions and choices
- make choices when given an opportunity.

We will describe later how these assumptions will be carried out in our interaction with the parent and the child.

When practitioners work from these assumptions, it is easy to see that building a relationship with a child is not an arduous task but the natural outcome of a positive regard toward the child. Thus, making connections with even the most difficult child is possible when we allow the child time to choose a path for him- or herself. Working with children need not be a long-term, difficult task, and utilizing their innate and natural tendencies and building on these strengths is easier, efficient, and more effective than trying to fill the deficit. This optimistic belief (at times described as naïve and Pollyanna-ish) in every child's ability to have a better future, when given the appropriate help in a timely manner, is what keeps us working hard and keeps us from giving up on any child.

Chapter 3

It's a Matter of Technique

HERE WE BRIEFLY DESCRIBE THE TOOLS THAT ARE COMMONLY USED IN SFBT. Since other publications have extensively described how, when, and for what purpose these tools are used (Berg & Dolan, 2001; Berg & Kelly, 2000; Berg & Reuss, 1997; DeJong & Berg, 2001b; de Shazer, 1991, 1994, Miller & de Shazer, 2000) we only briefly summarize the basic elements here. We realize that the therapeutic conversation is not a simple exchange of words but a complex, multifaceted exchange of glances, gestures, tones of voice, inflections, and many other ingredients that defy simple description. For a more thorough understanding of the conversational process, we strongly recommend viewing videotapes of actual sessions with children and their parents conducted by competent and skilled clinicians.

The usual topics that are addressed in an initial meeting between the client and the therapist are as follows:

1. What does the client want as a desirable outcome of contact with the therapist?
2. What reasonable explanation tells both client and therapist that these goals can be achieved?
3. What has the client achieved toward this desirable state of solution, even a small step?
4. What small step needs to be taken to move forward toward the goal?
5. How close has the client moved toward the goal?

There are four basic types of questions that will get your session moving toward addressing these points.

EXCEPTION-FINDING QUESTIONS

All problems have exceptions. Exceptions are those times when the presenting problem could have happened but somehow it did not. For example, 8-year-old Tommy usually loses his temper and lashes out at anyone around him whenever he gets frustrated, but somehow he managed not to do so on Tuesday morning when his classmate pushed him out of her way. Detailed inquiry about this exception revealed that whenever Tommy is in a good mood, he is more tolerant of other children and can even be quite helpful to his classmates and teachers. More inquiry about Tuesday morning before he arrived at school revealed that he and his mother had a very nice exchange about how well he was able to get himself ready for school, rather than the usual reprimanding and scolding about his dawdling in the morning. This information tells us that when Tommy has a cheerful exchange with his mother, he can be more patient with other children in the class. It means he has the ability to be patient and stay calm. The remedy is to find out how to repeat this successful strategy more frequently until it becomes a routine, habitual activity for Tommy through the cooperation of his mother and father. As we discuss in later chapters, with examples of dialogues, even serious and persistent problems have periods when the problems are less intense, or even a little bit easier to manage. Looking for these exceptions is critical to building further solutions.

SCALING QUESTIONS

We find that children respond quite well to communicating with numbers, rather than words, because numbers are something they can understand. A question requiring a number for an answer, what we call a scaling question, is simple for most children. With children, as well as adults, talking about a great variety of topics in numbers fits their way of thinking in incremental and concrete terms. Parents and teachers can teach children to adapt the scaling question and apply it to a variety of situations, to monitor their own behaviors. This type of question also makes most children feel competent and successful—it is very grown-up to carry on a sensible conversation with adults. For example, suppose the school counselor asks Tommy where he would put his mood on a scale of 1 to 10, with 1 standing for the worst mood where he will be certain to get into fights with other children, and 10 standing for his best mood, like on Tuesday morning when he was able to pretend that Debbie did not push him. At what number between 1 and 10 does he need to be to control himself? Tommy answers that he will need to be at 5 in order to have an OK day. How will he get himself up to level 5? How can his mother help him so that he will walk out of the house with a level 5 mood?

Once you have used this scale with a child, the follow-up sessions can be brief. You can simply ask the child, "Do you remember what we talked about last time? Where on the same 1 to 10 scale would you say you are at today?" Counselors who work in school settings where traditional therapy is difficult to do, perhaps owing to time constraints and an enormous number of cases, can use this tool easily. Some children might even volunteer their well-being while passing the counselor or social worker in the hallway. They can sign by making the number with their fingers. It is fun for children to have this kind of secret code with an adult without other children in the class knowing, because it indicates that the child has a special relationship with a counselor.

For children who like to move around, the therapist can say, "Let's pretend one side of the wall stands for 1 and the other side stands for 10. And let's pretend there is an imaginary line between the two walls that is marked 1 to 10. What number would you pick to show how much progress you made since you started coming to see me?" The child can move around and literally stand on the spot that indicates 6. The therapist can also have the child move one step closer to 7 and say what it feels like to be at 7. We provide a variety of adaptations of this scaling question for children and adolescents later in this book.

A Word of Caution

Scaling questions are not designed to measure a normative standard or to describe a bell curve indicating the "normal" or "abnormal" state; rather it is an internally accessed, subjective way to register a variety of concerns, such as how angry or frustrated the child feels, how happy or confident the child feels, how much the child feels loved by her parent, how safe the child feels with the father when she visits him, and so on. What a particular child feels at level 6 is very individual, and often we have no way to know exactly what that means to that child, but we do know that 6 is better than 4 or 5 but not as good as 8 or 9, and that the level will likely change to something else tomorrow or next week.

MIRACLE QUESTIONS

The original miracle question was developed with adult clients and is phrased as follows:

> I'm going to ask you a rather strange question [pause . . .] that will require some imagination on your part. The strange question is this. After we talk today, obviously you go home and you do whatever you usually do, such as take care of the housework, help your son with his homework, supervise the children, have dinner . . . and you will go to bed tonight. While you are sleeping, a miracle happens [snap your fingers], and the miracle is that the problem that brought you here to solve, just got solved because of this miracle. But this happens during the night and you have no way of knowing this. So, when you wake up tomorrow morning, you will notice something different about you and it will make you wonder, was there a miracle during the night? The problem is gone! Suppose this happens to you, how would you be able to tell that a miracle happened and the problem is solved?

This question works with regardless of the nature of the presenting complaint. It could be as serious as a suicidal attempt, depression, behavior disorder, violence, or abuse. The question seems to have the effect of transcending the problem, and the physical experience of imagining the solution clearly shows in the client's changes in expressions and postures.

Many children love this question when adapted to their experience—e.g., of the "tooth fairy" coming during the night and exchanging the tooth that fell out with something the child can use, such as a generous amount of money. A "fairy godmother" visiting and performing magic by waving her magic wand is also a very familiar character in children's stories. Some children delight in getting into an imaginary picture of their problems disappearing, followed by a magical transformation into a solution. And the therapist can help them to describe what others will notice has changed for them.

CASE EXAMPLE: MAGIC BOX ON HIS DESK
Consider 7-year-old Jason who was always getting into trouble with his teacher because in class he would throw a paper airplane in the air, fall off the desk with a loud thud, throw pencils, erasers, and other objects across the room or out the windows, and create numerous other little annoyances that wore the teacher down. When Jason was asked about his miracle question using a magic

wand, his immediate answer was that he would take all of his problems out of his pockets when he goes to class and store them in the magic box on his desk all day. Being a very smart little boy, he thought about his own answer for a while, and then he began to negotiate with the counselor and asked whether he is allowed to pull out one problem in the morning and one in the afternoon. The counselor decided that two problems a day would be a vast improvement over his current situation, and agreed to his proposal. Of course, his behavior improved in a rather short time, like magic.

As its name implies, the miracle question can be magical and there is no way to predict how the client will respond to it. Occasionally, some children and adults answer with big miracles, such as divorced parents reuniting, or even a dead older brother coming back to life, or a teenager might say he would have his very own metallic-blue sports car and not have to go to school. Rather than stopping this unrealistic dream, we suggest you pursue what difference having these "big miracles" would make in their lives, by asking follow-up questions. For example: "OK, so suppose you do have your parents living together again. I doubt that it will happen, but suppose they lived in the same house again, what would you do then that you are not doing right now?" The important point is not whether the fairy godmother is going to wave her magic wand, but how having the parents living together again is going to change the child's life.

Not surprisingly, many adults and children believe that these problems stop them from living their lives and performing their normal, everyday activities. This is understandable but, at the same time, terribly debilitating for the child to be stopped by such events as parents' divorce, father's absence, or other children making fun of them. On the other hand, it is tremendously empowering to feel they have overcome these obstacles and still continue to have "sleepovers" at friends' houses, play soccer, have lots of friends, and so on. Once they can imagine these miracle pictures, it is possible for them to begin to shape their lives because now they have a glimpse of how their life can be different.

COPING QUESTIONS

Designed to elicit even the smallest possible response that the client may have in handling even what seems like an impossible situation or a very trying and difficult event, some of the coping questions may sound like the following:

"How do you suppose you have coped with so many difficult situations you are just describing?" . . . "Most people would have given up long time ago. What keeps you going?" . . . "What is it about you that got you through such trying circumstances without giving up hope?"

These questions are mostly directed at parents and adults rather than children since they present concepts that are too complex and abstract for most young children. With teenagers, we change the question slightly and ask, "What helps you to get through these difficult times?" We find this coping question particularly useful when parents feel overwhelmed with other aspects of their lives such as marital problems, financial difficulties, illnesses that sap their energy, and then the child's problems increase the burden to the breaking point. Many parents describe how they feel like they have "reached the end of their rope." The reason we like this question is that even when the situation seems hopeless, both the client and the counselor or therapist can always find a very small thing the client has accomplished successfully, such as "managing to get out of bed this morning." What the client considers an insignificant success is magnified into something meaningful. Clients are often amazed to find that a professional would consider such a small accomplishment as getting out of bed important enough to spend a lot of time exploring it. Indeed, when clients begin to think about all the small things they did since forcing themselves to get out of bed, they become impressed with their own successes.

We also find this question useful with adolescents who see their life as a series of disasters. When professionals point out how the adolescents managed not to allow things to slide further, the adolescents become encouraged. Once they become hopeful about themselves, they begin to put their lives together and mobilize their energy and talent.

DETAILS, DETAILS, AND MORE DETAILS: EXPANSION AND FOLLOW-UP

Once you find the exceptions to the problems for your clients, their smallest coping strategies, pictures of miracles, or a certain number on a scale, it is crucial to build on the small solutions you discover and expand these small pieces into slightly bigger ones. For example, you can lean forward with an expression of amazement and ask a question such as, "Tell me how you managed to control your temper and not blow up the other day?" or "What else would you do when this miracle happens and the problem is solved?" or "What tells you that you are at level 5?" or "How long would you say you've been at level 5?" or "What else did you do to get through some of the tough situations you've been in?" Variations of these questions and expansion on the smallest successes encourage the client to look at more of his or her successes, thus making it difficult to dismiss the small success as not important or not good enough. The real work of building a solution lies in beginning with the smallest possible solution, looking at it from a variety of perspectives, and bringing in the perspectives of other important persons such as "What would your best friend say about how you managed to 'walk away,' as you say?" Bringing others' perspectives into conversation situates the child's success in a social context as well.

THINKING BREAK

In the beginning of the first session, we normally explain to the parent and the child that we will take a short "thinking break" toward the end of the session, and that after the break, we will give them some feedback about what we heard that might be useful to the child and the parents. Most clients are intrigued by this notion of a thinking break and often are eager to hear what our feedback might be. Some might be surprised initially, but most clients accept it as a sensible and thoughtful approach to their serious problems and concerns.

During the early development phase of SFBT, we discovered that taking some time out at the end of an interview with clients to think and reflect on the just-completed session serves a very useful purpose. The therapist's undivided attention during the sessions is given to observation and listening, and a physical separation from the intense interaction with clients affords emotional space to reflect on what was learned during the session. The therapist needs only a brief period, 5 to 7 minutes, during which time the clients return to the waiting room. Some children like to look around the waiting room, go to the restroom, get a drink of water, or even do some homework. Having used this thinking break for over 30 years, we are convinced that it is a very useful tool.

During this time of thinking, the therapist's focus is on reviewing the answers to the following questions:

1.   What stands out about this meeting? About the parent? About the child?

2. What useful information did I hear or resources did I observe about this child and parent?

3. What are the child and parents capable of doing that I can build on?

4. What do the child and the parent want from this contact?

5. What other resources does the child need from his or her environment?

6. What unique information or impression about this child or family did I notice that could become a building block toward their goals?

WAYS TO ORGANIZE
YOUR REFLECTIONS

After you quickly organize your information during the thinking break, the following outline can be used to provide feedback to the client:

1. *Compliment*: Point out positive observations such as the mother's attentiveness toward her child, the child's listening to the mother, the child's desire to please the parent, and many other traits that will be useful in moving to the next step toward building solutions. At times, the child's presence at a session may indicate a desire to please the parents, even though he or she may not agree with the parents' ideas of solutions. This is particularly true in the case of teenagers.

2. *Bridging statement*: Any suggestion to increase the frequency of solutions must make sense to clients in order for them to be motivated to experiment with the new ideas. Therefore, you need to offer some explanations for what the next step might be and a rationale for the suggestions that you will offer. For example, during a session with a client named Beth and her mother, Beth identified her wish to be more like a rabbit—quick, friendly, fun to be around, and having lots of friends to play with. Since Beth's solution was in line with her mother's wishes, the mother can become an important person to reinforce and support the rabbit's appearance around the house. This, in turn, will improve the relationship between Beth and her mother. This is the connection between the mother's or Beth's desire and the outcome desired by both Beth and her mother. Therefore, the following rationale and suggestion can be presented to Beth and the mother. "You both have told me there are already times when Beth is as quick as a rabbit, but this little rabbit named Sammy might need some help from everyone so that he doesn't become too shy to show up around the house. Therefore, I would like you (to mother) to pay careful attention to

when Sammy shows up around your house between now and next time we meet again."

3. *Suggestions for tasks*: Suggestions for tasks generally fall into two categories: (a) Do more of what works, which is the majority of time; or (b) Do something different, which we offer only under extreme circumstances, especially when teenagers are involved. In later chapters we provide case examples which discuss a variety of possible techniques.

SECOND AND SUBSEQUENT SESSIONS

After the first session, during which you have opened a potential for a small change, the next important task in subsequent meetings is to follow up on this emerging hope in clients that positive change is possible, build on their confidence that they are doing something useful and positive, and help provide a glimmer of what solutions might look like in practical, concrete, and behavioral ways. Like everything else related to SFBT, it is the combination of your convictions about people and the skills that will translate and communicate these convictions about them to your clients.

The important task for the therapist is to cultivate and follow up on these initial signs of hope about their life and their child. It is very important for the therapist to stay the steady course of moving toward the goals and not falling back into the deficit view of clients. When the therapist is not sure how to take advantage of even a small change, the client and the therapist can easily lapse into hopeless feelings. Therefore, we want to discuss in detail how to follow up on clients' responses in the second and subsequent sessions so that you can expand on small but significant changes. We can put the client's responses into three categories as follows:

"What Is Better, Even a Little Bit?"

The majority of clients are likely to respond to this question with surprise at first, become silent for a while as they search for the improvements, and then slowly begin to tell you about how life is a little bit better or how they feel a little bit calmer, more thoughtful of others, and improved in other ways. Again, the principle of bringing out the small details of successes allows plenty of time for the client to remember the week(s) since the last session. Many clients reply, "Nothing," initially, which makes sense from their perspective, since they have not thought about anything better. We find that clients answer this question in one of three ways: better, the same, or worse. We discuss how to respond to these answers.

Better

Since young children are not able to describe what is better using words, later we will discuss in more detail how to adapt this question when working with them. What we describe here is for the parents, adolescents, and some older children who can communicate with words. Surprisingly, when the therapist makes a point of asking, the majority of clients report that something is better. The following are some examples of "Wh" questions (what, when, where, who, how, *but not* why) that generate detailed information about successes:

- Tell me more about *what* you did instead of losing your temper?
- *When* did you realize that you needed to walk away and not get into a fight?
- *Who* was most surprised by your decision to walk away from Tom instead of hitting him?
- That must've been pretty tough to walk away from Tom when he was calling your mother a name. *Who* was more surprised, you or Tom?
- *When* your mother hears about this, *how* surprised would she say she is, on a scale of 1 to 10?
- *What* do you have to do so that you could do this again with Tom?
- *How* confident are you that you can do this again with Tom or other kids, on a scale of 1 to 10?
- *What* would raise your confidence one level higher?
- *What* else is better?

When clients report even a slight movement toward their goal, the first task is to help find ways to maintain this improvement. After the clients feel sufficiently confident in their ability to maintain the level of success, the therapist can discuss the next small steps for improvement.

Same

Some clients report "nothing is different" since the previous session. Rather than being disappointed with this answer, it can be viewed as positive, since "nothing is different" means there has been no change in the negative direction. That the client has maintained the level of previous functioning shows an ability to control his or her life. Some of the following comments would be helpful in this situation:

- Wow, amazing! It is generally difficult to stay the same day after day. *How* do you suppose you have done this?
- Suppose I talk to your parent (child), *what* would they say went better, even a little bit? *What* did you do this time that worked? In most situations, you would have jumped on other children. *How* were you able to control your temper?
- *What* level on your scale would you say you are at? *What* do you need to do to stay at level 4?
- *What* would change in your life when you can stay at level 4 for the next two weeks?
- *What* level would your teacher have guessed you were at since we met last time?
- *Who* will notice first when you move up from level 4 to 5?

Worse

On rare occasions some clients report that their life has become worse since the last session and again you need to ask about details for what made things worse. Indeed, disasters, accidents, illness, and other unpredictable events can happen in anyone's life. Respectfully listen to the client's description of unwanted events, keeping an ear open for any positive aspect of how the client handled the situation differently now than in the past, preventing the episode from being more disastrous. Variations on coping questions can be very useful here, to suggest that the client has not made the bad situation into something worse:

- *How* did you get through such a difficult week when so many things went wrong? Many people in your situation would not have handled it as well as you have. *What* helped?
- *What* was most helpful about what you did? *What* would your best friend say you did that was most helpful?
- *What* was most useful about helping you stay as calm as you have managed under such difficult circumstances?
- *How* come things are not worse?
- *What* do you need to do so that you can maintain your current level of functioning?
- Suppose you could raise the level just a little bit higher, say from 2 to 3. *What* would change for you then? In *what* way would your best friend say you will be different then? (Note: Occasionally some parent or child might report that there is no "best friend," making

it impossible to answer this question. Ask the client to "imagine (or pretend) you have a best friend," then continue with the question.

Each subsequent session can follow a similar format until the client reports that there is a small improvement, that things are better, and that they are confident of maintaining the improvement.

Chapter 4

Assessing Your Clients,
Agreeing on Goals

Grownups love numbers. When you tell them about a
new friend, they never ask you questions about the essential things. They never say to you: what does his voice
sound like? Which games does he prefer? Does he collect
butterflies? Instead they ask you: How old is he? How
many brothers has he got? How much does his father
make? Only in that way do they get the feeling they know
him.

—*The Little Prince*

ONE OF THE KEY POINTS IN WORKING WITH INVOLUNTARY CLIENTS IS TO
work with what is important to them, not what the professionals believe
is important for the client. Even though we already mentioned that
the child is by and large an involuntary client, in many ways, parents
feel they also are forced to seek help, not out of their own will but
because of their love and concern for their child. Thus, it is easy to
view the parent as "involuntarily volunteered" to seek help for their
child's sake, not for themselves. The reason we are emphasizing the
importance of listening for clues about what is important to the parent
is that even though parents care about their child, not all parents love
their child in the same manner. To some parents, having a well-behaved
child is a mark of their success as a parent; while other parents may
measure their success in a completely different way.

Many parents we meet, regardless of whether they are proud of
their own parenting or not, always report that they want to be a better
parent than their own parents were to them. We are heartened by this

desire to surpass their own parents, and it gives us hope that with each passing generation, we will try a little harder to do a better job.

ASSESSING THE CHILD

The most common information a therapist obtains upon first meeting a child is quite standard: name; age; how many siblings; grade in school; whether parents are separated, divorced, or single; what kind of work the parents do; and so on. This information is considered important according to the logic of grown-ups, but children do not attach the same degree of significance to it.

Noticing something special about a child's clothing, hair, or toys the child brings along are important clues about getting to know the child that tell you how to connect with the child. So too are the things the child notices in your therapy room, the way the child moves, and so on. In some situations, if the child does not show you these little clues, do not rush into the business of the session. Most children like to tell you what and with whom they like to play and what kind of games they like best. You can ask about a favorite toy. When the weather is nice, you might ask children to name their favorite outside games. When children respond to these questions reasonably well, then you can move on to involving their parents by asking them: what the child is good at?; what would the teacher say the child is good at?; what about his or her friends?; what is the child's favorite meal, TV shows, animals, or colors?; what surprises the parent about the child and what does the child like to do to surprise the parents?

Assessment of the child is usually accomplished by observing, for instance, how the child handles the challenge of a new game or how the child moves. (For example, does the child climb the stairs one step at a time or is the child able to alternate between two legs when going up the stairs?) Observations of such behaviors tell us what the child is capable of doing and how well the child is coordinated. (Is the child able to perform at the level of development accomplishment?) The assessment of the child also should feel natural, that is, instead of feeling like the child has to perform certain activities or a task for the therapist, getting into a natural, spontaneous movement is the best way to learn about the child's abilities, instead of disabilities. See Chapter 7 for a complete discussion of assessing a child with uncommon needs.

Assessment of a child's competence and strength is a continuous process of revision, just as it is with adults. For example, whenever you pick up a little idea that indicates what the adult wants instead of what he does not want, these little bits of information are added to your previous knowledge. The same is true with children: every behavior you observe that tells a new or different story about the child is helpful. Consider, for example, a child who was referred for ADHD (attention deficit hyperactivity disorder) assessment. In the interaction with the child, a perceptive therapist notices exceptions to this description, that is, the child may show a fairly short attention span to certain activities, while at other times is not distracted by a phone ringing and is able to concentrate on drawing a spaceship. It is also a good idea to offer several different tasks to do, over several sessions, in order to discover in what area the child shows mastery of skills and talents. When you discover a child who is competitive, this may be a resource. Another child may become intimidated and slowed down by competition, and then our effort is directed at discovering what other traits the child has that may speed things up a little.

Another important task is observing how children organize their activities. For example, if a child becomes more creative when the pressure is off, it is a good idea to offer a greater variety of material to choose from to match his style. Is the child able to decide and make choices on his own or does he become frustrated easily when offered help? Does the child like to do things according to her own rules or is the child able to follow directions? The speed with which the child behaves is also useful information. Many children, especially those who are referred for ADHD, are much more cooperative when adults slow down the activities and they are told about the change of plans well in advance. Playing games with children provides us with good information about how confident they feel. We find that young children do well with "open" games such as finding hidden objects in the room or finding something blue (red, green, etc.) in the room, but as soon as they get into competitive games that are predesigned and they must follow only certain rules, they become lost. Knowing what kinds of games a child can cope with is useful information for the parents and teachers.

Most of all, assessment of children entails learning about *what* is important to them, what capacities and abilities each one brings to the situation: it could be having friends, having their parents be proud of them, not being made fun of, feeling like they belong to a group. This information tells us where to focus the initial attention. The second important piece of information is *who* is important to the child—with whom is the child bonded?, to whom does the child want to be close?, and with whom does the child feel comfortable? Knowing these resources for the child will give us a clue on how to proceed and who should be in the therapy room as well as who is the adult most responsible for the child's care. Assessing a child's personality means, most of all, working with the special characteristics of each individual and working with these to find solutions, rather than trying to change the nature of the child.

ASSESSING THE FAMILY

By meeting a child with the parents for the first time, you begin the assessment of both the parent and the child simultaneously. As we mentioned before, working with children always means you have two clients: the child and the parent (in most situations). In most instances, except when working with a very belligerent teenager or a child who requires closer assessment for 2–4 sessions alone with the child, we tend to work closely with the parents. However, since we already stressed the importance of family to the child elsewhere, here we briefly pay attention to assessing the parents and family. Of course we ask questions that will orient us toward what the parents want from treatment and what the child wants. While doing so, we are all trained to be keen observers and listeners.

Family assessment usually can be best accomplished through the following methods:

- Asking questions
- Observing the interaction between the parents
- Asking the family to engage in some activities together (more on this later).

What to Ask

Since we have addressed and will describe more of the useful questions to ask, we will limit our discussion here. The following are some useful questions to ask during family assessment.

- Explore details of exceptions: What do the mother/father do in response to them?
- Was the response spontaneous or deliberate?
- What do parents believe to be most useful about exceptions?
- What is the influence of other members of the family? How are they helpful?
- What would other members of your family, grandma or grandpa, for example, say would be most helpful for your family?
- What would your best friends say you do that is most helpful for your family?

- How determined are the parents to teach the child to reach a perfect 10 in their achievements?
- How are the parents able to surprise the child?
- Do you like to be seen in public with your child?

What to Observe

The following is a list of nonverbal interactions you may want to observe, between parents, as well as between parents and child:

- What do I see in this family that tells me they can achieve their goal(s)?
- What interactions do I see, eye contacts, gestures, timing of parents' intervening in the interaction among the children, that shows me their ability to lead?
- How do mother and father take turns with the children? What is the trigger that causes them to react?
- What do I see the mother do to invite or allow the father to intervene? (In most families, mother is generally more active in intervening, and many mothers express the wish that the father would more actively intervene.)
- What do parents do, individually or together, to empower the child?
- What do I observe in this family that tells me that parents are able to be selective? (Successful parenting requires parents to be selectively deaf, blind, and mute.)

What Family Activities Help

Sometimes it is helpful to invite the family, especially when young children are involved, to do one of the following activities. If you initiate any of these activities, it is useful to tell the family that you will look for helpful interactions in their family and will share these observations with them. We want the family to experience successes so that we can help to build on these successes with our help and on their own.

- Draw a picture together.
- Have the family put a puzzle together.
- Have one member hide an object and the others look for it.
- Build something with wooden blocks (everybody gets the same number of blocks).

- Act out certain feelings, like feeling hot, cold, happy, sad, angry, etc.

All of these suggestions look good on paper but reality can be quite confusing at times. Therefore, we want to describe how therapists must listen with a special set of ears based on strong convictions and turn what could be a negative reaction to parents into a useful one as the following case shows.

CASE EXAMPLE: USE OF THERAPIST'S DILEMMA

As Mrs. Watkins was making an appointment, she made it clear that she was culling at the insistence of her 9-year-old son Greg's teacher. The teacher believed that Greg's antisocial behaviors of beating up other children and having frequent fights interfered with his ability to learn properly and as much as he was capable of.

When I (TS) went to the waiting room to greet Greg and his parents, Greg was talking to his father on the cell phone explaining where to find us. I invited Greg and Mrs. Watkins into the office and began to learn a little bit about what Greg likes to do. I learned that he likes to play with Legos, he prefers playing inside the house to going outside, and even though he has two friends he plays with occasionally, he would like to have "real" friends. He is good at art but does not like to go to school or even watch TV. When asked to rate how much he likes to go to school on a scale of 1 to 10 (10 stands for the most anybody could like going to school, and 1 is the opposite), he rated himself at 3. When asked what he wanted to have changed in his life, he mentioned that he would like to have more friends.

After 15 minutes, Mr. Watkins arrived and I began negotiating the goals Greg's parents have for therapy. Mrs. Watkins immediately said that she was coming to please the teacher since Greg never gives her any trouble at home. Her second idea was to find out how to help Greg jump one grade up because he has expressed this wish to his parents many times. Mr. Watkins was confident that his social problems were not as serious as the teacher described and he explained that teachers nowadays are not as well trained as they were when he was in school. He also noted that his son's solution of using fists made perfect sense. According to the father, friends were not as important as a good family and he certainly had one; therefore, he would like to see Greg skip his grade and advance to the next one.

Discussion: I began to realize that I was getting irritated with the parents. What in the world are they thinking? All Greg wants is not to go to school. He just wants to stay home and play with Legos, and the father endorses his son's way of using fists when he gets irritated at other children. No wonder Greg has no friends! How can these parents believe that skipping a grade would serve their son? I tried to stay calm and kept asking for more information that might shed more light on their logic.

The following information emerged from further discussion:

1. *Greg had repeated the first grade because he was considered insufficiently mature, emotionally and intellectually, to learn. Mr. Watkins thought this was a mistake and he should not have listened to the school psychologist who recommended this, and that Greg was an underachiever and he certainly was capable of doing better.*

2. *The manner in which Greg dealt with his brother's death a year ago in an accident is proof that Greg was very mature. Mr. Watkins explained further that Greg can express his ideas in a manner that even his father could not. I was surprised to hear about the death of their other child.*

3. *Greg's father was convinced that the social problems, if there were any, could be easily solved by moving one grade higher.*

4. *Mrs. Watkins thought she could help Greg do his extra work at home since mother and son are very close and he listens to her well. It would take about an hour and half, and at most two extra hours, of work beyond what they were doing already. While the mother talked, Mr. Watkins took Greg in his arms like a baby and nursed him by putting his finger into Greg's mouth, and Greg started to suck it like an infant. Of course, I was becoming increasingly irritated and observed something quite disjointed between what I was hearing and what I was seeing. While Mrs. Watkins spoke, father and son seemed to tune out the mother. They seemed so involved with each other, as if the outside world did not exist. I was aware of becoming angry at the parents, and it is very unusual to have such strong feelings during the first interview.*

5. *When I asked Greg how he thought he would jump one grade higher, he had no idea at all and his only comment was that he did not want to work too much for school. I explored with the parents whether there were other options, and they replied that they had thought about a private school where more individualized teaching was possible. Both agreed that even though they could afford it, they would not like this solution because of Greg's social problems! Before taking a thinking break, I asked the parents what the teacher's reaction to this skipping a grade was. The parents reported that the teacher ignored their question and only insisted that Greg's social problems needed to be solved first.*

Thinking Break: Recognizing my unusual responses to the parents, I had to think about my irritated reaction to them in a very solution-focused manner. I was really glad to have this opportunity to take some time and figure out how to use the information in a helpful manner. Because I had such a strong negative reaction to the parents (about the manner in which they discussed their dead child, how unrealistic they were about Greg's ability to master moving up a grade, and how they treated Greg as an infant, among other things), I was at risk of not listening to the parents, thus getting into a power struggle with them, as the teacher seems to have done. I had to remind myself that even though the parents' goal of advancing one grade sounded unrealistic, I had to respond in a respectful, collaborative manner, and not become reactive to them. So, I began making a list of things I heard and observed:

- *Parents want to take their child's wishes seriously*
- *Parents want to see their child succeed*
- *Mother is willing to invest more time with Greg*
- *Mother's positive relationship with Greg makes it possible for him to listen to her*
- *Father has an unusually close relationship with Greg*
- *Even though the teacher turned down their idea, they seem persistent*
- *Instead of insisting with the school, at least the parents are willing to discuss the question of Greg jumping a grade with me; there is some openness to look at other options.*

After careful thought, I gave the following descriptive feedback to the three: "I'm very impressed with how you (to the parents) both want to do what is best for Greg and it is impressive that Mr. Watkins, you are concerned about both sides of Greg's development, the emotional as well as the intellectual side. I am also impressed with Greg's ability to listen to his mother. It seems to me that skipping one grade up would mean a lot of work for the whole family; especially for Greg, it would mean more school work. Therefore, I would like both of you to observe very carefully all the little signs that tell you that Greg is ready to take on this extra work in school. In order for me to assess more clearly Greg's ability to manage his moving up a grade, I would like your permission to meet with Greg alone for three sessions so that I can assess his strengths and needs."

The parents agreed and I met with Greg and also visited him in his class. I asked to meet with the parents only for one meeting to report my observations, and began with the report of strengths that I saw, particularly how Greg was doing good things with other children in the class. I also noted the handicap that Greg seemed to do well in a small group but as soon as he was confronted with many children, he began to protect himself by fighting, even though there was no obvious reason to feel attacked. Mr. Watkins replied that this was the first time they felt their wish was taken seriously, especially about the jumping one grade. They had thought things over and decided to look for a private school for Greg.

This case study is a beautiful example of how important it is to listen to the parents, even when they seemed so unrealistic and inconsistent. The teacher's response to such an absurd idea would not be out of line for most of us, but the therapist turned things around by listening to her own voice with an ear for discerning solutions rather than judging the parents from an expert's position. It certainly sounds easy and simple, but even the most experienced and skilled therapist can encounter situations where one can get caught up in a power struggle that would not be helpful to the parents and children. The real expertise lies in how to listen to the clients and look at everything from their perspective, not ours, and yet not see the situation exactly as the client does. The ability to see similarly with and differently from the client is what makes us useful to clients.

CHILDREN WHO DO NOT
RESPOND QUICKLY

Some children may take a little bit longer to respond to the therapist's reaching out to them at the first or second meeting. The most helpful thing a therapist can do is to normalize this cautiousness and reassure the parents that their child will eventually decide to talk when the child finds the right moment. Be prepared to wait the entire first session with some very reluctant children and, in such cases, it is a good idea to carry on a normal conversation with the parent or caretaker, especially about what the child is good at—e.g., positive personality traits, habits, what kind of food he likes, favorite games. During this period you observe the child's nonverbal cues and see whether he is interested in joining the conversation. You can engage the parents in their desire for the more positive interaction they wish to have with their child. Even the very young child is very attentive to adult conversation, and some children clearly become calmer when parents mention something positive about them. Even though the child is not participating actively, you can find out what the child is capable of doing, such as help with the baby sister, read, get dressed without help in the morning, help set the table, and so on. These kinds of conversations become an indirect way to compliment the child and the parents.

In Chapter 7, where we describe techniques of working with children with uncommon needs, we will address ways to give "bad" news to the parents about their child's limitations such as developmental delays, and also show how to arrive at this assessment in detail. We will also discuss ways to help parents and schools plan to maximize the child's abilities.

GOAL NEGOTIATIONS:
GUIDE FOR SUCCESSFUL OUTCOME

Often described as goal-driven activities, SFBT insists that the criteria for termination must be negotiated as the first step toward successful outcome. Any concept of successful outcome can only be measured by its criteria and definition of where the client wants to be. Since the client is the consumer of our services, we believe the client is the best judge of whether our joint work has been successful. The following section describes in detail how to negotiate a successful outcome.

Most adults—such as teachers, nurses, medical doctors, parents or caretakers, family members, even baby-sitters—who refer a child for therapy have a fairly good idea of what is wrong with the child. They might even have some good ideas of what is needed to remedy the problem. Yet, when asked to explain the kind of behaviors they would like to see, they instead frequently regress to asking "why" the child is behaving that way or what the child is doing wrong. Therefore, it is often the therapist's job to translate this problem statement into signs of solutions or goals. This is achieved by asking the adults to describe what they would consider the signs of a successful outcome in concrete, behavioral, and measurable ways. When the adults begin to notice these changes, many in turn behave in a way that is supportive and encouraging to the child.

In order to be helpful, the negotiated goals between the caregiver and therapist should have the following characteristics. They must be:

- described as a presence of solution(s), not an absence of problems
- described as a beginning of a solution, not an end of the problem
- concrete, measurable, countable, specific, and behavioral
- realistic and doable for the person involved
- described in interactional terms, and in social context
- thought to take hard work to achieve
- important to the client.

Negotiating the outcome of therapy at the beginning conveys an optimism to the parent that the problem can be solved. It sounds rather simple to do but it actually requires patience and persistence on the therapist's part, because most adults have been preoccupied with the nature of the problem and have only a vague sense of how they would like things to change. After all, they have lived with the problem for quite some time, and by telling the therapist the details of the problem, they are trying to be helpful. Here is a typical dialogue between a therapist (T) and a mother (M) at the beginning of the goal negotiations.

T: So what needs to happen here today so that you can say to yourself that it's been helpful to come and talk to me?

M: Melody has this terrible temper problem. She's been a rather difficult child from her baby days and she can lose her temper at the drop of a hat. What's more difficult is that as she get older, she seems to get worse instead of better. We thought that her growing up a bit would help her control her temper, but it is really getting worse. Now we are hearing from the school how she is the same way with other kids and she is even starting to hit, shove, and bite other kids.

T: I can see that you have very good reasons to be concerned about Melody. So, what would you like to see her do instead of shoving, hitting, kicking, biting, and losing her temper?

M: Maybe it's genetic. Her father was like that, really hot tempered and had no patience at all.

T: I wonder what you need to see Melody doing instead that will tell you her temper problem is getting a little bit better.

M: I want her to learn to take "no" for an answer and be nice to other kids. She is so aggressive that other kids don't want to play with her during recess.

T: So, it sounds like you would like to see her play well with other children, have more friends, and follow rules.

M: That's it. She needs to learn that there are rules everywhere, that she has to learn to get along with other kids and grown-ups, and that she has to listen to people.

T: Those sound like reasonable things to ask a 6-year-old. So what exactly will you see her do that will tell you she is learning to play with other kids, accept "no" for an answers, and listen to grown-ups?

M: I don't expect her to listen to adults all the time, but once in a while she will listen to the teacher, to me, and her grandmother, and not try to get her way all the time.

As this conversation shows, the mother is beginning to become more concrete and more specific describing Melody's solutions. Being persistent produces two benefits: the goals begin to become more realistic ("not listen to adults all the time, but once in a while") and concrete; having described Melody's behavior in terms of a solution, the mother is more likely to notice things Melody does that tell her she is making an effort and making progress. Clearly, when the mother begins to see Melody's effort to please her, the relationship is likely to improve, which is likely to encourage Melody to behave even better.

"Understanding" the Reasons Behind the Child's Problems

It is reasonable and rational for adults to want to understand the "reasons" or "causes" behind a child's problems. We all want to make sense of something as incomprehensible as why a child would not want to listen to a parent. It is also reasonable to believe that there is some causal relationship between the problem and a historical event or trauma that may have caused the problem. Our clinical experience shows, however, that once the discussion begins to move toward what went wrong and how the problem may have originated, it is difficult to shift the conversation to a future desirable state of solutions. Therefore, it is useful for the therapist to have some guide to know when to shift the conversation to a future desirable state of life for the client. As the following dialogue shows, such request can be used as a starting point, not an end, of goal negotiation:

M: I need to understand why Devon is so obstinate and always wants to get his way. None of my other children are as difficult as Devon.

T: Of course, you would like to know why he is this way. Do you want to just understand it or do you want him to do something about it?

M: That's a good question. I guess I want him to do something about it. I want life to be a little bit easier, to get along with him, and not have him fight with me about every little thing that he has to do. It gets to be pretty exhausting trying to explain to him all the time.

T: So, suppose he learns to accept that there are certain things he has to do without fighting with you every step of the way. What would he do instead?

M: Well, first of all, he would not give me those big sighs with this disgusted look on his face, and his eyeballs going up to the ceiling. When he does that, I just feel like slapping him in the face and I end up walking away so that I don't hit him.

T: So, what would you suggest he do instead?

M: He could have a pleasant look on his face and maybe just go do it. Maybe that's asking for too much, but why can't he be like other kids?

T: So, suppose he does, with a pleasant look on his face, just go do it. I'm not sure about how likely it is that this will happen, but suppose he does. What would change between you and Devon?

M: I will feel like going out of my way to do more things for him, like cooking his favorite dinner, maybe even allow him to go to the "sleep-over" with his friends—things that I know he likes to do.

As you can see, in a fairly short time, the mother not only identifies behavioral indicators that she will consider as progress but also is able to include herself in the solution. If the mother is receptive to looking into how she can change along with Devon, the treatment can be much briefer, because when the mother's interaction with Devon is positive, he is also more likely to respond positively to his mother's wishes.

How to Handle Multiple Goals

You may become overwhelmed when you hear multiple problems reported by many sources, including parents and referring profession-als. If you feel this way, ask the parent or the caretaker to set priorities to help you get started. For example, listen to how two different therapists propose setting the goal. The first therapist spoke as follows:

> I can see that lots of people are interested in making sure that Jonathan gets the right kind of help and soon. I think it is a good sign that many people think there is hope for him. So, of all the concerns everybody has, including yours, where do you think will be a good place to get started so that you can say that he is heading in the right direction?

Another variation in negotiating the goal is as follows:

> You mentioned lots of problems about Jorge and you certainly have had some tough times with him. I can see that you need some relief right away from the many years of living with so many difficulties. Obviously we can't do everything at once, so what small signs do you need to see that will let you know we are heading in the right direction?

Even though both sound similar, the emphasis on the need to negotiate "small signs" and the "right direction" reflects how the therapists are sensitive to pick up on the adult's primary concerns. The therapist who is working with Jonathan emphasizes how many people have hope that he can change, while the therapist who works with Jorge emphasizes how long the parent (or caretaker, teacher, etc.) has suffered with Jorge's complicated problems and acknowledges that it is about time for the parent to get some relief from it. But note that both therapists emphasize small steps and heading in the right direction to indicate to the parents that they will need to look for small changes, not fantastic or amazing changes.

When Parents Expect the Child
to Change First

We are frequently asked, in seminars, consultations, and training sessions, how to manage situations when the parents expect and, at times, demand the child to change his or her behavior first before the parent is willing to give the benefit of the doubt. It is understandable for parents to believe that once the child's problem is corrected, their lives will become easier and their relationship with the child will change for the better. This does happen quite often and we have seen that even a small change in a child can make a remarkable difference in the parents' life. Yet, we have also seen the opposite: when the parent changes, the child becomes easier to live with. This has taught us that no matter who begins the change process, each person involved in the social context has to change to adapt to the other's change.

This concept is difficult to put into practice when the therapist is faced with very provocative teenagers or with children who are very discouraged and have nothing positive to say about themselves. Some children and adolescents are very difficult to manage in a session. They are not cooperative and seem to defy every effort the therapist makes to get along and feel positive toward the child. It is important to recognize that the more difficult the child or the parent is to engage, the more desperate their experiences are, and the more they need to be validated and supported. It is important not to take their difficult behaviors personally but to view them as a form of communication that expresses how angry, hopeless, and desperate they are for some sort of help.

When you try to see everything from their point of view, while maintaining the posture of curiosity, a child's difficult behavior becomes easier to accept. Therefore, first you must accept what they say. For example, when a parent says the child has to change first, you need to accept and try to understand everything from the parent's perspective. Consider the following dialogue:

T: So, suppose your daughter does all the things that you would like her to do, as we have been discussing. What would she say about how you will be different with her?

M: You know, that's just it. Sometimes, I feel like I don't even know my own daughter because I can't imagine what might be going on in her head. But I suppose she will say I will be calmer, talk to her nicely, and maybe even look at her in the morning and say, "Good morning" to her. But you know it is really difficult to do because she is so nasty to me from the moment she gets up until she falls asleep.

T: So, what would she say she would do when you say "Good morning" to her?

M: It's been so long since I've said that to her. She will probably be wondering what's wrong with her mother.

T: So, after she figures out that it is still the same mother, what would she do that she didn't do this morning?

M: She will be calmer herself, and more pleasant to be around, not spitting her words out at everybody. And she will have her breakfast and get ready to go to school on her own without my having to nag her.

The therapist must learn to selectively listen for the goal in every exchange. Even though the mother lapses into problem talk quite often, the therapist leads the mother gently to talk about the details of solutions. We find that the longer the client has been seeped in problem talk, the longer it takes for the client to begin thinking instead about personal wishes.

Changing Goals

It is not that uncommon or unusual to negotiate the goal in the middle of treatment. This does not occur because parents are unsure or ambivalent about themselves or their children's progress, but, as one mother explained, "Until I solved this problem, I didn't know I needed to change the next problem." Using the scaling questions, which we will describe later, one mother described her dilemma by saying, "Until I got up to 5, I didn't even know what 6 might look like, but now I think I do." When the pressure of immediate stress is overwhelming, it makes sense that clients would have no room to think about a bigger picture of how their lives can be better. For example, until parents have the feeling that they can handle the pressing issue of their child's urgent problems, feeling like they are constantly "putting out the daily fires," they have difficulty sorting out the priorities. But once they feel that they are overcoming some obstacles and can see the larger picture, they can pinpoint the bigger issue that will make a somewhat bigger difference. Therefore, it is important for the therapist to listen to their ideas on how achieving different goals would contribute to making their life a little bit easier.

Chapter 5

Let's Get To It!

NOW THAT WE HAVE DESCRIBED SOME BASIC TECHNIQUES TO APPLY TO SESsions, we can discuss how to actually proceed. This chapter will address practical questions regarding how to structure the session, how to work with parents, and even what equipment and toys can be used with children.

GETTING STARTED

Who Should Come to The First Session?

This question is raised often by the parents, the referring person, those who work with children, and many therapists as well. When a parent asks this question, our general stance is to say that "whoever will be most helpful in finding the right solution for the child" would be welcome to come to the session. This person usually turns out to be the mother or other important person to the child. Some adolescents bring their best friends or other adults they feel are close to them, such as a special teacher, counselor, clergy member, or neighborhood adult. Generally we invite the parents to decide who should come since they know their child best.

Frequently, the decision of who should come to the first session is made by the referring person, such as a teacher, lawyer, parent, nurse, judge, or social worker. The referring person may recommend that the whole family should come or that only the child be brought to the therapist, or child and another should come, and so on. It is important to respect their opinions and work with decisions that were already made, even though you might disagree that the entire family has to undergo the inconvenience of finding a baby-sitter or getting help with transportation from a neighbor. Sometimes, the entire family shows up for the first interview and if the therapist views it as the family's attempt to be helpful to the child being treated, it allows the therapist to compliment all the family members on their good will toward the child and their willingness to be helpful. Unless the circumstances of the referral make it necessary to do otherwise, we like to talk to the parent first, since generally it is the parent who makes important decisions that affect the child.

It is important that therapists have sufficient flexibility and willingness to work with whoever requests services, and have the ability to make the most of whatever information is presented. No amount of information is ever complete, and we collect useful information as it emerges: sometimes in bits and pieces, other times in floods of words or mountains of paperwork and evaluations or histories sent from the referral source.

When working with adolescents, you may find that they prefer to come alone or bring a best friend instead of a parent. We also have had parents come without the teenager because the child has refused to show up in anticipation of being blamed, lectured, thought of as "mental" or a "psycho," or believing that seeing a "shrink" is a sure sign that they are not "normal," thus making it difficult to fit into their social circles. It is entirely possible to help teenagers without insisting that they show up for a session, especially in those situations where the parents are afraid of the teen's potential for violence or are concerned that the behavior might become worse when the adolescent is extremely upset. Again, we would like to emphasize that since we make an assessment for solutions, which is quite a different focus than assessing the problem, this is possible. All parents have a fairly good idea of how they want things to be different, and what solutions might look like, and so do children and adolescents.

Between the Phone Call
and the First Session

As soon as the appointment is scheduled, we usually mail the following to the parent and referring person.

* Information about what to expect from therapy; office hours; the fee; phone and fax numbers; e-mail address (optional); and some information about the therapist's credentials and area of expertise.

- A questionnaire designed to elicit parents' concerns and perceptions of the child's problems and resources. (See Appendix.) Although we ask parents to bring this questionnaire with them to the first session, many forget or misplace it. It is therefore a good idea to have extra blank copies on hand at the first meeting.

We expect that the parent and the referring person, such as the teacher, who knows the child best, will become our most valuable resource person. As you can see, the questionnaire is designed to elicit the child's successes, strengths, skills, and accomplishments that perhaps adults and the children themselves do not recognize yet. We find that, surprisingly, many parents begin to see their child in a slightly different way when they arrive in our offices.

Explanation of What Will Happen

Even though you may have sent written information about what to expect the session to be like, at the first session it is a good idea to explain once again what will happen during the session. This is important because we cannot count on all parents to have explained this to the child. The following introduction is quite commonly used to orient both the parents and the child.

I suppose you are like most other children who come to see me and I'm sure it was difficult for you. I can imagine you wanted to stay home and do something else, like play doing your favorite activities or toys. This is perfectly normal because all children I meet think that. Maybe this meeting will become a little bit easier for you when you know what is going to happen to you today. First I would like to get to know you a little bit, like what you like to do, what you are good at, and things like that. The second thing is to find out what you would like to have changed in your life and what your parents would like to see different. Most parents and children want to change different things, and this is quite normal also. I am interested in finding out everybody's point of view. I will talk to you a while, then I will talk to your parents for quite a while and you can go and play or draw a picture. It is perfectly OK for you to listen to what grown-ups are talking about, if you want to. When we finish talking, I will take a short break and think about all the good things you are going to tell me. When I come back to the room, I will ask you to sit on this chair again because I want you to hear what I have to say.

When Parents Request that the Child
Be Seen First

Occasionally parents request that the therapist see the child alone first, and, if it is reasonable, we try to accommodate. However, when such an arrangement would be too overwhelming for the child to handle, thus ending in tears or a fearful look on the child's face, we must be open to change the plan. It is reasonable to ask that the parents stay in the room with the child until they believe that the child has calmed down enough and they feel it is the right time to leave, because they know the child much better than we do. You can talk with the parents about their "good reason" for asking the child to be seen first, and all the positive qualitites of the child can be learned during this phase. In general, the child will visibly relax and calm down, and will then feel comfortable enough to look around and become curious about the new surroundings. A therapist can seldom meet with a very timid child without the help of a parent or caretaker who is familiar to the child. If verbal communication is not possible with the child, you can always find something the child might be interested in playing with; you can always break into a familiar song or nursery rhyme with a doll nearby. Remember that children cannot, and should not, be rushed into closeness or intimacy by an adult; they need to take their own time and even very young children have to make their own choices.

When to See the Parent
and Child Separately

When working with parents and adolescents, the decision of whether to meet with the parents and the teenager separately is fairly easy. When parents are so frustrated with their teenager that no matter what the topic of conversation is, the parent repeatedly returns to the child's problems or appears to be preoccupied with the child's problems for various reasons, it is time to see them separately. Likewise when several attempts to change the topic to what the child has done well or to some positive changes the child made since the appointment was set are unsuccessful, then it is best to see them separately. There are times when the child is irritated and it seems impossible to create an atmosphere of cooperation and respect for each other or with you. It is easy to see the adolescent or child's reaction to a parent's complaint:

lowering the head, slouching more, downcast eyes, no participation, and a look of resignation and despair are hard cues to miss.

Sometimes, the tension between the child and the parents is so obvious that they almost behave as if they cannot stand each other. Just separating them from one another frequently gives you enough room to interact with each party; seeing that they are capable of being different with you is a good indication that they are capable of being different in other social contexts.

Rather than continuing a painful exchange, ask the parent to step outside into the waiting area and ask to talk to the child alone. It is embarrassing for children to be berated and scolded in front of strangers who witness their humiliation for the first time. If such a scene repeats at home, at least the child can get away, walk out of the room, go to another room and shut the door, or even walk out of the house. But it is difficult for children to escape when they are sitting in your office.

CASE EXAMPLE: VIDEO GAMES

Peter, age 15, was brought to therapy against his wishes by his parents who were fed up with his staying up all night and then not being able to get up in the morning to go to school. On those days when he does barely manage to get to school, he sleeps most of the time, then, in turn he stays up all night playing computer games. His grades were suffering and of course the school was very concerned and upset about him. His parents brought him to the session, convinced that he was addicted to computer games. His father was very angry with Peter, and he kept reciting the offensive behaviors that he reports had gotten worse during the previous couple of months. His father alternated between scolding and berating Peter and blaming his mother for doing a poor job of raising the child. The mother did not say much, out of fear that it would escalate the father's frustration. She said that she was afraid that one of these days the father and son might end up in a physical altercation because Peter is getting big.

Peter hardly said a word; his head went lower and lower and it was obvious that he was in a great deal of pain. Realizing that a continuing tirade from his father and silence from his mother was not productive, nor useful, I (IKB) asked the parents to go back into the waiting room and I spoke to Peter alone. As soon as I said to him, "Obviously you have some good reasons to play computer games so much. What are some of your good reasons?" Peter immediately burst into tears and reported that he had been hit by his older brother and his father, who were greatly upset with him. He reported that playing computer games was the only spot in his life where he found a little bit of peace and fun in an otherwise very bleak life.

Peter reported that since his parents set up the appointment three days ago he had started going to school and was trying to concentrate on studying.

He made these changes on his own, and of course we talked quite a bit about his wishes for changes. He agreed to return to the session by himself the following week, with his parents' permission.

After a short consultation break, the therapist first complimented the parents on their patience, their desire to see Peter do better in school, and their faith in him that he can do better in school. Obviously the father was so frustrated because he could see the potential in Peter; even though Peter had not gone to school for weeks, they still had confidence that he could catch up with his schoolwork. Therefore, we asked the parents to keep track of all the little signs they notice that Peter has turned the corner and is beginning to be more like his usual self that he had lost for a while.

When to Get the Parent
and the Child Together

It depends a great deal on how the case is moving, but our general rule is that we are in frequent contact with parents, since they accompany their child for each appointment. It is a good idea to ask the parents to look for successful mastery of exceptions—such as whether the child's temper is under control, when the child is calmer, listens better, or is getting better reports from school and so on—so that the parents feel like they are working together toward improving the child's behavior. So, when to put the parents and the child together? We think it is a good idea to meet together when there are noticeable changes toward the positive directions, both at home and at school. When the family experiences successes, the conversation in the session is more likely to be around what the child and parents are doing to make things go better, and it is easier for the therapist to give credit to both.

Normalizing While Assessing
the Child

When a child seems hesitant and afraid, it is helpful to have the parent in the room with the child. Children need all the reassurance they can get, and even then some children are timid and reluctant to venture too far away from their mothers. It is always important to *normalize* the child's reluctance as a good trait and/or comment on how secure and safe the child feels with mother. Instead of reassuring the child before the child is ready to hear it, a therapist can slow down the process by asking about what special talent the child has, what are some favorite toys, what is he good at, what has he learned to do already, such as counting numbers, recognizing different colors, learning to read, and discerning shapes. Recently I (IKB) was talking to a 5½-year-old boy and I asked him what he was learning in kindergarten—does he know his alphabet, his numbers, and colors and so on? He proudly pointed out that he was learning "math." He was very careful about making sure that I learned his age correctly as "five-and-a-half" when I guessed he was 6 years old. These little traits a child shows us even in these brief interactions can be useful in teaching us the best way to work with the child. For example, in my later conversation with the same little boy, I made sure that I used the word "math" instead of "numbers."

Some children are the opposite of timid and shy. They are excited about seeing everything new, may charge into the room, touching everything, and trying new toys. Some children take things apart and, of course, are unable to put things together again. All these children certainly can be thought to be curious, "shows how bright he/she is," "he is a doer," and can also be "a handful" for parents to keep under control. It is a good idea to test the parents' responses fairly early in the interview to assess how they understand the child's problems, whether the behavior is viewed as a deficit in the child, a willful defiance of the parent, or whether the child is acting against the parent because, for example, "he is angry at me for divorcing his father," as the parent may assert. This is where we begin our intervention because we offer parents and the child ever so slightly different ways to view the child's problem and see how the parents react to our comments. This gives us more clues on how to relate to different parents.

It is easier to assess the parents because they can explain to you what they do and don't want the child to do. Many parents insist on a child's sitting still in a chair like a grown-up and answering all the questions you might ask, while others are indifferent or unable to manage the child's behavior. Others are thoroughly fed up with the child's difficulties, and it is easy to see when a parent is disgusted with the child. You can again normalize the parent's reaction to the child and be sympathetic about his or her difficulties. We find that this is more common with parents of adolescents, because they often have had to deal with the child's problem for many years and also because a teenager is able to criticize or defy parents' authority or wishes more openly and in a more exaggerated manner than can a younger child.

Conflicting Goals

One of the strongest features of SFBT is its insistence on discussing the criteria for termination as the treatment begins. Frequently this is the first serious topic that emerges during the early stages of treatment, especially with parents or caretakers, since it is they who define the child's problem, and are upset or uncomfortable enough to initiate the request for service. Since the discussion of how to negotiate workable goals is covered extensively in Chapter 4 and by many writers in the SFBT field (Davis & Osborn, 2001; DeJong & Berg, 2001b; de Shazer, 1994; Hoyt & Berg, 1998), we will touch only briefly on this topic and limit our discussion to the management of conflicting goals.

It is certainly normal and understandable for parents to believe that once the child's problem is corrected, their lives will become easier to manage. It happens quite often, and we have seen that even a small change in a child can make a remarkable difference in parent's lives. At the same time, most children, especially adolescents, believe that their lives will improve only if their parents change: for example, if mother did not mention the daughter's poor eating habits, did not nag the son for not keeping his curfew, and a host of other conflicting demands for each other. In other words, it is normal for the parent to say that the child needs to change, while the child would state a desire for the parents to change. When we therapists are faced with a provocative and defiant teenager or a parent who has clearly crossed the boundary of not respecting their teen's privacy, it can be difficult to remain objective. If therapists limit their views to who is more responsible for problems, for example, then it is easy to lose objectivity and side with either parent or the child. This would certainly contribute to a loss of credibility with both sides, thus losing one's effectiveness. The teenager may feel "ganged up on" and may not show up for appointments, while the parent may feel blamed and may pull the child out of treatment.

Conflict between the goals of supporting parents and supporting children will occur more often when working with adolescents than with younger children, because younger children are usually not able to articulate their frustrations in as coherent and, at times, hurtful a fashion. Therefore, younger children are more likely to express their frustrations in behavioral ways, such as throwing a tantrum, throwing things, punching others or things, and so on.

CASE EXAMPLE: BATTLE OVER FRIENDS

Heather, age 12½ years, attends a middle school, likes horses, rap music, and of course, her social network of friends, which is the most important thing in her life. Being the youngest of the group of friends she hangs out with, she feels she is well taken care of by them. She came to the first session with her mother upon her family doctor's recommendation, following Heather's two suicide attempts.

Heather (H):   It is very important that I can go out every evening. But my parents don't let me go. They don't understand that this is like breathing to me. I have to go out, otherwise I can't live.

Mother (M):   Please tell the truth, we especially don't like the people you meet; they all drink alcohol and smoke marijuana. They are just not the sort of people we want you to meet and they are a bad influence on you. You were not raised that way.

Therapist (Th):   It would be helpful for me to know what you would like to see come out of this meeting today, mom first, then you, Heather.

M: We want Heather to give up drinking, smoking pot, and to stop threatening us with a knife whenever we don't allow her to go out. She has to stay home. You know, since she started to smoke pot, she has changed so much. It all comes from her smoking that drug. Before she was such a wonderful girl. She listened to us and was helpful around the house.

Th: I see there are several goals to reach. Which one would you consider to be the most important to get started?

M: Heather has to stop smoking pot, of course, right now.

Th: OK, how about you, Heather?

H: I want to go out every evening and not be told when to be back. I want my parents to stop criticizing my friends, and stop carrying on about my smoking pot. You know I hate to live at home. I want to get away, just like my sister did when she was my age. She was in the mental hospital for over a year and I also deserve to have some time off from my parents.

This is a fairly typical situation where both sides seem to have drawn the line in the sand and demand that the other side move first, to the point of the daughter attempting suicide twice. The mother is convinced that her daughter's troubles began with getting mixed up with the wrong friends and of course getting into drug use. Not only is the mother worried that she is losing control over her daughter's choice of friends and activities, but also she feels helpless about what to do about it. The daughter is feeling quite trapped in a situation with her family and sees that the only way to escape from what she perceives to be a prisonlike existence is to either end up in a psychiatric institution like her sister has or take drastic measures like suicide attempts. The only solution that makes sense to her is to break out of this oppressive home.

Viewing both sides' perspectives as valid and understandable is the most useful stance to take. It is important to stay neutral. So far, however, both sides are negotiating about what will be absent from their lives, rather than what will be present in their relationship. As the SFBT approach to therapy prescribes, the presence of a solution, not an absence of problems is the criterion for a good goal. Therefore, this kind of impasse is the beginning of further negotiation in which the goals need to be further and further refined until the two parties can arrive at a consensus on what they really want their

*everyday lives to include. The following segment is the beginning of a negotia-
tion about what both sides want, and what kind of difference these solutions
might make in their relationship. It is important to refocus on the relationship
between the parent and child, thus avoiding assigning blame to either side.
Remember that assigning blame quickly degenerates into conflictual dialogues,
as the following example shows. Notice how the therapist here bypasses assigning blame or discussing past grievances and quickly moves into discussion
about the desired changes in the relationship.*

Th: So let me ask you this question. Suppose you were to stay in one evening
     next week, I don't know how you will do this, but just suppose you did
     that. What difference would that make between you and your parents?
H: I don't know . . . (long pause) Maybe they would give me a little credit
     again.
Th: What will your parents do to show you that they are giving you a little
     credit?
H: Maybe they will let me listen to my music in my room real loud, not
     like right now, I have to listen to my music only using earphones. It's no
     fun.
Th: Suppose they let you listen to your loud music. What difference would
     it make?
H: Not a whole lot.
Th: Say some more about what will be different between you and your
     parents, when you stay in one evening next week.
H: Next morning we would not scream at each other at breakfast.
Th: What will you do instead?
H: I don't know.

*Notice that Heather did not object to the idea of "staying in one evening"
when the therapist introduced the possibility. This is the first shift in the
mother-daughter dialogue, and surprisingly, the daughter is able to entertain
the possibility of staying home one evening a week. This kind of subtle and
incremental shifting of thinking and making small choices takes infinite patience on the part of therapist. As you can see, this small shift in the content
of the conversation slows down the process of blame-defend-counterattack that
has been going on. In fact, when the topic changes, it is often very difficult
to return to the same old blame-attack interactional patterns. A considerable
shift occurs during the next segment of conversation, where the use of scale
is introduced to help clients to assess their own situation.*

Th: Heather, on a scale of 1 to 10, where 1 stands for there is no chance
     and 10 means there is every chance that your parents will let you go out
     every evening, where do you stand right now?

H: 1.

Th: That's pretty bad. What are you going to do about this?

H: I don't know, I just have to go out, I told you that is the only way I can live.

Th: I see that you are in a very difficult situation. Tell me something, although you are on 1 on the scale, there must be a good reason for you to keep fighting with your parents every night?

H: There is no good reason, I'm just desperate. It is so difficult at home.

Th: Well, Mrs. Andrews, how likely is it that you will allow your daughter to go out as she wishes? Again, on the same scale between 1 and 10?

M: She knows us well, it is still just at 1.

Th: Heather just said that she is desperate. Suppose there is something you can do to make her feel just a little bit better, what would that be?

M: I think we should ask her sister and brother to tell her off, about the pot smoking.

Th: Suppose she gives up smoking pot, what difference would it make?

M: All the difference in the world! She would be normal again.

Th: What would be different between the two of you when she is normal again?

M: Well, she will care about school and the grades she is getting, she will listen to us, and not run away.

Th: So, suppose she does all those things, what will be different between the two of you?

M: We used to cook together, and you know, she has a wonderful sense of humor. I like her jokes.

Th: So, that's what you would really like to see happen, that you can cook together again, laugh at her jokes, she can make you laugh, and things like that.

M: Yes, of course!

It took a while to arrive at what mom really wanted, that is, to go back to the "normal" way of doing little things like cooking together, laughing at the same jokes, and so on. A scaling question is used to assess how each was willing to back down from their drawn line and by sidestepping, instead of confronting head on, the mother and daughter were able to find a common goal of being and doing "normal" stuff that they once knew how to do.

We want to point out that this common problem of conflicting goals can be easily negotiated so that they can arrive at a third solution, as the following example shows.

CASE EXAMPLE: BATTLE OVER DOING DISHES

This case involves a single, working mother of five children who initially wanted her 15-year-old son to "just understand" how important it is for him to take his turn washing dishes on the designated evening after school. The son, Nick, also mentioned that he wanted his mother to "understand" his position better so that the outcome would be that he would not have to wash dishes on the evenings when he goes to his dad's house and eats evening meal there. His reasoning was that since he did not dirty any dishes, he should not be made to do as many dishes as other evenings when his turn for the dishes came around.

Therapist (Th):   So suppose Mom understands your feelings about it, your opinions about it, about this issue. What would change?

Nick (N):   I think her reactions toward me, for the future. How she would react; maybe not now, but how she would react a week from now or any time later.

Th: Say some more about how your mom would change.

N: Okay. For example, I get home and I'm just coming from soccer practice and I had school all day and all this other stuff I have to do. If I go over to my dad's, and I didn't use any dishes over at mom's, then I don't think I should have to do any dishes. I didn't dirty the dishes.

Th: Well, you have good logic there. So then once Mom understands that, then what, she will not make you do the dishes on the night that you got to visit your dad?

N: Right. Or we could come to an understanding that I should have less dishes.

Th: (To Nick's mom) What about for you? When Nick understands this, why he must participate in this helping out with the chores, what difference is it going to make for the two of you?

Mom (M):   It will slow down the bickering, you know, back and forth a little bit. "No, it's your turn!" "No, it's not!" And for him to understand that everybody has a turn whether he's gone or not. Home is still home and he may not have eaten on Thursday, but here it is Friday and there's still dishes that have to be done. That's the rotation. The rotation is what it is. If it's his turn he should just do them, whether he was there or not.

Th: So you are interested in less friction in the home.

M: It would make things a little more smoothly.

Even though the dispute between mother and son began as an issue of doing dishes or not doing dishes on Thursday, the therapist was able to listen to both sides of the issue, stayed neutral throughout the conversation, and it turned out that what both ultimately wanted was to have the household "run more smoothly." This is the kind of goal that both sides can easily agree on, since this will benefit both mother and son, and more importantly, there are many different ways to achieve the goal of having the household "run more smoothly." Thus, the issue of doing dishes on Thursday receded into the *background. We would like to point out that had the therapist prematurely made a suggestion for a quick solution, such as getting a dishwasher, or even using disposable paper plates and tableware, mother and son would have missed the opportunity to learn that what the mother really wants is a smooth running household. In addition, had the discussion stayed with the dishwashing issues on Thursday, one or the other side would have felt defeated or have won the debate, which is not a very good long-term solution. This is the kind of situation that could easily trigger another similar dispute, with a different topic next time.*

"What Difference Would it Make Between the Two of You?" or "How Would That be Helpful to You?"

When parent and child have different goals, these kinds of questions are very useful to diffuse both sides, thus making it possible to arrive at the real difference. Whenever there are differences of opinions or options, most people, including parents and children, tend to immediately turn the issue into a "right or wrong" one, instead of accepting the genuine differences that could potentially lead to an alternative solution. In the heat of arguments or intense emotional reactions to issues, it is easy to forget that both parties want some sort of "difference that makes a difference," and not just a recycling of old issues. Notice here we are paying attention to the relationship, that is, the space between people, not one right or wrong party, but we are interested in the relationship "between" the parent and the child. It is important to remember that we are not interested in solving the internal psychological issues of either parent or the child, but the quality of the relationship between two people who care about each other. This kind of nonblaming stance allows room for the parent and child to think of ways to benefit both sides, not fight a win-lose battle.

Again, notice the phrase "How would that be helpful to you?" assumes that whatever the client (parent or child) is trying to do is something that is helpful to the other person or to herself or himself, and the therapist is interested in finding out the HOW part of help the client is seeking. Again, this is very different than asking "why" questions which often can be interpreted as blaming or fault-finding, thus triggering immediately defensive responses.

In the following case example, we describe at length how one can negotiate the treatment goal even with a mother who is very frustrated with her inability to feel that she is a good mother. Rather than being put off by a parent who feels hopeless about her child, the therapist pursues and negotiates the goal with both mother and the child in the same room, balancing the adult's need to talk and a child's need to discuss her alternative ways to solve problems.

CASE EXAMPLE: FAST AS A MARMOT

Sarah, age 8, was described as a child with "terrible" behavior problems at home and at school. After an explanation about what to expect, I (TS) tried to learn what her mother (Mrs. Heinz) desired as the outcome for the session.

Therapist (Th):   What needs to happen today so that you can say it's been worthwhile for you to come here?

Mother (M):   You know, Sarah is just terrible; she never listens to me or the teacher. She is a very naughty girl. Even as a baby, she could never be quiet; she was restless and made me feel like I could never please her; she made me feel like I'm a bad mother. She cried all the time and when her younger sister came along, she started to torment her little baby sister.

Th: I understand that you want to be a good mother to Sarah and it's not been easy and you want Sarah to listen to you.

M: That's right, it's been hell; she is ruining my life with her stubbornness, and now my boyfriend wants to leave us because he can't take any more of her stubbornness. She's had a sleeping problem for a long time, and she is allergic to several things. I am always taking her to the doctor; now he says her tonsils have to come out because she is always catching a cold. Schools says she is good at reading but hopeless in math; she can't remember the numbers and multiplication, even if I practice with her for hours.

Th: OK, let me understand the information you have given me so far. From what I understand, Sarah was a very active baby, not easy to please. She is a strong-willed child with lots of ideas and she is having problems with math and multiplication in school. I also heard that you want to be a good mother, and you spend many hours trying to help her learn. She has some allergic reactions and may face tonsillectomy. Wow, what a list of information in such a short time. It is very helpful to have parents who know how to observe their children carefully, and I can tell you that it will be very helpful for me because it is important to notice small things. Tell me, what difference will it make when Sarah starts to listen to you? We don't know yet how she will do that, but just suppose she does.

M: She will make me feel good, I would know she appreciates me as a mother. You know, I'm working so hard in order to be able to offer my kids good things that I didn't have as a kid.

Th: Tell me a little bit more about what will happen between the two of you.

M: I will smile more at her and I will joke with her as I do with the baby.

Th: What would Sarah do differently then?

M: I'm sure she will be less jealous and stop teasing her sister.

Th: What else?

M: *Maybe she would have more self-confidence. You know, she has very little self- confidence. But no wonder, she always messes up situations and never does what she is told.*

By the therapist's careful choice of what to pay attention to and what to ignore, the mother was able to think about how she wanted her difficult situation with Sarah to change. Surprisingly, she had some concrete ideas of what will happen to her and Sarah, including some connection between mother's smiling more and Sarah's improved self-confidence. If the mother was alone in the room, of course one could continue with her vision of change, including her answer to miracle questions. When working with a child, however, it is important to bridge what the parent wants with how the child makes sense of what mother is talking about, and this bridge building can be accomplished by having the child visualize the solution. Also the visualized solution must be important to the child as well, not only to the mother.

Th: *Sarah, I'm going to ask you and Mom a very special question, a question that needs some imagination. Look at this magic wand. Imagine you go home with your mom and there you do whatever you have to do, maybe meet your girlfriend, do your homework, like you do every evening. Then in the evening, you have dinner and then go to bed. . . . While you are sleeping a magic event happens because of this magic wand and the problems that brought Mom and you to see me today are gone, poof . . . just like that. But because you are sleeping nobody knows this has happened during the night. Tomorrow morning as you wake up, what will be the first little sign that this magic wand worked?*
Sarah (S):   *I don't know.*
M: *Don't be silly, you are just too lazy to think.*
Th: *I told you it was a special question. It is quite normal not to know and you will have some time to think about it. Even grown-up people do need some time to think about it.*
S: *I would have my red pullover on my bed and I want it so much.*
Th: *What else?*
S: *My sister would feed the guinea pig for me and then we would have breakfast together.*
Th: *What else?*
S: *Mom would not force me to eat toast and butter, maybe I will just drink my milk.*
Th: *Tell me, Sarah, when you find the red pullover on your bed, find out that your sister fed the guinea pig, what will you be doing then?*
S: *I will know Mom likes me and I will not have my bad temper.*
Th: *What will you have instead?*
S: *I will be in a good mood.*

Th: *Wow, will you? Tell me, what are you doing when you are in a good mood?*

S: *I'd laugh. I like to play with my sister and sometimes I do what Mom tells me.*

Th: *Tell me, how will the breakfast be different when you are in a good mood?*

S: *I don't know, maybe not shouting. And Mom's friend will not nag at me.*

Th: *What about later in the day, how will you find out the magic happened?*

S: *The children at school will play with me and I will be good at numbers. I want to have a girl friend at school, like the other kids have, but nobody wants to play with me.*

Sarah further described her miracle as involving exchanging Pokemon cards with other children, playing games with Annie and Becky after the lunch hour, and her teacher not constantly telling her to concentrate. After commenting on Sarah's ability to answer such difficult questions, the therapist excused Sarah to go and look at some of the other toys in the room while she talked to her mom next. Mrs. Heinz's miracle was: Sarah would get up on her own, wash herself, and feed the guinea pig without any arguments. The mother explained that she herself would be calmer in the morning, and therefore, would not need to smoke to calm herself down; breakfast would be peaceful, and she would kiss Sarah good-bye before she goes to school. Sarah would listen to her and would be willing to do her chores like putting away the dishes from the dishwasher, tidying up her own room, and so on. The therapist then invites Sarah to join her again in the talking area.

Th: *You just heard how your mom will find out the miracle has happened. The most important thing for Mom is that you will listen to her and you will do the things that she asks you to do. What I heard from you is that you want to be in a good mood and have friends. Here, I have a basket of animals. (Therapist spreads out the animals on the floor and sits together with Sarah.) Suppose you were one of these animals. You are a good listener, and very quick and you do things right, and you are in good mood most of the time. Which animal would go best with that?*

Sarah starts to take the different puppets in her hand, then tries to make the decision; clearly she likes the horse.

Th: *It looks like the horse could be the one. Tell me a little bit about horses.*

S: *You know I have a horse named Blackey and I go horseback riding every week. He listens to me very well, he really makes me feel good. But actually he is not fast at all. No, I don't think that's it.*

Th: Okay, have another look. Maybe you will find an animal you like better.

M: She never can make up her mind; she is very slow.

Th: You are right she takes her time, but to me it seems that she has been
       listening carefully because she wants to make sure that she finds an animal
       that is quick and listens well.

S: I think I got it! I would take the marmot. You know, last summer we
       went to the mountains for our vacation and we saw them there. They
       always watch out, listen to any sound. If there is something they don't
       know, they whistle and then run into the next hole. Yes, that's it. They
       are very good listeners and so fast. And you know, they are in good moods,
       too, because they have time to lay in the sun, just doing nothing, and I
       watched how they play with their friends. I think they have a good life.

Th: That seems like a good choice. Let's put back all the other animals in
       the basket and then you may put the marmot on your hand. I want to have
       a little chat with it.

Sarah followed the direction as she was told.

Th: (Addressing the puppet) What is your name?

Marmot (Sarah):   My name is Tommy.

Th: That's a nice name. How old are you?

Marmot (S):   Nine.

Th: Do you know Sarah? Sarah has just picked you out of all the animals,
       do you know why?

Marmot (S):   Of course I know. Because I can listen very carefully, I am
       quick and I care about sisters and brothers. Because whenever I whistle,
       everybody knows danger is around and they can go to a safe place. I like
       to be helpful.

Th: Wow, you really seem to be a good animal. And ever so helpful. Tell
       me, Tommy, how did you learn all this?

Marmot (S):   Hmm . . . I don't know. It's a secret. It was hard.

Th: Yeah, I suppose is, but it seems you made it.

Marmot (S):   Yes, Mom says I am the quickest child she has. She is very
       proud of me.

Th: Do you think Sarah could be a little bit like you?

Marmot (S):   I don't know . . . it is hard . . .

After the therapist explored the times when Sarah already was attentive and
fast like a marmot, it was time to take a short thinking break and come back
to mother and daughter with some feedback about what the therapist had
observed from her interactions with them. After complimenting Sarah for
working so hard during the session, the therapist told her how impressed she
was with her imagination. The therapist also complimented the mother on

having such a creative and cooperative child who can express herself so well, especially considering her age. The therapist also told Sarah's mother how she can see that she is working very hard to make Sarah's life better and it is clear that she really wants what is best for her child. The following is the suggestion to the mother and daughter:

Th: *Sarah, it seems to me you could make a big difference when you become a little bit like Tommy. As Tommy said, it will take lots of hard work. So, between now and next time we see each other, I suggest that you get to know Tommy as well as you can. You may find out a lot about marmots and how they manage to enjoy life and at the same time be so attentive and fast. Mrs. Heinz, I would like you to carefully notice when, where, and how Sarah behaves a little bit like a marmot. And, as I realized at the beginning of the session how good an observer you are, I'm sure you will even notice a change after only a few minutes when Tommy is around the house.*

It was Sarah who came up with the idea that she will listen carefully, enjoy a good life, and have friends like a marmot does. She was creative and smart enough to have found an animal that combined both her mother's wishes and her own and came up with a marmot. To behave like Tommy is definitely a different and easier way to think about achieving her goal than turning a naughty girl into an obedient one, as the mother has been trying so hard to do without success.

Again, rather than feeling like we are forced to choose between helping parents get what they want for the children and siding with the child, through negotiation, the therapist was able to combine what both wanted and thus came up with a helpful task that is new to both. We believe this is the first small building block toward constructing a different future.

NETWORKING WITH
OTHER PROFESSIONALS

A number of experts are often involved in helping children who need special solutions. Phone calls, e-mails, and in-person conferences often may be necessary. Generally, working with children means coordinating various professionals' activities so that everybody does not confuse already overwhelmed parents and the child. Thus, therapy may be more labor-intensive in this sense and often takes longer than working with adults for a variety of reasons. When networking with other professionals, it is very likely that most of those you will encounter will be coming from the "problem-solving" framework. Therefore, they will likely look for and assess problems first. The following are some important points to remember.

1. *Be sure to keep in mind your goal with the child and parents.* Your goal becomes the guiding principle for how to stay focused on doing what is best for the child and the parents. It is very easy to become distracted from the goal, and the conversation can easily degenerate into problem talk about the child or complaints about parents. Neither of these are very productive.

    If you are attending a meeting of professionals, always ask about the purpose of the meeting and remind the others gently if the conversation becomes negative. For example, a chair of the meeting might say that the purpose of the meeting is to express "concerns" about the child's behavior. As you would do with parents and other caretakers, it is always helpful to ask for further clarification of how such expressions of concern would be helpful for the child. In one such meeting with the school, the child's teacher finally expressed her idea that the mother and her live-in boyfriend should go to therapy themselves and that the child should be placed in a foster home. Of course the mother became very offended and immediately began to blame the teacher, saying that the teacher did not know how to teach and manage her class.

2. *Reframing as a useful tool.* When you are faced with such tight situations, reframing their hidden positive motivation as an effort to help the child is very useful. In the previous case example, therapist immediately began to say that it was apparent that they all thought about what is best for the child and want the best chance for the child to succeed in school, and it would be worthwhile to investigate which approach might be the most useful. The adults began to calm down and became refocused on the goal of the meeting.

3. *Always compliment other professionals and always give the credit to someone else.* Nagging parents or teachers can be easily complimented on their good observations, on their interest in seeing the child succeed, and ensuring that the child has a good future. If the child begins to do better since starting therapy with you, you can always give the credit to the parent and the teacher for having laid all the important foundations for the child to finally bloom. We can say that what we have done is to give the child a chance to show how she or he learned from the parent or the teacher.

    Whenever parents report to you that their child came home

from school and told them what was enjoyable about school that day, such as certain art class activities, learning new music, learning to swim, or seeing a video in class, make sure you suggest that the parent contact the teacher and to share the good news their child brought home. By giving the teacher this positive feedback, the parent is influencing positive interaction between the teacher and the child. Teacher recognizes that the child is not always complaining about school, but the child is showing interest and paying attention to what she or he is learning and the parent is paying attention to the child's learning and how effective the teacher is already.

4. *Summarize and periodically remind the child of the professionals' good intentions.* Also repeat and summarize the child's strengths and successes periodically during the meeting.

5. *Make liberal use of tentative language.* This will increase your chances of being heard and elicit cooperation from others. Examples of tentative language are: "It seems . . . " "It sounds like what you really want is . . . " "I wonder . . "Perhaps . . . " Could it be. . . . "

Chapter 6

Communicating with Children on Their Own Terms

SINCE CHILDREN COMMUNICATE THROUGH ACTIONS, VISUAL IMAGES, PLAY-
ing, games, and many other creative activities, we devote this chapter
to the variety of ways the therapist can utilize to unleash these resources
that children have. You will notice that all the activities are designed
to enhance the children's sense of competence, expression of their will,
offering choices, and, most of all, giving them a sense of control over
their environment. The ultimate goal is to empower them so that they
will feel successful, confident, and have a sense of mastery—all of
which makes the child more in control of his or her life. We want to
describe some equipment and materials that we have found most helpful when communicating with children.

PROVIDE A COMFORTABLE SETTING

Ideally every therapist would like to have the nice setting and all the
equipment we will list here, but these are not absolute necessities. Keep
in mind that the toys children seem to like the most are the ones that
allow them to create things themselves. For example, I (IKB) remember
the best toys my daughter had when she was young were the very
large cardboard boxes that I got for free from our neighborhood appliance store. I usually brought the box into my house and placed it in
the family room, and then we would cut out the door and windows
and decorate it with crayon and magic markers to look like a house.
I placed a used blanket on the bottom and draped an old sheet or worn
out blanket over it, and it became a secret hiding place, with a "Do

Not Enter" sign posted in the front. Lots of neighborhood children would come over and play in it for hours, day after day. When "the house" got worn down, it was time to go to the appliance store and get a new one.

A Word About Toys

By design, I (TS) have only a few toys. I prefer to have unstructured materials that help me to enter a child's specific world. For example, I have a plentiful supply of cloth, construction paper, and colored felt tip pens. The cloth can become a river; one can create a Pokemon out of it, use it as the veil of a fairy princess, or a crown for a king or a queen. The material you select to have around must serve a specific purpose—that is, to enhance your communication with the child. Undefined material allows a child's creativity to emerge, unlike, for example, those plastic action figure toys with which children may become easily bored.

Using undefined material means children will be creative and construct their own toys. Most children are proud of what they have come up with and want to show it to their parents and other important people. I keep an instant camera handy so I can take a picture of children's creations that they can take home to show to others. I believe this step helps to build a bridge to the next session we meet, as well as to the family.

Quite often I (TS) volunteer at a refugee center near my office. It is designed to serve refugees primarily from former Eastern Bloc countries, and, because of a lack of adequate space at the center, the director's office doubles as our children's group room. I usually bring along some balloons, colored magic markers, crayons, some construction paper and a small ball tucked in my carry-all bag. As we will describe here, even these few items can serve quite nicely in working with children.

Obviously your office needs to be comfortable for children of all ages; this means you should have enough space for children to move around when they need to, for those children who are active or like to get down on the floor. (Note: We also met parents who do not allow children to get down on the floor. It is important to respect these rules parents have for their children.) It goes without saying that your office should be easy to clean up after a day's use, and ideally it is nice to have windows so that children can listen to birds, look out at the sky or clouds, and even flowers and trees, if they wish. However, these amenities are not essential to a good therapy session. Since children's attention spans are much shorter than those of adults, it is helpful to have a variety of potential material for activities available.

A rather large room can be divided into three distinct areas: a talking area with comfortable chairs; a play area around the bed; and an activity area around a table. The talking area has a normal adult table with six chairs and a little table with four little stools, designed for young children. Children are always given the choice of which table they want to use, and some children insist on sitting at a large table to show how strong or big they are, even though it is a struggle. A "play area" is located on the table and it has drawing paper, colored pencils, scotch tape, and blunt scissors. When dealing with very young children, each area can be designated as "play land," "doing land," and "talking land" and I may lead a young child by the hand and move from one area to another. I find it helpful to have clear, visible, and separate areas, not only because toys can be kept out of the talking area, but also because this kind of separation elicits such nice cooperation even from very young children.

Secret Hiding Place

In one corner of my office I have an inexpensive bunk bed. The top part of the bed has a mattress on it but I took out the bottom half of the bed and placed a cushion on the floor on which a child can sit down. I made a little curtain that parts in the middle of the front of the lower half of the bunk bed, and this area becomes a secret hiding place if a child wants to go in there and hide while I talk to the parents. Some children who are not sure about participating in the session find comfort when they can hide while they listen to the adults talk about them (mostly good and positive things) and they have control over when they are ready to come out and become visible again. Beside the bed there is a doll house, a stable with wooden animals, a basket with colored wooden blocks, a basket with animal hand puppets, and two standing coat hangers with other puppets.

Because I sometimes meet with the family separately, there is a second room, much smaller than the one described above. In it I have sand, a dart game, and some children's books. Other items that are not essential but nice to have available are:

- *Writing or white board.* A fairly good size writing or white board that can be easily erased is very useful for the child to scribble (will be described later), or draw pictures. This white board should be hung on the wall low enough so that even small children can reach it, even while sitting down.
- *A large message board.* I have a large message board made of cork on one wall. Children are asked whether they want to leave the

pictures they draw in my room or take them home. Many children choose to leave the drawings in my office so that when they return, they can continue to work on them, or change the pictures. Some children choose to take them home and then decide to hang them up either in their own bedroom or on the family refrigerator.

- *Couch and some comfortable chairs.* A sturdy couch or sofa and 2 or 3 comfortable chairs where the parents can sit is necessary. Some young children may decide to sit on their mother's lap initially until they become comfortable with the surroundings.

Children and Eye Contact

Recognizing that young children have boundless energy and need to move around or fidget a great deal, even in the "talking land" it is a good idea to keep little things available that children can fiddle with in their hands, especially while they are talking. Even adults find that the most natural and comfortable way to discuss serious topics is not to make or maintain eye contact, but to sit side by side, or perhaps go for a walk. This is the reason the most intimate conversations occur while couples drive in a car or look at the distant view while sitting on the porch. Therefore, do not expect young children to maintain eye contact. They usually look down at their shoes, their hands, or even the floor. This is also true of adolescents. It is more helpful to take a walk together with adolescents and do what we call "walking and talking." Teenagers feel more comfortable walking around while thinking about some difficult questions they are often asked.

Ringing Phones

It is certainly nice to have the luxury of an assistant who answers all your phone calls, but, I (TS) do not have such an assistant, so the phones are answered by voice mail. However, many children are very surprised when I do not answer the phone during the session and some even insist that I do. It is amazing to see the expressions on their face, realizing that they have not received such undivided attention from too many adults.

CHILDREN AS SOLUTION FINDERS

A colleague of ours, Brian Morgan, tells this story of how he was inspired when faced with the task of talking to fifth graders about mental health issues during national mental health week. Brian was the director of the local community mental health center at the time, and he had a friend who taught fifth grade. Knowing that Brian was active in the community, this teacher friend invited Brian to talk to her class about what mental health is, why it is important for children to understand mental health issues, and how to become mentally healthy.

At first Brian panicked. How do you explain what mental health is to fifth graders? "Such a complex and complicated concept," he thought, and wondered how he was going to connect with a classroom full of 10- or 11-year-old children. Then he remembered that he was learning about the solution-focused approach at the time, and he began to wonder how he could incorporate things that the children were familiar with to teach his lesson. They all lived in a beautiful rural area of northern Washington State where mountains, apple orchards, and horse breeding are all very well known. By observing these surroundings, Brian became inspired and felt he now knew how to approach the children about mental health: with something they knew well and at which they were good.

Brian introduced his talk by explaining to the children that he was going to ask them about something they were very good at and knew how to do. Of course they were very curious, so he had their full attention. Brian asked the curious children how many of them had cats, dogs, or horses, and of course all the children's hands went up in the air. Then he asked how they know when these animals do not feel well, since the animals don't know how to talk. Hands began to go up and the children began to describe how they can tell by looking at them whether they were thirsty, tired, sick, happy or sad, glad to see the children, and so on. Brian asked the class who could come up to the front and show the class how these animals looked when they were thirsty, hungry, tired, sad, or happy. Some children used their entire body and facial expressions, while some others in the audience would instruct the volunteers to change their posture, stance, hand and leg positions, and facial expressions, until they got it just right. When the class was satisfied, Brian asked the class to describe what they did to help the animals that did not feel well. Of course he was properly impressed with the children's knowledge of animals and, being a rather outgoing person, he hammed it up a bit. The children loved him as much as he loved them. Then he encouraged the children to describe how they took care of those animals that did not feel well. They all had lots of ideas about what they would do to take care of the animals when they were ill, thirsty, hungry, hurt, or unhappy.

Next he moved on to the topic of the plants, flowers, trees, vegetables, or flowers their parents raised in their gardens. Again, the children had lots of ideas and a variety of remedies for sick plants, trees, flowers, and so on, including the use of nitrogen and other chemicals in fertilizers that Brian was not even familiar with.

Next Brian asked the class how they could tell when their friends were not feeling well physically and emotionally. Some children volunteered to be the child "not feeling good inside" and the class again assisted "the child in need," making suggestions for gestures, facial expressions, and postures. The children were very involved in the topic and also were so enthusiastic about showing how much they knew, describing their many ideas of how to help when their friends were sad, upset, angry, lonely, or did not have friends.

This topic was extended to include their family members, neighbors, and relatives. The teacher herself enjoyed the hour very much and invited Brian to return for another discussion session the following week. Brian eventually returned three more times and got into discussing the techniques of how to help their friends, including allowing the children to show each other and Brian how they listened to those friends who needed special help. Brian reported how impressed he was with these fifth graders' sensitivity, ability to listen to what the others were saying, and thoughtfulness.

The teacher was so impressed with her own classroom of children that she later made a special arrangement for Brian to visit the class once a week for an hour during the entire semester. We, just like Brian, are convinced that children have the intuitive knowledge and ability to empathize with those in trouble. Once we respect their abilities, their knowledge, and things they care about in a respectful way, these intuitive capacities can be elicited.

Playing, moving around, talking about what they know best and what they are familiar with is the primary way that children communicate. When they are asked to show how much they know about their surroundings, most children behave as did the children in the class that Brian met. Therefore, it makes sense to utilize visual images, both creating and changing from one picture to another, to build bridges between the children's world and the adult's. This also fits very nicely with the solution-focused philosophy to view all clients, including children, in the same manner. Some of the techniques we will describe in this chapter we learned from the children who needed our help, some other techniques we heard about, some we experimented with, and some were inspired by reading children's stories and folk tales.

We are convinced that you, too, will discover, in some very personal ways, how to develop your own techniques once you become familiar with the principles behind the solution-building thinking. There are, in fact, no limits to your imagination and creativity. The examples in this chapter are intended to help you begin experimenting with various techniques.

NAMING AND VISUALIZING
THE CHANGE

A few years ago, the museum of ethnology in Zurich had an exhibit showing photographs of the ordinary, everyday lives of children of all ages from all over the world. What was unusual about this exhibit was that all the photographs were taken by children. I (TS) was deeply touched by what the children chose to show other children and adults, and what they thought was important to them. The exhibit inspired me to make the connection with the children I see in my office day in and day out. It occurred to me that pictures are a very good way to remind the children of what is good about their lives. The use of pictures also helps children focus on making their visual images more vivid through pictures so that they can be reminded of their own dreams and hopes for themselves.

As you will notice in the following sections, it is always helpful for a child to have a name for a solution, and this is followed up with some concrete idea of how the change from problem to solution will occur. The name and the picture of how the change will occur have to be meaningful to the child's life and make sense to him or her. The solution should also take into account what the important adult in the child's life values as an important goal. This helps to turn an abstract word, concept, or expression into something the child can grasp in a concrete way. Listen to how individual and personal these images are for each child.

As soon as the goal becomes clear during the first session, the therapist can invite the child to come up with figures, animals, events in nature, sports, movies, or well-known children's story characters, that would characterize the desirable change.

For example, most children between the ages of 7 and 10 can easily answer when asked to pick an animal that represents themselves, their problems, or the desired state they would reach when they change their life. We find that most children can respond easily to this and really become involved in the transforming process in a very personal and individual way. As a therapist you can help the child find an animal that matches what is "normal" to him, as the following dialogue illustrates.

CASE EXAMPLE: FINDING THE RIGHT "FIT"

Mathew gets into lots of difficulties at school and at home. In spite of the teacher's constant reprimand, he moves around a great deal, cracks jokes, and makes faces that cause other children to giggle. Mathew is described as hyperactive.

Mathew (M):   When I am the class clown I behave like a monkey I have seen in the zoo. When I am quiet and concentrate on my work, people tell me that I am normal.

Therapist (Th):   What animal would you say is most like you when you are normal?

M: A sloth, because these animals move very slowly and they are quiet.

Th: Do I hear you right? A sloth is most like you, a normal animal?

M: No, that's not it. It's the opposite of a monkey. Like me, just like me, normal, normal, well, a normal animal is a cat or a dog.

Th: Which would you prefer, a cat or a dog?

M: A cat.

Th: A cat is normal in what way?

M: Well they sleep, they sometimes jump around, they can be very concentrated when they are catching a mouse. To me they can do all the different things that are needed.

Th: That could mean it would be helpful if you could turn from a monkey to a cat? Is this the thing to do?

M: Yeah, then I would be like most of my friends, you know, just like everybody.

It is amazing how well Mathew was able to figure things out in his mind and express his thoughts clearly, thus describing how he saw his difficulties. He was very aware of his difficulties with friends and recognized that he is different from other children. Being an only child, he needed some help to fit into a social group and to be viewed as "normal." Mathew lives in a rural area where cats and dogs are very common. To become like a cat really meant to cope with the feeling of being average, and not to stand out.

Shantele, 7 years old, is very shy and afraid of recess at school because of big boys who constantly tease her and make fun of her. She initially described herself as a little mouse and wanted to become a very courageous tiger. Tigers were important to her, because she said she had recently seen a movie about tigers in Africa.

Brad, 9 years old, was referred because of his aggressive behaviors toward his siblings at home and other children at school. According to his teacher, he did not follow rules at all, and was always disorganized, losing his home-

work, his pencils, notebooks, shoes; he just didn't know how to plan his work. Even though I spent some time with Brad, he seemed to be having a hard time finding any way to articulate his visual images with animals. So, I took the basket of hand puppets of animals and we sat down on the floor together. He still had trouble choosing any animal that he thought represented what he wanted to become. Based on what I had observed in the time I worked with him, it occurred to me that Brad did much better when he had an opportunity to touch things. Therefore, I asked Brad to take each puppet in his hand, feel the texture of the cloth, and take his time. That helped! After some time he decided to turn from a stingray to an owl. What was interesting about working with Brad was that the stingray puppet was made of slippery material, while the owl puppet was made of fur and feathers. In this case I was sure the difference in the tactile sensation between the two puppets was most important. To Brad, changing from a stingray to an owl meant turning from something slippery and cold to something smooth and warm.

Brittany, a 10-year-old, wanted to become more relaxed and friendly with others instead of bursting out frequently in a bad temper. I met her soon after the Fourth of July holiday, when watching fireworks in the park was very popular. Brittany explained her thinking in the following way: "I want to turn from a volcano to a sun. The fireworks called volcano make quite a noise and 'spit' out sparks. The sun is less spectacular but very pleasant to look at, like a big red ball." She came up with this idea from her recent experience, and it was obvious the volcano and the sun were quite meaningful to her.

Betty, a 15-year-old teenager, said that she would like to turn her relationship with her mother into "a rubber twist game." To her, playing the rubber twist game was connected with being very flexible and having fun.

Claudio, a 12-year-old boy, was considered to be at a high risk of dropping out of school, in part because he was afraid of the other children who were older, bigger, and had more friends. His idea was to change from a blue Chevy into a red Ferrari. He explained that the Ferrari has many gears, can speed up very quickly, and is admired by everybody whenever he cruises by.

Some children can easily find a visual image, while others need some help. The help a therapist provides is to name categories of symbols which might be meaningful to the child. Likely categories include: animals, sports, games, movie stars, rock stars, star athletes, characters from stories, motorcycles, cars, and cartoon characters.

Many beginning clinicians wonder whether it makes a difference which way the child imagines the changing process—for example, changing from a mouse into a tiger, or changing into a tamed tiger from a wild one. But it does not seem to make a great deal of difference how the imaginative change occurs as long as children can identify the changes taking place. Our impression is that most children like to think of an obvious and dramatic change; therefore, you may hear from children that they visualize changing from one species into another, either from a ferocious, brute force into a gentle, loving one—a scared mouse into a brave tiger or very fast rabbit.

We believe it is important to accept the child's vision, imagination, and wishes. Even if a therapist's personal preference is a mouse, a tiger, a cat, or a dog, it is important to accept the personal and unique meaning the choice of animal has for each child.

Younger Children

Children at the age of kindergarten or younger often need more direction and guidance than older children. It is best to make the suggestions to young children in a tentative language so that they can reject or change it to fit their ideas, as the following examples show. We want to emphasize how important it is that your tone of voice, inflections, and other linguistic techniques convey your sincere wish to elicit the child's responses and that you are not imposing your own views. Puppets that move are very useful when working with younger children. For example, a therapist can make a little crocodile puppet that stands on a stick with a little home-made cage made out of lightweight cardboard. The crocodile can pop out of its little cage that sits in the middle of the stick, and a child or the therapist can hold up the stick to indicate an animal is hiding in a cage. The following is the dialogue a therapist can carry on while using the crocodile puppet on a stick.

T: It sounds like you have an anger-crocodile at home. And this crocodile comes out of the cage whenever it decides to become angry. What do you think?

Child (nods her head): Uumm.

T: Is that right? This crocodile has to be tamed and has to start to listen to you, Shannon!

At other times, you may get the impression that the child strikes you as a little turtle. A therapist might take the turtle puppet in hand and say:

T: To me it sounds like you are like this turtle when you get scared of other big boys. And her head sticks out only once in a while. It seems like it would make a difference when the turtle poked her head out a little bit and started to look around.

Having acted out the steps of sticking her head out a little with a turtle puppet, you can hand this puppet to the child to experiment with. Soon the child is able to start taking the role of the turtle and giving it his or her own voice.

WORKING WITH HAND PUPPETS

Hand puppets are very helpful tools to initiate and carry on conversations with children because they make it easier to visualize situations. They also assist the therapist in talking to the children throughout the treatment process. Using puppets is similar to helping a child enter into a fantasy world and reach a state of dissociation, but always under the child's control.

When you work with hand puppets, you must remember one thing: Once either you or the child has a puppet on your hand, the puppet becomes your conversation partner. Once you take on the persona of the puppet, look at the puppet, react to the puppet's movements, talk to the puppet and not to the child. This is very important because it helps children to stay in the role of the animal they chose at a safe distance from themselves, while at the same time experiencing parts of their own behavior or the behavior they will strive for in the future.

The following questions might generate some useful conversation with the puppet:

- What is your name? How old are you?
- Do you have friends? What are their names?
- What do you like to do? What is your favorite game?
- Where is your favorite place to stay?
- What are you good at?
- What is your favorite food?

In a case where the chosen animal is a turtle, you might ask:

- What is the good reason to hide your head under your shell?
- How do you find out it is time to pop out your head again?
- How do you know the right time has come to hide in the shell?

If the child has chosen two animals, make sure you talk with both of them. In the case of Brad, whom we met before, this becomes more clear as we continue our conversation.

T: Hello! Wow, what wonderful colors you have!

Stingray (Brad):   Isn't it beautiful? I have gray with blue spots on my back, and yellow on my stomach. But you did not say anything about my tail. I have a very powerful tail. I can keep all my enemies away with it. Look at this. (Brad swings the tail of the stingray toward me.)

T: Oh, your tail scares me! How do you know it is time to use it?

Stingray: That's easy, most of the time I use my tail when I get bothered by fishes when they make too much noise, when they come too close, when they don't want to play what I want to play, and especially when they tell lies to the grown-ups, and I get told off afterward, even if I haven't done anything wrong!

T: It seems with your tail you try to make your life easier for yourself, more like the way you would like it. Does it work?

Stingray: Sometimes yes, but not really. They say I am a very dangerous animal, everybody stays away from me and I have nobody to play with. That's boring. Nobody likes me! I would like to be appreciated like my brother. But I am proud, and I am so strong!

T: I see. So you like to be strong, you like it better; when it is quiet, you would like to play with others and you like to be appreciated by the grown-ups. By the way, there is another animal here, and his name is Henry. Did you know him?

Stingray: Yes, I know, but I have never spoken with him, I don't want to talk to a weak owl.

T: That's OK, I will now talk to the owl. Maybe you can wait a moment? Maybe I will be right back!

I ask Brad to put down the stingray, and put on the owl puppet.

T: Hello, good afternoon. I see you have your eyes wide open. Can you see well?

Owl: Not too good right now, but at night I can see every little animal on the ground. That's good to catch mice, you know.

T: I see, and what a wonderful feather coat you have, all in white.

Owl: I am not any ordinary owl, I belong to a very special breed.

T: Tell me, what are you good at?

Owl: You know I can sit very quietly without moving, I can observe carefully, people ask my opinion because I am very clever.

T: That means other animals can come and see you and ask you questions. Do they also play with you?

Owl: Of course they do, because I give good advice, everybody likes me.

T: It sounds like your life is pretty good. Do you know Brad? He also tries to have a good life. But at the moment he is not very successful. He is a stingray with a very strong tail and he needs to straighten up his life, but it doesn't seem to work too well. Do you know the stingray?

Owl: This idiot? He always messes up the situations. The only thing he knows is to beat up everybody with his tail.

T: It sounds like you don't think very much of the stingray.

Owl: No, I don't like him.

T: How would you do it?

Owl: I told you, observe carefully and be friendly.

T: You mean you could be more successful that way?

Owl: Oh, for sure.

T: That sounds interesting, You know, Brad is in a difficult situation. The teacher tells him off at school, and at home there is one big fight. But tell me, do you think the way the stingray is doing things is not appropriate?

Owl: I don't know.

T: Have you ever talked to the stingray?

Owl: No, why should I?

T: Well I just thought, in fact, you both want the same thing: to have a good life. You do it differently, though.

Owl: Hmm . . .

T: I think the way you do it would please the parents and the teacher. It seems to me the stingray just shows how angry and bothered Brad sometimes is. The part with the tail may be helpful to get rid of the anger, but you are right, it puts Henry into difficult and messy situations.

It is very obvious that Brad moves in and out of the roles as he plays with puppets, and he soon slides out of the dissociation when he says:

Brad: Yes, I have a big anger!

The therapist asks Brad to put the stingray on one hand, and the owl on the other hand. Then the therapist speaks to both of them:

T: Did you hear that? It sounds as if Brad would like to become a careful observer, friendly, have friends to play with, but also has to get rid of a huge anger. Would it be possible that you two could talk to one another: as you, owl, are good at observing, being gentle and so on, and you, stingray, are good at getting rid of anger. Maybe you could come up with a very good idea between now and the next time we meet.

We hope this dialogue gives you a good idea of how to work with hand puppets, building toward solutions that children generate.

STORIES

Most children love stories. In many ways, stories are a good way to communicate with both adults and children. Children like to hear about other persons, animals, toys, or any creatures that experience events, difficulties, and triumphs over struggles similar to what they have to deal with. Children find it fascinating to hear how much pain or inconvenience the hero of the story has to go through to find solutions. Yet, it is nice to enjoy the difficulties and successes from a safe distance. Telling and listening to a story together is a very intimate experience—sharing fantasies, dreams, and many other human emotions while learning about life together.

There are differences in the level of intimacy you may want to manage, depending on the level of intimacy the child wishes, needs, and can handle. For example, rather than reading a story out of a book, you can tell the same story from memory, with different animated gestures, changes in voice inflection, and postures in order to help children to be in a certain frame of mind that allows them to create their own visual images. It is also very helpful to tell the stories sitting side by side with the child, or even touching or hold the child, as most parents discovered long ago.

Children between ages 11 and 14, however, often prefer to draw pictures or scribbles while listening to stories. Many children this age and older seem to listen best and concentrate better while they are engaged in doodling or keep their hands busy doing repetitive activities.

Picture Books

Picture books tell a great deal to a child much more effectively than using words. It is helpful to look for and collect books with your "resource" and "solution-focused" needs in mind. The books you choose should tell stories that you like yourself and can identify with, because the story has to make sense for you in order to be effective with your listeners. You will soon realize that out of the hundreds of books published every year, perhaps you will become familiar with somewhere between 10 to 12 books. You don't need to have a large library of children's books at home or at your office. We believe, instead, that it is enough to find a few picture books that you enjoy, and whose illustrations and stories fit your personality. Deciding which story to tell a child during your session will depend a great deal on what you have discussed during the session and what goal you are trying to achieve.

Using Picture Books or Stories as Your Feedback

As we mentioned elsewhere, a thinking break is part of the session and a wonderful way to summarize the entire session and provide a memorable message for the client to take home with them. Following a compliment about what you have observed, heard, and learned about the child, you may wind down the session as follows: "While I was thinking about the good things you have told me about yourself, a story crossed my mind and I would like to tell it to you," or some variation on this to fit the child's needs. You may ask permission to do so and wait for the agreement, even though it is very rare that any child or parent would refuse to hear a story. After you finish reading the story, make sure that there is no discussion about it—just read the story and then end the session. There should be no discussion about what the story meant to the child; trust their intuitive ways to understand the meaning and to find useful ways to incorporate this story to their life situations. Our experiences have borne this out many times over.

Story Construction

You may not always find an exactly matching story to fit each unique situation you encounter in your practice. Therefore, it may be helpful to make up stories for your client's individual situations, and we want to give you some guidelines for making up a story to fit a child.

All fairytales, even adult stories, have a certain pattern. This becomes very clear when you read any one of the Harry Potter stories, and you can immediately see why *The Adventures of Harry Potter* is so appealing to children of all cultures and languages. It is helpful to have this pattern in mind when you begin to create your own stories. Like any new lesson, we assure you that you will become quite good at it with practice.

The main character or hero (protagonist) is in some sort of trouble and, in order to solve the difficulties, the hero has to perform a task. In order to reach a goal, the hero must go through dangerous and difficult situations. The enemy (antagonist) tries very hard to stop the hero from succeeding by creating all sorts of obstacles for the hero to overcome.

There are helpers like wise men or women, dwarfs, giants, speaking animals (such as lions, monkeys, snakes, and owls), and talking plants (like a huge oak tree, bushes, but seldom flowers). These helpers possess a lot of power, energy, and wisdom; they often have good ideas and advice for the hero. They sometimes may allow the protagonist to have important tools like keys, swords, or secret maps as a special gift, but they are to be used only in very specific ways. The helpers help as long as the protagonist is willing to make some effort, take risks and do things without knowing exactly why it has to be this way. The protagonist must carry out the secret rituals exactly as told, even when they seem to be wrong or a mistake.

In fairytales, the hero never reaches his or her goal right away. There are always setbacks and unexpected disasters that make it look like the hero might give up. These setbacks or failures come in threes, before the protagonist finally achieves the goal. The story ends with awesome rituals and signs of success—for example, marrying the most beautiful princess, becoming rich, becoming the most powerful person in the land (like a king or a queen who rules for a long time, stays wise and good, and helps others).

How to Construct a Story

The protagonist represents the client for whom you are creating a story. The protagonist should have some similarities with the client, such as where this person lives, age, gender, and also similar behavior patterns and ideas. It is important that there are enough differences, that the story stands on its own and is not a summary of the child's life. The helper can be selected out of the client's favorite comic figures, animals, or plants. The helper may have the same strengths as the client and clearly possesses a trait or personality that is similar to the client.

The antagonist is the "personalized" problem in the form of an animal, robot, evil person like the witch, (as mechanical gadgets, or a hurricane in a story told to a hyperactive child). Once you establish these three main characters, you can start:

1. Introduce the outline and background for the story. Describe the surroundings, the time of year, the weather, and the activities that are taking place such as celebrating Christmas, or a birthday, or the weather was perfect for a picnic, or hiking in the woods.
2. Introduce the protagonist by describing the character's strengths, and what other people appreciate about him or her.

3. Introduce the antagonist in terms of how that person is creating havoc in the life of the hero. Describe the problems in as concrete a manner as possible so that the client can form a clear picture of the problems the hero is facing.

4. Have the protagonist be quite desperate, not knowing what to do.

5. Let the protagonist think of something that was helpful in the past, or let the helper appear, asking the protagonist whether she or he needs help.

6. Have the helper give the protagonist advice. The directions provided with the advice are not easy to fulfill and have to be followed exactly as given. No shortcuts or alterations are allowed.

7. Have the protagonist gain courage. On the way to achieving the goal, the protagonist believes he or she is smarter than the helper, thus altering the advice.

8. The protagonist fails and has to start over again, maybe under even poorer conditions than before, like climbing a mountain without shoes or possessing no warm clothing in the snow.

9. After two or three further failed attempts, the protagonist tries very hard to concentrate on what the helper warned him or her about. The protagonist can find a little trick not to get lost on the way, like counting, singing to overcome fear, keeping his hands in his or her pockets, and so on.

10. Finally the protagonist reaches the desired goal.

11. Have the protagonist realize a difference within him- or herself—feeling a great sense of calmness, having a clear way to think about his or her problems, being able to see or hear better, having more friends, and so on.

12. End the story with a special ritual where the strength and endurance of the protagonist are celebrated.

CASE EXAMPLE: VANESSA'S STORY

Vanessa is a very bright, outspoken 8-year-old child, who wants to be first in her class. Vanessa's mother, Mrs. Klaus, told her story of her difficulties with Vanessa with an exhausted, worn-out expression, saying she had reached the end of her rope with her daughter because Vanessa never goes to bed before her parents do. The mother explains that ever since Vanessa was an infant, she could not allow her parents to have some time to themselves. This was true in daytime or in the evening, but evening was particularly difficult for the mother and the mother was desperate to have some private time with her husband. During the first session with mother and daughter, I created the following story for Vanessa.

Once upon a time, a very nice little girl with fair hair and a voice like a nightingale lived in a big house near a small town. There was a little river in front of the house where the little girl named Vanessa used to play. Vanessa liked to stay outside and have fun, but she had no friends and no other children to play with. This was a big problem which upset her very much. Vanessa thought about how to have friends to play with and thought, "What if I can have a nice dream and tell other children in my class about it like other girls in my class do? I wonder if that would help?" "Forget it!" she told herself, "You can never make it to the dreamland first because you always get there last. And by the time you get there, all the really fascinating dreams are taken by other little girls."

But deep in her heart she knew that to be among the best dream tellers in the class, she would have to be happy during the night and also during the day. Then other children would like to listen to her stories, play with her, and be interested in what she did.

Vanessa was very sad. In order to become an interesting dream storyteller, she had to go to bed early so that she could be the first in the dreamland. But how could she manage that? She could not go to sleep early because she was used to finding out about everything that was going on in her house. Not knowing all the details of what was going on in her house with the grown-ups would be a horror to her. Then she thought, maybe she could make friends in a different way rather than telling stories about her visit to dreamland and all her fascinating dream stories. She went on thinking about both sides on and off, but it was useless. She just could not come up with which she wanted more, but the voice in her heart became stronger. It kept saying, "Come on, Vanessa, be the first in dreamland and your problem is solved! You want lots of friends so much!"

Next day, she sat throwing little stones into the river. There was no smile on her face and she was very sad that she had to play by herself. All of a sudden, a white owl flew around her and asked, "Nice little girl, why do you look so sad?" Vanessa told her problem and also her wish to be the first to arrive in dreamland so that she could pick the most fascinating dream story to tell other little girls, but she could not do that because of her difficult dilemma of missing out on grown-up things. "Well," answered the owl. "It seems to me you are really stuck. I will think about your problem. Come back here tomorrow at the same place at the same time and I will be here again." "Thank you dear owl," said Vanessa. "I promise I will be here tomorrow."

Next day, Vanessa almost missed the meeting with the owl because she had to help her mother clean up the kitchen. As quickly as she could, she ran to the river and arrived there breathless, but just in time. The owl was already waiting for her. "Listen," said the owl with his deep voice. "I have been thinking a lot about your wish. It seems to me there is a way that your wish may come true. But it is not going to be easy and you have to make some effort." "That doesn't matter," replied the girl, "if only I can tell a nice dream story in school."

"OK, you have to listen very carefully to what I am going to explain to you, Vanessa. You have to go from this village to the neighboring village, and there you have to climb a little hill, which is behind the church. On top of that hill you will find a key under a white stone laying under a big pine tree. You should take this key and put it under your pillow when you go to sleep. But you must be very careful because there is one rule to follow. When you walk along the path from your village to the next one, and while you are climbing the hill, you are not allowed to turn back and watch what is happening behind your back." Before Vanessa could thank the owl, he had flown away. On the way back home, Vanessa repeated what the owl had said to her. "Well, that's easy," she thought, "I am sure I will manage fine."

Vanessa had to wait until the following Wednesday when there was no school in the afternoon because of a teacher's conference. Right after school she had her lunch and, having done her homework, she was on her way. She walked out of her own village and started heading for the hill that would get her to the next village. She could already see the church of the neighboring village when she heard some music. First she did not pay attention to it, but it became louder and louder and she began to wonder where it was coming from. She turned back to find out and saw two men playing guitar sitting under a tree. Vanessa quickly continued on her way and went up the hill, huffing and puffing, until she found the white stone, but there was no key underneath.

She quickly became very angry and she wanted to blame the owl when she realized why the key was not under the stone. It was not until that moment she remembered that she was not supposed to look back on the way up the hill, and she realized that she had forgotten about this rule the owl told her. Now the anger turned toward herself. After a while she tried to comfort herself by saying "I will try it again next Wednesday." The following week it was a most wonderful carriage with two white horses that attracted her attention. They came from the village she had to go to. When they passed, she felt she just had to turn back and take another glance at this wonderful picture. Of course, again there was no key under the stone when she arrived at the crest of the hill.

Very sad and discouraged, Vanessa returned to the river and sat down and started to cry. After a while, something in her heart like a dream told her: *You have to have a trick to keep you focused and give up paying attention to what is going on around you.* She came up with an idea. The following week she would count numbers on the entire way up the hill and would always look down at her own shoes. She followed this plan and refused to be distracted as she made her way from her village to the hill with the white stone. This time it worked! The key was there!

The key under her pillow did a wonderful job. She entered the dreamland along a rainbow and dreamed the most wonderful dream. It was the best night Vanessa ever spent and it was also a success when she told her dream at school.

The next evening Vanessa wanted to put the key under her pillow again. It had disappeared, even though she carefully had placed the key in the corner of her bedroom shelf. Next day she went down to the river and hoped to find the owl. Fortunately the owl came and Vanessa could ask where the key had gone. But the owl did not answer this time. The owl just looked at Vanessa. While looking into those big dark eyes, Vanessa felt a wonderful strength, a golden feeling, and she knew the answer herself! *I have to be very concentrated and not listen to what is going on. I should not be eager to know what others do. If I just stay in bed, feel the light blanket, smell the smell of the pillow, and touch the fine fur of my teddy bear, then I will make it and have nice dreams again.*

CASE EXAMPLE: MIGUEL'S TRAUMA

Twelve-year-old Miguel and his younger brother were adopted from Chile when Miguel was 7 and his brother Pedro was 5. His adoptive mother was very concerned and upset that Miguel would never allow her to touch him—because Miguel just did not trust her or had difficulty emotionally bonding with her—even after many years of being cared for and loved by his adoptive parents. On the other hand, the mother reported that Miguel's brother Pedro, age 10 now, had made a good adjustment to the new life, was doing well academically, and was getting along well with family and friends.

These circumstances troubled the adoptive mother a great deal because she knew that the boys' earlier life had been extremely difficult and she was determined to do her best for her two boys. In the first meeting I (TS) learned that, in Chile, Miguel had to watch his brother Pedro getting beaten up by his aunt and uncle to the point that he was hospitalized three times.

Miguel's answer to the miracle question was that he would become friendly with his mother, would play nicely with other children, and have friends of his very own. In a scribble game (to be described in detail later) with me, where we each took turns adding one line, Miguel's pictures consistently turned out as depictions of either prisons or hospitals.

I decided to use one technique of story telling where I start the story and then ask the child to finish the story exactly the way he wants to finish it. So, I started to tell a story:

There were two sisters. One was two years younger than the other. Both were very pretty, with fair hair and blue eyes. They were brought up in a very hostile family and nobody really cared about them.

One day, the younger of the two girls became very ill. She was so sick that she had to be brought to the hospital several times. There she was looked after very well, she got lots of toys to play with, people smiled at her, and she had enough to eat. Meanwhile, the older sister stayed home all on her own without her younger sister, she was not allowed to go visit her sister at the hospital and nobody would tell her about her sister in the hospital. She had no idea how her younger sister was doing, whether she was safe at the hospital, or was getting enough to eat.

She was very lonely without her younger sister, very miserable and worried about her. In a way, the older sister had a harder time and was more miserable than the sister in the hospital. Nobody took any notice of the older sister because, everyone assumed, she had to be glad that she was not sick and in the hospital; everyone thought she should be happy because at least she was healthy. Nobody even noticed that she did not get enough to eat, was not playing, and was very miserable. After all, a broken heart just didn't count to the grown-ups.

Miguel had been listening to the beginning of my story with a very pained expression on his face. When it was Miguel's turn to finish the story, he could not and the session ended there.

When Miguel returned the following session, he began to describe how he did not like to watch his brother get beaten up by his uncle. This was the first time he ever talked about this experience of his earlier life and, once he began, it was as if he didn't know how to stop talking. Miguel poured out his heart with lots of emotion. His father was in prison, his mother ran away, and Miguel and Pedro had to go to live with their aunt and her husband. They were all so poor that Miguel and Pedro never had enough to eat. By the time they became 4 or 5 years old, Miguel and Pedro were out on the streets selling fruit to earn money. What made things worse for Miguel was that his brother Pedro started to wet the bed at night and this was the reason his uncle beat Pedro. Both boys were eventually given up for adoption and they came to live in Switzerland.

The following session, Miguel wanted to finish the story that we began two sessions ago. He said the ending of the story would be like this:

Somebody, some grown-up person, would spend an afternoon with me and take me fishing and listen to me; the grown-up person would talk and we would have something to eat together.

Then we started to draw pictures of Miguel going fishing with someone and that someone turned out to be his adoptive mother. We had a total of eight sessions.

Construct the Story with the Child

There are two different approaches to creating a story with the child:

1. You may begin to tell the story you made up for the child and when the protagonist is in big trouble, allow the child's favorite figure—such as a cartoon character, sports hero, a robot, or superhero—to arrive. Then you can ask the child to finish the story.
2. You can construct a story with the child by taking turns: the child tells one sentence, then you add the next sentence and so on until the story is finished.

DRAWING PICTURES

As you have noticed, the work with puppets still requires some language skills on the part of the child, but picture drawing is a form of expression that does not involve sophisticated language skills. Many children find it familiar to draw pictures because they seem to do it almost intuitively. You may suggest the child make any drawing he or she wants. The following are some suggestions of topics for solution-focused picture drawing.

Ask children to draw a picture of:

- what they do well
- favorite places, dog, family, best friend, or anything they like
- what they want to be when they grow up
- what is important to them
- when everything is OK in their lives
- an animal that makes them feel good or happy
- the day after the night the fairy godmother comes and waves her magic wand and shows all the problems that upset Mom are gone (or 10 on the scale)
- their families when the problem does not involve them.

Throughout the session you can ask the child to draw pictures when it seems to fit nicely with the information that was generated and when you believe the child is close to the next step. For children it is often easier to make it clear through a drawing what the next step will look like than describing it with words.

It is particularly important that you ask the child to draw a picture of a specific situation or event, such as when the child is no longer bothered by the tummy aches, bed wetting, family conflict, or loss of an important person. Remember that drawing a picture is not designed to pass time; rather, we find that it often turns out to be a very important step toward achieving the goal.

Solution-Building Cartoons

Crowley and Mills (1989) have written about the magic of cartoons in their work with children. I was fascinated with their work and began to adapt their techniques to fit the solution-focused approach with children. I find this technique very helpful for children who can follow instructions but either prefer to work nonverbally or are unable to express their intense emotions in words. Cartoons have appeal throughout the world and to children of all ages. The specific technique featured here follows a six-step approach that eventually leads to a desirable state for the child.

1. The picture in the first panel represents the problem.
2. The second picture panel shows the mighty helper the child wishes to have that will successfully deal with the problem.
3. The third panel shows a solution the child worked out together with the helper and which creates an exception to the problem.
4. The fourth shows what is different for the child when there is an exception.
5. The fifth picture focuses on the future when the exception becomes a reality again.
6. The sixth picture is a sign that shows the child's thanks to the helper.

Step-by-Step Instruction
for Drawing Cartoons

We now want to describe a more thorough set of instructions you can give to create this solution cartoon and that is tailored to fit the child.
How to instruct the child:

1. Give the child a sheet of construction paper, draw a line across half of the sheet and divide into six panels blocks as shown in Figure 6.1.
2. Ask the child to draw, in the first panel in the top, a picture of the problem. If it turns out to be complicated, the child may just draw the matching form and color representing the problem.
3. Ask the child to think of a mighty figure or a hero—such as Batman, Robin Hood, other similar figure—who will make the problem disappear, and draw it in the second panel block. The figure can be from a favorite story, animal, or machine that will best help to make the problem disappear.
4. Ask the child to dream a little dream and think of a good present (gift) to offer to the problem so that the problem does not bother anyone anymore. Ask the child to draw the picture of the perfect present in the third panel on the top row.
5. Ask the child to draw the situation after the problem has accepted the present and the exception has become true. This goes in the first panel on the bottom row.
6. Ask the child to have another little dream and imagine a future time when it may be necessary to call this helper again. Then ask the child to draw that situation in the second panel in the bottom half.
7. Ask the child to thank the helper by drawing a little sign of thanks. This fills the last empty panel on the bottom row.

Pictures 2 and 3 require the most patience, as they demand a process similar to answering the miracle question. The child has to get in touch with his or her inner resources, and this can be a challenging task. It may take some time and the child will need your respectful and sensitive help. Questions such as: Which figure do you think is very powerful and can handle tough situations?; Which animal do you think could cope best with the situation?; Can you remember a story where somebody was in a difficult situation and all of a sudden, somebody comes along or something comes up, and everything turned out fine? As a therapist it is important that you facilitate this search for a solution and foster the hope that changes are possible, as magical as they may be. You are offering the child an opportunity to think outside of the box.

**Warning: Do Not Intrude on the Child's
World of Imagination**

Many therapists can easily be seduced by the desire to understand the child's thinking and thus become tempted to interpret pictures about what the child maybe thinking, what it might mean, or what the child is trying to say. This could unwittingly lead you to be distracted from your task and ask many problem-solving or diagnostic questions. We believe this will not only be distracting from your focus on helping the child to design individual solutions, but we also believe it is disrespectful. We find this technique so powerful because it allows children to connect quickly with their own resources without having to use words. We believe this technique draws on a more intuitive understanding than an intellectual or discursive knowledge. All children are intuitive about what feels right to them and what does not. We see the children's pictures as their nonverbal expression of their intuitive understanding.

Of course, it is natural for adults to be curious about what secret meanings a child's pictures may hold. However, in order to discuss the "meaning" behind it, we must engage the child in talking to us in an understandable manner. Thus, asking children to describe what their pictures mean is asking them to rise to the level of linguistic sophistication that they are not able to meet. It is better to trust the impact of the pictures and consider the six little drawings as a wonderful present from the child.

CASE EXAMPLE: COMFORTING BLANKET

Ron, an 8-year-old boy, was brought to therapy after the death of his newborn sister. The family had arranged a rather unusual funeral ritual, where the dead infant's body was kept for several days in the room where Ron slept before the burial. He developed a serious sleep disturbance, was very withdrawn and noncommunicative, and had great difficulty concentrating in school. When we first met, he was listless and losing interest in friends, his school work, and his surroundings. He said very little during the meeting and, indeed, was not interested in his environment. Instead of talking to him, I asked him to draw the cartoon pictures as we described above. The pictures showed the following:

First panel: Ron drew black clouds with sharp edges, representing the problem.

Second panel: The shape of a bear that looked like a panda.

Third panel: A very colorful blanket.

Fourth panel: The cloud is all but covered with the colorful blanket.

Fifth panel: A bed in his bedroom and three poplar trees standing near the graveyard that he passes on his way to school.

Sixth panel: A heart in bright red.

After the session, Ron agreed to show the cartoon to his mother. I asked Ron whether he would like to make a colorful blanket, like the one in the picture. He was very enthusiastic about it and his mother thought it to be a wonderful idea also. During the several afternoons following the session, mother and son began painting the fabric they had chosen with the most cheerful colors. Afterward, his mother lovingly sewed the cloth together into a very special blanket. Ron took this blanket to his bed and began to have a restful sleep at night.

This was one of those rare occasions when a therapist is given an opportunity to transform the resource for expression into an action with an immediate positive result. We want to remind you that not every case leads to such a dramatic outcome, but, in this case, involving the mother in creating the solution together had a dramatic outcome for Ron. We believe it is important to remember that change can also be effective without an activity as involved as the one just described. Our experience shows that even a small change can make a big difference when the solution is meaningful to the child and the parent. Our hunch is that this cartoon making process reminds the child of possible solutions, and this must be terribly reassuring not only to a child but also to adults.

CASE EXAMPLE: SCARY SEIZURES

Sam, a 10-year-old boy, was diagnosed with ADHD. He also suffered from epileptic seizures for which he had been taking medication regularly. Thanks to the recent changes in his medication, his seizures were under control, which was a big relief to Sam and his parents. However, his aggressive temper had continued to be a problem for him at school. He was socially isolated, and his main problem was that other children were afraid of him and therefore avoided him or made fun of him. When Sam's fear of the older children who made fun of him became too intense and overwhelming, he became verbally and physically aggressive. He preferred to stay inside the classroom during recess, and even during lunch hour he sat alone in a corner while the other children swapped foods, talked, and planned sleepovers or going to movies together. Often he came home very frustrated and in a bad mood because of what had happened in school. His bad temper would explode and he would become aggressive toward his younger sisters and brother. His mother felt overwhelmed and often did not know what to do to soothe and comfort him. Because he was unable to articulate his frustration when he became so upset, I decided that it would be best for Sam to make pictures instead of trying to talk. He drew the following pictures (see Figure 6.1):

First panel: The problem, Sam tormenting his doll. He said, "I usually go after my brother."

Second panel: The helper, the Pokemon Picatchu.

Third panel: The present for the bad temper, a huge magic pill.

Fourth panel: The change, Sam tells me he will feel like a famous race car driver.

Figure 6.1. Sam's cartoon charting his imaginative way of addressing his frustrations at school.

Fifth panel: The moment he needs help the most, the school playground where he goes during lunch recess.

Sixth panel: The sign of thanks, a Pokemon ball that he wants to offer to Picatchu.

This example illustrates the wonderful capacity children have to come up with unique solutions. It was clear that feeling like the famous race car driver would make a big difference to Sam. I asked Sam to show me what he would look like when he walks around the stadium looking like his favorite race car driver Schumacher. I asked Sam to walk up and down the room and to wave saying goodbye, like Schumacher would. When Sam got into the role of the famous and triumphant race car driver, with his head held high as he looked around the room with a confident smile, he shook my hand very strongly as he walked out of my office.

Interactive Picture Drawing: Tools for Empowerment

Drawing a picture can also be a form of conversation for children, adolescents, and families, as well as a tool for talking between two or more people. We want to describe several such interactive ways that children can be involved in talking with the therapist, parents, and even with their entire family.

Turn Taking

This is particularly suited for younger children because there are only a few rules to remember while drawing pictures together with others. Youngsters love its simple and spontaneous activity, and it is flexible enough to allow talking while drawing pictures.

How to instruct the child:

1. Have two sizes of drawing or construction paper, large and small. Ask the child to select the size.
2. Ask the child to start a picture using only one color at the beginning. As soon as a different color is needed, the child has to hand the picture over to his or her partner (therapist, parent, sibling, etc.).
3. The partner adds to the initial drawing until the third color is needed. Then the partner person must hand it back to the first person.
4. The drawing goes back and forth until both the child and partner agree the picture is finished.
5. Discuss with the child where is the best place to hang the picture, whether in his or her home or in your office. If the child decides to take it home be sure to ask where in his or her home is the best place to hang up the picture.

Family Picture Making

The idea behind this task is to involve the members of a family in this creative process. While the family members are working on this project, observe the helpful interactions among them, such as sharing, cooperating, having fun, being polite to each other, or talking to each other. Make sure you mention your observations and give feedback regarding all of things you have observed about how well the family works together.

How to instruct the family:

1. Tape a big sheet of paper on the table. Prepare many different colors of magic markers, crayons, or pencils. If you decide to use water colors, it is helpful to take recycled egg cartons and fill each egg cup with a different color.
2. Ask the family members to make a picture simultaneously, that is, each person helps to make the picture at the same time. The

family can have a little discussion in advance about what they are going to draw and who is going to draw what.

3. If you feel this could be too complicated for some family members, ask each member of the family to start at a certain point (such as the center of the paper), and work outward toward corners; or ask them to begin in the four corners and work toward the middle of the paper.

4. Remind the family that the finished product will be a surprise for everyone.

5. While they make the picture, sit back and enjoy the family members cooperating with each other. Make comments and give feedback on the respectful and cooperative behaviors you observe—e.g., their willingness to change/adapt or to cooperate with each other (if it is true).

6. Again, ask the family if they want to take the picture home and where would be the best place to hang it up.

Scribble Game

D. W. Winnicott was a well-known British child psychiatrist who wrote extensively about the use of a scribble game from his psychoanalytic point of view (Winnicott, 1970, 1971). This game can be easily adapted to the solution-building approach. The basic idea of scribbling is to create spontaneous and unplanned reactions to a scribble. As the name indicates, the goal is not to create a masterpiece but to have fun and see what comes out of it. This allows children to be relaxed. Often the anticipation of the next move enhances children's curiosity and creativity. We find that children are often very surprised and proud of their own creativity; and the partnership with adults enhances their confidence. Even though Winnicott saw this game as a diagnostic tool for understanding the unconscious processes of a child, we view this technique as a tool of communication that works well with children.

This game works better when each participant uses a single color throughout. For example, the child might pick red, while you may pick black. Both of participants stay with the color of choice until the end. How to instruct the child:

1. Ask the child to make any kind of scribble on a sheet of paper.

2. Ask the child to hand the paper over to you after finishing one stroke of any shape. Your task is to add to the drawing by integrating the scribble the child originally made. Pass the drawing back and forth between you until you decide the work is complete. When you have finished your drawing, put your names in one corner.

3. Take a new sheet of paper and now it is your turn to start the scribble. Once you complete your scribble, hand it over to the child.
4. It is now the child's task to add to the little drawing, as before, by integrating his or her marks to the original scribble.
5. Create five or six drawings (or as many as you think will be helpful).
6. Spread out your several different creations, like a little picture exhibition.
7. Ask the child which picture he or she likes best from your series of scribble drawings.
8. Ask the child what he or she wants to do with the selected drawing. You may suggest that the child hang it up on your office wall or that he or she take it home.

Many beginning therapists, or those who work with children without prior experience, often ask how many turns each participant should take to complete the scribble. There are no strict rules about how many turns are needed; however, the general guideline is to continue until you and the child have arrived at a closure and feel finished. Occasionally you learn that a child can be very concerned about making a perfect scribble. If you find this to be the case, instruct the child to just draw something on the paper with eyes closed, thus allowing the child permission to be spontaneous and imperfect. It helps to keep the scribble activity simple and failure-proof.

Some children may spontaneously start to talk about one or the other drawings. It is a good practice to follow the child's lead but, again, resist any temptation to make interpretations or analyze what the child meant by these scribbles. Frequently this game offers a chance for the therapist to discover and connect with the child's strengths and resources. In a tentative manner, you may want to casually mention to the child: "It seems very helpful for you to take your time," or "It looks like you have lots of good ideas, and you want to start right away and surprise yourself." Many children comment about this game saying that they did not know they were such a good "painter."

Making Up a Story

On some occasions, especially when the therapist feels that this way of communication is useful, you can ask the child to choose one of the pictures and use it to make up a story that you and the child will compose cooperatively. Your can follow these brief guidelines on how to create a story based on the scribble.

Figure 6.2. An example of a product of the scribble game, signed by Anja.

1. Ask the child to choose a favorite picture from the several scribbles that you have drawn together. Put the picture between the child and you.
2. Start to make up a story inspired by the picture by saying the first sentence (e.g., "Once upon a time there was an angry face . . . ").
3. Ask the child to add the next sentence.
4. Pick up the thread and add your piece of the story.
5. Continue this back and forth process for a while, until one of you finds the end of the story.

The complete story, like the finished picture, is an object to be admired and an opportunity for further conversation between yourself and the child.

GAMES AND PLAYING

Playing and being creative within a framework where children experience their abilities and strengths is helpful. You can contribute to a child's empowerment experience through a variety of games. Many activities may serve this purpose, but, whatever you do with the child, it has to be fairly similar to what the child wants. We will describe some activities that we have found to be helpful, and describe the context that fits a child's needs.

Mix and Match

The idea behind this game is to offer children a chance to be creative by showing them they can create many different colors.

First, use recycle empty egg cartons and pour watercolors in each cup: red, yellow, white, and blue, and so on.

How to instruct the child:

1. Ask the child to make a guess in advance as to how many different colors there will be.
2. Ask the child to make as many different colors as possible out of the four colors provided—red, yellow, white, and blue.
3. Tell the child it is OK to mix all the colors, even the new ones that came out as a result of mixing.
4. Have the child paint a ball or an Easter egg in every color that he or she has created.
5. Have fun and enjoy the child's creativity and discovery of "hidden" talent.

Power Hands

This technique encourages children to have a conversation about their abilities and strengths.

First, take a fairly big sheet of paper and ask the child to put down both of his or her hands on the paper. Draw the outline of the child's hands. If the child is very young, you may tell one of the nursery rhymes you know, one for every finger that is touched.

How to instruct the child:

1. Let the child decide which finger to start with.
2. For each finger drawn on the paper ask the child to find what she or he is good at.
3. Take the finger the child has selected; shake hands with it a little and ask: What is your thumb good at?
4. Have the child name the activity, for example, football or jump rope.
5. Ask the child what color matches the selected activity (e.g., football) and have the child color the finger in the chosen color.
6. Depending on the child's age, the child may also write the word corresponding to the activity (e.g., "football") or draw a picture of a football in the finger.
7. Have the child go through all ten fingers in the same manner.

In the end you will have ten fingers on the paper, each in a different color and each a different strength. In order to close this activity on a positive note, you can ask the child to put two hands together, making sure all fingers touch to form a roof. Then ask the child to press on the tops of the fingers. You can then say in a soft, soothing voice: "Carry a magic little house of power along with you; whenever you need to feel strong, push your fingers together like that and feel the strength."

The Most Wanted Person

Most children between the ages of 8 and 12 are fascinated with stories about cops and robbers, good guys and bad guys—the FBI's most wanted list, and so on. This game is based on their natural curiosity and intense interest in this subject, so that you can create a game of "warrant of goal" instead of a warrant of arrest. In "warrant of goal" you write out a description of the child as well as everything the child has already learned (so far) about what he or she is good at.

On the first page provide:

1. A picture of the child, taken with the instant camera in your therapy room.
2. A personal description: color of eyes, hair, height, weight, any special marking or special features (e.g., corn rows, dreadlocks, a braid, or special clothing or shoes).
3. Date of birth.
4. Favorite activities.
5. Favorite music.
6. Favorite food.

The first page is a personal assessment. Often children like to write down these facts in different colors, make little drawings, or illustrate the first page with special stickers or markers.

Page two includes what the child has already learned. This page is very helpful to make it clear what the child's abilities are.

1. Ask the child to put down very simple things they learned, such as: like to walk, to dress, to make the bed, to swim, to play basketball, help with dishes, take care of brothers or sisters.
2. Ask about child's interactional skills, such as: learned to make friends, defended friends when someone treated his friend unfairly, walked away when someone calls him names.
3. Ask about basic skills in school, such as: knows numbers, knows alphabet, knows how to read, knows how to sing, knows how to wait in line patiently, learned to take her turn, is polite to adults, learned to play a musical instrument, learned to ride a bike, learned to twirl a baton.
4. Ask about the child's skills at home, such as: how to make toast, cook eggs, clean shoes, hang up or fold clothes, pick up towels from the bathroom floor, empty the dishwasher, set the table, knows how to use the washing machine, sweep the floor, pick up shoes from the entry way.

The second page should illustrate and make evident a whole list of skills. Children are often amazed at the long list of things they know how to do. You can spend some time talking with the child about what was easy to learn, what was more difficult, and how she or he learned to be good at particular skills.

Page three includes the next thing the child would like to achieve and what kind of abilities listed on page two would be helpful to achieve these new skills. Ask the child what he or she would like to add on page two in one week, one month, or two months. You may need to listen and observe carefully so that you do not force the child to over-reach for something that he or she may have difficulty achieving. Ask the child what the parents, the teacher, or other grown-ups could do to be helpful. Frequently, just by going through this procedure children come up with a clear idea about how to make the next step.

Case Example: Math and Swimming

Sheila was a very bright girl of 10, yet she had a great deal of difficulty with math. Her teacher kept reminding her about her intelligence and generally thought of her as lazy. Sheila also was very frustrated with her difficulties and she was finally able to explain to the therapist that the most difficult part of math class was when she had to read descriptions of problems in sentences. She realized that when a math problem was represented in numbers, she could solve it very fast, but reading the problem written out in words got her into big trouble. She began to panic every time she had to read the math book. She explained that she would become so anxious that, even with the book in front of her, she wouldn't know what the question was. Before anyone realized it, Sheila's little problem grew into a very big problem and she began to develop many psychosomatic problems, such as stomach aches, headaches, shortness of breath, and sleeping problems.

When we began to do the "Most Wanted Person" list, on the second page she listed her swimming skills. When asked about this, she explained in detail, with a great deal of animation in her body and enthusiasm in her voice, how she learned to swim. Swimming had not been easy for her, she explained, and the steps she took to learn to swim were very clever. She explained that at first she had to watch the water closely, then stick her hand into the water. To overcome her fear of the water, she kept repeating the words, "I will be able to breathe" over and over to herself. She reported that this helped to calm her down and pretty soon she was in the water and breathing, too!

Sheila thought about it for a while and then decided that she could solve math word problems in a similar way. She thoughtfully explained in the following manner: "I have to look at the sentence and read it through. Just like I learned to swim by touching the water, I have to touch the sentence. You know what? That means I have to want to know what it means. The sentence I have to have in my head is: "I will understand what is written down." Sheila learned to solve math problems rather quickly.

What a smart child Sheila is! And of course we met so many Sheilas.

Below are some brief descriptions of other games that can be useful when working with children.

Hot and Cold
(Looking for Hidden Objects)

Purpose: General empowerment for children who have difficulties being "a sore loser" and for children who need to learn when to ask for help and feel OK about needing help from others.

How the game is played: You select a little object like a little ball, a small toy, a mitten, or anything small enough, and show it to the child. Have the child decide who will be the first to hide the object and who will be the first to find it. You discuss with the child in advance that help is available, but it is up to the person who has to look for the object to decide the moment she or he wants help. The common help given is to say "warm" or "hot" when the child gets closer and say "cooler" or "cold" when the child moves away from the object.

Make sure you take turns because it is a great feeling for the child to see you facing the same task and the same challenges.

Simon Says (Commanding Game)

Purpose: Teaching children to listen, to concentrate, and to be attentive.

How the game is played: Depending on the child's age, you want to give somewhere between 3 to 10 instructions; for all ages the instructions must be enjoyable as well as easy to understand, remember, and then perform. At the end, the child evaluates his own success as to whether he followed all the commands in the right sequence. For example, the instruction may go like this: "Sam, I want you to go to the door and open and close it gently; then you are going to stand on the red chair and sing a song; you will then go to the other room and throw three dart arrows, then come back to the therapy room and draw a picture of a house." It is important that you as the therapist also take a turn to fulfill the commands the child gives you. Be prepared for how difficult it is for children to give orders since it is rather unusual for a child to give commands to an adult. Instead, they are always told what to do, so it is good for them to experience giving orders to an adult for a change.

Let the Fingers Look

Purpose: Assist the child in learning how to be careful, to slow down, and to approach any task in a sensitive, concentrated way and to show the child that it is possible to do things in different ways. According to the age of the child, you gather 10 to 20 different objects (e.g., a pen, wooden animal, a safety pin, a shell, button, thread spool, bottle opener, and many other small objects) and put them into a bag.

How the game is played: Have the child close his or her eyes while you cover the child's eyes with a soft cloth, large handkerchief, or scarf, and tie it gently to make a blindfold. Pull out one object at a time from the bag, place it in the child's hands, and ask the child to identify the object only by touching with both hands. Lay down in a row all the objects the child has identified correctly. In the end, the child removes the blindfold to see what he or she correctly identified by touching only. Now you can take turns by asking the child to remove a number of objects from your office or desk and put them in the same bag while your eyes are blindfolded. You then remove the blindfold and try to identify the items. You and the child can participate in the game together by identifying how many items are still missing.

Reading by Touch

Purpose: Enhance the child's ideas about learning differently, paying close attention, and improving concentration for tactile sensations.

How the game is played: Ask the child to sit with his or her back toward you, facing the opposite wall. Use the child's back as a writing board, computer screen, or blackboard. First go through the motion of cleaning the blackboard or computer screen by wiping the child's back. Indicate where is up and where is down (up is toward the neck and down is toward the waist).

How complicated a drawing you want to draw depends on the child's age. For a younger child, draw a picture of a house, the sun, a flower, a girl or a boy, and ask the child to identify the picture on the blackboard (computer screen, etc). When the child already knows the letters of the alphabet and numbers 1 to 10, you may want to write a word by spelling it out on the child's back and asking the child to identify the letters. At times you can end the session by writing the word "good-bye" and use it to compliment the child for his or her ability to pay close attention to body sensations.

Backgammon

Board games are good tools to teach children necessary safety skills that may be difficult to explain because the concept is too abstract. For example, Joyce was brought to therapy because she had been molested by a stranger in a local park. It was clear that she had some special needs because of her limited intellectual ability to figure things out for herself so that she can protect herself. Learning to play backgammon gives you and the child a nice opportunity to talk about safety repeatedly without being intrusive. A base rule in backgammon is that stones standing alone can be caught easily by the opponent. By playing this game several times, Joyce began to understand what self-protection meant and it was much easier to translate the concept to her everyday life, including her interactions with strangers.

Abalone

Brandon was a bright boy in many ways, yet his organizational abilities did not match his intellect and he was constantly criticized for being disorganized. Trying to use visualization with animals or puppets did not work with him because he could not find any meaningful visual images of what he wanted to have different in his life. Then I (TS) remembered that he told me how well he played the strategic game of abalone. So, I decided to play the game with him and during the game asked him how he was planning different moves. Abalone is a game similar to chess and it requires several important skills such as the ability to concentrate, to see the larger picture, make decisions, and plan ahead. It was very clear that he was always planning the next move and "thinking ahead," which also seemed to be the key for him in matters related to school. Brandon did not realize that he already had all the useful skills to do better in school until we started to play abalone. The only difference was the context. As if by miracle, he realized that he already possessed all the skills necessary to be a good student, and that he only needed to transfer these skills from one place to another. During each of the six sessions we met, we always played abalone; of course he beat me each time and from session to session his school work became much better organized.

SCALING

Even though we have already discussed the usefulness and applications of the scales with children in Chapter 3, we want to add several useful techniques to your toolbox. The techniques lend themselves very nicely to scaling questions and children's ability to master them.

Children like to be active, take things in their hands, and move around. We have to remember these facts and transform the scaling questions into little actions. We like to remind you that there is no limit to your creativity in adapting basic techniques to working with children. Here we list some examples children seem to like quite a lot.

For those children who do not yet know the numbers these games are useful:

The Success Tower

Take a basket fall of wooden cubes in different colors and sizes and sit down with the child. (With younger children it is best to sit on the floor with them.) Ask the child what went well between last and this session.

For every positive event the child remembers, instruct the child to place a cube on the table, stacking one on top of the other. Also ask mother and father, if they are present, what they think went well. When there are no more events to mention, go through all the cubes again by naming what cube stands for which success. You may want to have the child take picture of all the successes with your instant camera and then discuss who will get to see the photo. Some children like this way of measuring the progress and are eager to collect the success pictures.

Balloons

Balloons are very helpful to visualize the progress of all sorts of things such as growing courage, listening to mother, picking up a room, learning to gain control over a bad temper, and so on. Tell the child that a balloon without air indicates the first visit with you. Ask the child to inflate the balloon to the extent that the child thinks the courage (or whatever the still that needed mastery) has increased. Have the child let out the air again and ask how he or she managed to gain this amount of "courage." Then have the child inflate the balloon again and while he or she does so, you repeat all the helpful facts you just heard. Find out whether the child, mother, or other adult can think of even more helpful behaviors that can be cited. Ask the child to inflate the balloon to the level that the he or she thinks would be helpful and then the level that would signify mastery of the skill in question. Playing with the balloon this way focuses the child's attention while you are asking "scaling" questions.

CASE EXAMPLE: FEAR REDUCTION

Nathan, who was 6½, was so frightened to enter the office of the therapist (TS) that he clung to the doorknob and would not venture into the office. Seeing this frightened child, the therapist immediately pulled out a bright red balloon and started to blow it up. Surprised at this unexpected event, Nathan stopped being scared and let go of the doorknob and started watching the balloon inflate. The therapist twisted the top of the balloon so that the air would stay inside and handed the balloon to Nathan, pointed to the balloon and said, "Nathan, this is how much you are afraid to come inside and talk to me. I want you to hold the top of the balloon with both hands and let out the air so that the balloon becomes the size you want. It means you are still afraid but you can still come inside and sit with me and your mom, so you and I can talk together." Nathan held the balloon in both hands, slowly let the air escape from it so that the balloon became about half the size that the therapist made initially, and said, "Here, now I can come in and talk."

Moving Around the Rope

Take a rope and lay it on the floor of your therapy room. Define together with the child which end of the rope represents how bad the problem was when either Mom or Dad first called to make an appointment for the first meeting, and the other end of the rope, which stands for the day when it is no longer necessary to see the therapist. Have the child jump along the rope on one foot (or move along its length in some other playful way) to the point where he or she is today. Put a name down where the child stopped. Explore how the child got so far and discuss every helpful step and behavior the child has achieved. When no more new information comes up, repeat all the steps the child has taken to arrive at that point of the rope. If possible, take an instant picture of the child describing each of these accomplishments as he or she moves along the length of the rope. Write each accomplishment on the back of the appropriate picture.

Painting the Hand

Show the child a common poster picture with five different faces that range from a first face with an angry expression to a last one with a smiling face. Ask the child to select the face that matches his or her mood today. Paint this face with watercolors on the back of the child's hand, placing the eyes right below the fingers and the mouth toward the wrist. Now ask the child about all the good things he or she did. For every single item the child mentions, you paint a finger in a different color and in a different pattern. Have the child put the hand on the table (preferably on a white background) so that you can take a picture. The painted fingers look like multicolored hair. Many young children love the effect and of course want to take the pictures home and post them where they can be shown.

Heaven and Hell (Jumping Game)

Almost every culture has jumping games for children; therefore, most children should be familiar with this game, which is particularly useful for active children. The bottom, or the floor, on which the child stands indicates hell (or how bad the problem was when the child's parent or the teacher called) and the top indicates heaven, (or the day after the miracle). Have the child jump to where he or she has moved up on the way to heaven. You can repeat this game at the beginning of each of the following sessions as well.

Success Picture

Using a flip chart, ask the child to think of all the helpful things that happened since the last session. You can also ask all the adults present in the session to describe and draw pictures of the child's successes since the last meeting. Using questions that indicate how the other important persons in the child's life perceive things (also called relationship questions, to be discussed in Chapter 8 on adolescents), you can also ask those present in the room to relate how others who are not present would report how the child did since the last session. Again, ask them to draw pictures of the list of those success stories. The child can take the finished picture home, and you might want to discuss with the child and the family where in the house they might want to display the picture.

For children who know numbers this scaling game is useful:

Jump in Different Directions
Along the Numbers

Have the child write down the numbers 1 to 10, each number on a separate sheet of paper. Place these sheets on the floor in numerical order. Ask the child to jump as far as he or she thinks has changed toward 10. Ask the child to jump one number higher and then ask how he or she will make it happen and what would be the consequences of such improvements—"What would your mommy (or daddy) do?"; "What would your teacher do?"; "Friends, brother or sister, or other important person in the your life?"

EXPERIMENTS

We are often asked whether it is helpful to suggest an experiment or a homework exercise to a child. Our view is that it helps in the same way that such suggestions are helpful to adults—that is, such experiments take the therapy into the client's real life outside of the therapy room. In other words, experiments or homework assignments become an extension of what took place in the therapy session.

We want to review and list some of the guidelines and principles behind the suggestion of homework in general, including working with teenagers and adults.

- The experiment must be related to what the client wants as negotiated during the first interview.
- The experiment must be doable and usually a small step toward the client's goals. It is important to "go slow."

- The main purpose of the experiment is to elicit different reactions from those important in the life of the child. The experiment or homework alone rarely makes the difference; it is the *response of others toward the child performing the experiment that counts.* Thus, when a child's new behavior is known only to the child, it creates only a limited effect. Instead, we want to generate a ripple effect that involves the observations and reactions of the persons important to the child.
- If you cannot come up with an idea for an experiment, do not force yourself to come up with one: frequently a compliment alone is sufficient to generate new behavior.
- Most of the experiments fall into the category of "doing more" of what works.
- The number of experiments that propose the child "do something different" should be extremely small. These exercises are useful to break a chronic pattern where everyone is frustrated.

Flip a Coin

Most children (teenagers also) like this activity. It works better if you use a foreign coin (from a collection of foreign coins) and have the child choose one. The experiment begins with the child flipping the coin the first thing in the morning upon waking up. When the child gets heads, the child performs one kind of secret, novel activity; when the child gets tails, the child gets to have his or her usual day. Parents are to guess which side of the coin turned up each morning, but the child is to keep this information secret. This experiment can last about a week before a child loses interest.

Children like to surprise their parents. Find out from the child what might really surprise the parents (e.g., making breakfast, picking up the room without being told, polishing shoes, taking the dog out for a walk). Children often need some small help to figure out what might be the secret surprise that they can perform on their own without supervision of or prodding from parents. Having this little discussion with the child increases the chance that the child will actually create a new behavior, which in turn will elicit new responses from the parents. You may need to alert some children to look for "surprised" responses from those who are important to them, such as what faces mother might make, what father might say, or what new things they might do.

Pretend a Miracle Happened

A variation of "coin toss" is to "pretend a miracle happened." This experiment surprises children as well as those around them. After having discussed the details of a miracle with a child, the child is asked to pick a day on which the miracle will occur. (The day is to be selected without the help of a "coin toss" or other random method.) On this special "miracle day" the child will pretend that the problem is solved—for example, other kids are not taunting him in the playground during recess; she would behave as if she did not hear other children's comments about her haircut. The child's job is to find out who noticed that he or she was pretending that it was a miracle day, and what he or she did differently when the other kids noticed the different behavior. This experiment of pretending as if the miracle the client visualized during the session actually happened provides the child with a real-life opportunity to test his or her own ideas for solutions. Rather than waiting for the miracle to really happen, the child will get a "sneak peek" of how things can be when the problem is solved.

General Observation Task

Shaping and enforcing a child's positive behavior is generally accomplished through selective listening, talking, and paying attention to certain desirable behaviors. Undesirable behaviors are to be ignored. The more the parents pay attention to a child's negative behaviors, the bigger the negative behaviors become in the minds of observers. In order to enhance and increase positive behaviors, it is important that the parents participate in noticing the child's emerging positive behaviors. A therapist needs to give specific suggestions to parents on what to observe so that they can recognize the changes taking place with the child. For example, an observation task for a child might be, "Between now and next time we meet, I want you to observe very carefully what face Mom makes and what she does every time you start your homework without her telling you to do so." To a parent, you might suggest, "Between now and next time we meet, it would be very helpful to watch for when Tommy's anger crocodile stays in his cage," or "Observe when the wise owl shows up around your house."

Here are two observation activities for parents or caretakers.

Hit List

Ask the parents to put up a sheet of paper somewhere in the house. Every time they notice something their child does that impresses them, they are to write it down on this paper. The child may also write down things the parents did that were helpful.

What Goes Well

For every time the child listens and follows a direction of the parents, put a marble in a glass jar. The parents can spend few minutes with the child at bedtime and discuss what each marble stands for and what the parents observed that the child did well during the day. When the jar becomes full, the child gets a special reward. It is a good idea for the parents to discuss the reward with the child in advance. Our experience tells us that the reward is more effective when the parents do something with the child—special activities such as going to the park, playing basketball, going fishing, throwing and hitting baseballs together, swimming activities in the evening, going for a walk in the woods at night with flashlights—rather than buying material things.

DO SOMETHING DIFFERENT

When a parent tells the child to perform routine activities or chores and the child frequently does not listen parents need to respond in an innovative, novel way. Instead of becoming frustrated, many creative parents remember that children like surprises, so they find creative ways to remind children about the chores and responsibilities. Children can easily ignore reminders when repeated many times, and even describe their parent as "nagging." To avoid this "nagging" behavior and to be more effective, the parents need to do something entirely different to catch the child's attention—for example, sing the reminder, write the message down on a large piece of paper or flashcard and flash it when it is least expected, whisper the words as if it is top secret, or lead the child by the hand without saying a word. Here we list some other Do Something Different (DSD) activities that parents can do to catch the child's attention.

Pretend a Miracle Happened

Although it is useful for adults and teenagers to pick a convenient day for when a miracle is to happen, this is often too abstract for most children. You might want to suggest instead that the child pretend during the coming week that the "angry crocodile cannot go out of his cage" (using the image the child has used to visualize his or her problem), and the parent is to find out on which day the crocodile has been locked up in his cage. Parents participate in this activity by paying attention to how many days the crocodile was locked up and what was different around the family when the anger crocodile was quiet inside the cage.

It seems reasonable that most parents and children think that they have to wait for the problem to be solved before they can begin to behave in the way they want to—for example, smile more, be more active, or reach out to other kids with a smile. Instead of waiting for the problem to disappear on its own, pretending that the problem is already solved gives the child a head start. This would speed up the process of feeling more confident, having more friends, getting good grades, and so on. We believe the true empowerment of a child lies in the experience of taking charge of his or her problem and making life go the way that he or she wants.

We often tell the child not to warn the parents which day he or she will pick as the "pretend miracle happened" day because when it comes as a surprise, the parents are more delighted with the child and more spontaneous activity is likely to occur between the parents and the child. When the parents are aware of this general instruction, and because the child has complete control over which day he or she chooses to pretend, most parents naturally become very curious and are on the lookout for a pleasant demeanor. Many parents are tempted to discuss the child's good behavior and to point out such good behavior was what the parents were waiting for. Parents can easily revert to "nagging" and remind the child how difficult he or she has been. In order to circumvent this tendency, we suggest to parents that they not discuss the experimental tasks we recommend.

Parents need to learn to discreetly recognize and reward the child's positive changes. Therefore, we often suggest to parents not to have a lengthy "heart-heart" talk with the child about his or her success; instead they should wait until the next therapy session where the details of the success will be discussed in detail.

Surprise Hug (or Other Surprises)

Sometimes described as a technique of "pattern interruption," this exercise is a very good tool for those frustrated parents who report that they "have tried everything we can think of." Rather than waiting for the child to change, the parent can help speed up the process of change as well as take credit for helping the child to change. In turn, this can contribute to a rapid resolution to the problems. Repeated patterns around a child's temper tantrum, arguments around homework, and other more serious problems such as stealing and lying can respond nicely to this technique.

When parents respond to their child's behavior in a very predictable manner—such as reprimanding, scolding, or feeling exasperated—this may create dissonance in the child's understanding of his or her behavior. But when a child instead receives a surprise hug or a note tucked into the lunch box he or she may wonder what the parent might think he or she did that is positive. This can trigger the child to search for all the successes or good things he or she has accomplished recently. The child then expands the search to other situations such as school, visiting friends, dinnertime, being a good sibling, and a host of other possible things that he or she might have done to deserve a hug. By not explaining the reason behind this surprise show of affection, a parent can help the child to become curious about his or her own positive behaviors.

Suggest to parents they should hug their child out of the blue, say, "Honey, you made me feel great by the way you did something," and walk away. If the child is surprised by this action, the parent should just pretend nothing unusual happened. If the child wants to know what the hug was for, the parent should just smile and say, "Honey, this is a secret; maybe you will find out someday." The parent should then change the conversation.

Along the same lines, you can make the following suggestion to the parent who complains about the child's messy room or other irritating habits that wear down their patience. Have the parents place a chocolate heart, picture of a heart, or other common sign of affection in a place where it is very difficult to overlook, such as under the bed linen, in his or her lunchbox, or in the child's favorite shirt pocket. The chocolate heart or a picture of a heart should have a note attached to it that reads: "I hate your mess and I feel upset about it every time I see it, but I definitely love you, Jim [or Jane]. Love, Mom [Dad]."

Magic 5 Minutes

Ask the parents to spend 5 minutes each day with their child. This should be done regardless of how the day went and without letting the time be interrupted by a phone call, the doorbell, or even TV. Suggest to the parents that they consult the child on how to spend this magic 5 minutes. Some children have come up with these ideas: give a massage, tell jokes, make a drawing, play card games.

Power

Ask the child's father to have a little play physical contest with his son (or daughter if she is physically active) every day—e.g., battle with cushions, arm wrestle, shoot baskets. It is not important who wins the game, but the ability to control the fight is important. Make sure a kitchen timer is set so that you will know when to stop.

Responsibility

Ask the parents to give the child a "big" responsibility. Frequently we hear parents say, "We only ask our child to do little things, but even then he does not do it." Perhaps this is the point. Children want to do important things such as cook a dinner, do the shopping, paint a wall, or take care of a sick parent. Doing important tasks now and then allows the child to feel important and capable of making a contribution to the family.

The Wonder Bag Surprise

Have the child and the parents write down five wishes, each on a separate piece of paper. Put the two sets of wishes in "wonder" bags and exchange the bags. (The bags can be very simple, brown paper lunch bags will suffice.) Every week one wish is picked out of each bag and the child, as well as the parents, have a whole week to fulfill the wishes. Remind the parents and the child to write down wishes, not orders.

DO MORE

This broad category of techniques we call "Do More." Here you will find many little techniques (or tricks) that have been used successfully for generations. Rather than inventing a new wheel, we like to suggest that you learn from parents what they have found works with their child and then get them to "do more" of what works for them. Many parents we meet do not recognize that they have a treasure chest full of little techniques and tricks, and we just want to describe five little techniques that you can use with a child immediately.

Little Trances and Anchors

Find out from the child situations in which he or she felt confident, strong, and successful—e.g., singing, talking in front of the class, helping someone, or playing football. Invite the child to imagine very clearly the situation, including the colors, the sounds, the smells, the body sensations, tones of voice he or she heard. Ask the child to give a name to this particular situation.

Ask the child's permission to touch his or her wrist and ask the child to close his or her eyes. While you are holding the child's hand, you can lead the child through the situation you just discussed by saying: "I ask you to go into the situation [use the name the child gave to the situation] and while you can see yourself running after the football, you listen to all the noises from around you; and while all the different sounds are coming from around, I want you to pay attention to what you can hear in yourself, the words you are saying to yourself. And you may discover and notice all the different sensations and this typical feeling of being in a successful situation."

Instruct the child to touch his or her wrist between now and the next session to get in touch with the positive and successful feelings whenever it is needed.

Tighten Your Butts!

We learned this little technique from a special education teacher named Margaret Shilts who, for 26 years, has taught children with special education needs. In that time, she developed many useful techniques that she uses without recognizing how wonderful they are. When her class of children become restless and irritable, she distracts the children by telling them to "Now tighten your butts five times!" Margaret explains that this activity is not noticeable to others and helps to refocus the children on managing their own behaviors.

Magic of Rubbing Your Thumb

This technique (from Shilts again) also calms down a roomful of restless, even "hyperactive" children. You direct the children to focus on rubbing their thumbs and index fingers together. They can do this under the desk, with their hands in their pockets, or with their arms hanging at their sides without drawing attention to themselves. We found this to be a wonderful way to calm down children, even in a group.

Hands on Your Head

Another special education teacher came up with this little trick to help children to focus in an active classroom setting. When a roomful of children seems to become noisy or boisterous, instead of yelling at them, the teacher flicks the light in the room on and off. She trained the children to put both their hands on their heads when the room becomes dark. This prevents the teacher from having to yell at the class.

Safe Place

Some children tell you that the day after the miracle they feel calm and safe. You can ask the child to imagine in detail the safe place. You can lead the search for a safe place by saying: "Close your eyes and let yourself be surprised by the pictures coming up. You may discover a place you know, maybe in nature or somewhere in a house you know. You may discover a place you have not been but just comes up in your imagination and it can become very meaningful to you. Just let yourself be surprised by the pictures you have. When you think one of them stays with you, you can start to describe it to me." Again, you lead the child to notice the colors, the sounds, and the smells; the child should have a detailed description of the safe place. Ask about where the child is, whether he or she is standing, sitting, or lying down. Ask the child to take notice of the sensation of the texture of the materials or environment around the child. The picture should be be as specific as possible. This specificity will help the child experience the calm and safe feelings as soon as he or she re-imagines that safe place.

Chapter 7

Treating Children with Uncommon Needs

EVEN THOUGH WE BELIEVE THAT ALL CHILDREN ARE SPECIAL AND UNIQUE, there are children who require even more uncommon and specially crafted approaches in the therapeutic setting. These are the children who must learn to compensate for their problem by utilizing resources beyond those they already have. These resources may include: additional help; medications; specialized training such as physical therapy or speech therapy; and medical devices such as a wheel chair or walking aids. The more important resources for these children, however, are their family and their parents' commitment, love, and willingness to do whatever is necessary to provide the best help. Community and neighborhood resources and support are also important, as are the public financial resources to provide special programs, transportation, and special facilities in schools and in health care settings. The child's own personality—determination to become the best he or she can be, desire to be normal like other children, intellectual ability—also becomes a valuable resource.

We always try to make use of the child's native abilities and individual strengths. We also aim to find an individualized approach tailored to fit the child's views as well as those of the parents'.

Despite all the personal resources, there are children whose needs may never be fully met and who, in order to be productive and feel satisfied with their life, may require special services for their entire lifetimes. Therefore, we have decided to follow the usual practice of the field and, in a separate chapter, discuss these extraordinary children and their parents, all of whom have overcome some amazing obstacles and have learned to thrive despite of their uncommon needs.

In this chapter we list the questions most frequently asked by parents and caretakers, as well as audience members in workshops and training programs. We then offer our own thoughts and present helpful practice hints through case examples. We are not always successful as therapists (particularly when trying to help in these difficult cases), and we want to recognize this fact. We will share our agonizing moments when working with these unsuccessful cases. Later in Chapter 9 we offer some helpful ways to view such situations.

Throughout any contact you may have with a child with uncommon needs and their parents, it is always important to remember their heroic dedication and determination to face enormous challenges every day. The grace and humor of these family members are a lesson and inspiration to us all.

As we have done elsewhere in this book, here we provide guidelines for treating children with special needs by seeing their humanity and admiring them. As with any child, do not categorize them or focus on their problems.

1. Meet the child as a person first; ask about favorite activities, best friend, what he or she is good at, and so on.
2. Determine the resources found in the child, his or her parents, and his or her environment—e.g., what the child knows how to do, what the child excels in at school, and so on.
3. Consider what might be a "good reason" for the child to have a specific problem—for instance, and what the child might be trying to accomplish through stealing.
4. Look for another way to meet the child's needs so that engaging in this troublesome behavior is no longer necessary.

These principles are adaptable to almost all situations. Finding the individualized approach is where the therapist's creativity is called for.

ASSESSING A CHILD WITH UNCOMMON NEEDS

When meeting a child with uncommon needs, it is a good idea to have in your mind some outline of routine questions that you can adapt in a solution-building manner. With traditional assessments, the meeting is usually designed to push the limits of the child's capacity until the child will reach the point of not being able to perform the tasks. In this kind of situation, we would not be able to assess the child's full range of abilities and strengths, because we would be seeking to find his or her limitations. We like to compare what we do in therapy by means of the following imagery.

Suppose you are strolling through a wonderful garden with lots of different plants. Some are commonly seen everywhere and you know right away what kind of plants they are, while others are so exotic and unusual that you are surprised to find them. Some plants grow everywhere like weeds, while others only thrive under special conditions (e.g., in shaded areas in fertile soil, in full sun, only in sandy soil).

Unlike the view that assessment is an objective, unbiased, scientific study of facts, we believe that assessment is also very interactive. When we approach the child with an attitude of acceptance and encouragement, anticipating to be surprised by the discovery of what the child is capable of doing, not only is it easier to get the child's cooperation, but often the child performs to the best of his or her ability. Of course, we are also interested in the child's needs and limitations, so the important point is to be surprised by as many skills and abilities as the child shows us so that we can build on these when addressing his or her limitations.

Because a child's strengths may not become obvious when posing basic questions, you may need extra sessions, perhaps in the range of 2–4 sessions, depending on how serious the child's special needs. It is important to observe the child in different contexts, for example, perhaps without the hovering or worried mother. It is important to observe and interact with the child in different situations and times of the day and not draw general conclusions from an individual session (perhaps the child had a fight with the caretaker on the way to the first interview).

The following are some areas of observation that a routine child assessment will require:

- Large and fine motor skills
- Visual skills: visual perception, recognition, and reproduction of visual material
- Visual-motor coordination: hand-eye coordination
- Auditory capacity: recognition of sounds, reproduction of sounds, capacity for perceiving and memorizing words and numbers
- Attention span
- Psychological abilities: coping strategies with new room, new person, new toys; reactions to success, frustration; ability to sustain efforts; interaction with parents, therapist, and siblings
- Cognitive-intellectual skills: understanding of speech, context, and knowledge
- Planning of actions: ability to perform serious sequences.

CASE EXAMPLE: SUCCESSES THAT MATTER

Six-year-old Jack was a very difficult child for his parents to manage. He was very bright, with amazing language skills for his age, and he ruled the roost at home. The only child of a very young mother and a father in his second marriage who has two grown children from his previous marriage, Jack did well in kindergarten. Yet, Jack would not allow his parents to talk to each other. He would make sure that he disrupted their grown-up talks and never followed his parents' directions or orders. His father's approach was to give Jack a long-winded explanation of why he needed to listen to his parents. The father alternated these lectures with lavish praise whenever Jack did small things on his own, such as tying his own shoes, buttoning his own jacket, and so on—tasks that most 6-year-olds can perform quite well.

During the first and second sessions, Jack would often plug his fingers in his ears to show the adults that he was not listening. He did the same when his parents told me things they thought Jack was good at. I started to pay attention to moments when Jack was listening to what his parents were saying. I realized that he was very attentive whenever his parents complimented him on things he himself considered to be real achievements. It finally occurred to me that in their good intentions, the parents were praising the boy indiscriminately, complimenting him for every little thing he did. It seemed that Jack felt he was not taken seriously. After a thinking break, I suggested to the parents that they pay attention to what they would like to compliment the child for and whether they thought these were outstanding events for Jack.

By the third session, Jack stopped plugging his ears and his parents realized that their way of praising him was not helpful; in fact, it effectively undermined what they were trying to accomplish with him.

Focus on a Child's Abilities, Not Only on Disability

This is a theme we have repeated many times in this book. Therefore, we want to offer a case example involving Mathew. His case shows what a difference it can make when we work with the child's abilities, and not focus only on disabilities.

CASE EXAMPLE: BEATING CITY HALL

Mathew's referral was triggered by a recent violent outburst and a physical attack on a teacher. Fourteen-year-old Mathew was diagnosed with Prader-Willis Syndrome (PWS) by his pediatrician, whose care Mathew had been under for many years. This diagnosis is based on the following major and minor criteria. Major criteria include: hypotonia; excessive weight gain after the first year; obsession with food; characteristic facial features; and mild to moderate intellectual retardation. Minor criteria are: behavior problems; vio-

lent outbursts; obsessive/compulsive behavior; tendency to be argumentative, stubborn, and persevering; stealing and lying; sleep disturbance; speech articulation defects; and skin picking. His mother reported all of the mentioned criteria, except Matthew's being overweight. I (TS) was very surprised to see Mathew with normal weight and recognized this as a sign of success and an indication of environmental resources. I wondered, how in the world did he achieve this with hyperphagia and obsession with food?

Mathew was a champion for a normal weight PWS among the age group of 14–18 in Europe. I learned that all the food is locked up—his mother was the food keeper in the home, and the teacher performed this role at school. Apparently he was disciplined enough to accept this limitation on food, even though his sister, brother, and other children at school were allowed to help themselves. I was awed to think about all the hard work it must have taken to attain the degree of discipline and control that Mathew and his family had accomplished so far, because with PWS, one is not able to feel full but is always hungry.

During the first session I learned that Mathew liked to ride horses, attended the special school for intellectually challenged children, and he was the best in math in his class. In addition, he wanted to be a farmer someday. His answer to our miracle question (described fully in Chapter 3 that generates client's vision of desirable future) was that: "Other people would not get on my nerves, I will have fewer temper outbursts, and keep my weight." As I talked longer with Mathew, my assessment was that he seemed to be functioning at the intellectual level of an 8 year-old. It meant Mathew and I needed the help of puppets or other objects to visualize what he wanted; verbal contact alone would not be sufficient. So, I asked Mathew which animal he thought represented one that did not get bothered when others wanted to get on their nerves. His answer was "a horse," and we agreed that he needed to have a skin as thick as a horse's. I gave him a blanket and we decided that it was a "horse skin." He enjoyed playing wrapped in the "horse skin" and did not want to put it down until the end of the session.

I learned that his mother was a very strong person who obviously had done a marvelous job with Mathew, but she felt she was at the end of her rope and could not cope with life anymore. The situation was getting to be just too much for her. Her answer to the miracle question was that she would have someone to talk to about her worries and about different ways to handle the situation with Mathew. She also desired the security of knowing that Mathew had someone else to come and talk to when she could not cope any more so that the burden was not all on her shoulders but perhaps shared with a therapist.

I had been seeing Mathew and his mother once every two weeks during the past year. (As of this date, I continue to meet with the two.) For the first six months, we concentrated on building a "success tower" representing the *accomplishments of the previous two weeks. He always liked to have his picture taken with the success tower at the end of the session. There were small differences between his mother's and his perception of how he was doing: he called whatever he had done a "success," while his mother would described it as a "first step." Neither of them ever took issue with the fact that progress had been made.*

Recently, our focus has been on: (1) learning, as much as possible, what are the most favorable situations that make Mathew feel successful; (2) what Mathew can do to increase the likelihood of a successful situation; (3) what others in his life could do to be helpful.

Here is an example from school: The teacher learned about what the term "horse skin" meant to Mathew, and this secret code word seems to work much better for him than when the teacher told him to "calm down" or to "control your temper." It has become clear that being told to "calm down" was like being told off by the teacher and it has a way of escalating his temper instead of calming it down. During the past year, he has had no outbursts or aggressive behavior toward others, and the current goal is to maintain this level of self-control.

His habit of picking at his skin got to be quite severe for a while, to the point of his skin becoming infected. Mathew came up with the idea that he wanted to reduce "the building plots" on his body, and so he set up a competition between himself and the city of Zurich's public works department who repair the streets. He wanted to know whether the workers would finish their job of filling the potholes first or he would reduce the "building plots" on his body. As he made progress toward reducing the number of sores on his skin, his goal changed to having a "smooth skin" over his entire body before the city workers finished their street repair project. He beat City Hall! For the first time in a long while, he had smooth skin over his entire body and he likes to show off his body in warmer weather. Sometime later, he started to pick his skin again, but knowing that he succeeded once makes all the difference in the world.

SOLUTIONS FOR
DIFFICULT SITUATIONS

We are often asked whether and how we deliver bad news to parents about their children. Most people misunderstand our approach. They think that we do not emphasize problems because it somehow means that we avoid dealing with problems entirely or that we avoid delivering bad news for fear that we may devastate the parents. As we want to touch on a number of difficult issues in working with children, we hope it becomes clear that such misperceptions derive from our *emphasis* on solutions. We never deny or "pretend that a problem does not exist."

We always speak plainly to parents about their child, even when we need to deliver "unwelcome" or "bad" news.

We want to show, through the following case example, how to assess a child when there seems to be a difficulty, and then how to follow up with parents when it is your unpleasant task to deliver such news or possibly suggest a difficult course of action that parents can take.

CASE EXAMPLE: IS OUR CHILD "RETARDED"?

Milena, a 5-year-old ball of energy, was brought to therapy by her parents in order to address a very serious question: Was Milena retarded? Did she have ADHD (Attention Deficit Hyperactivity Disorder) and, if so, what kind of kindergarten should we send her to? What was wrong with her? Was there hope for her?

As usual, the first session was with Milena and her parents. Even before we walked into my office (TS), it was clear that Milena was active: she was looking at the children's books in the waiting room and she quickly said hello to me and went into the therapy room on her own. She moved from item to item, touching everything in sight. Somehow I had the impression that this was her way to reassure herself.

I asked Milena to sit down and explained what was to come. She listened to my words, but I sensed that these words did not mean much to her, or there was no indication that she understood them. I started to ask Milena some questions, but she was having difficulty comprehending or answering my simple, age-appropriate questions. I quickly realized that she might respond better to activities rather than to talking. After obtaining permission from the parents to spend some time playing with Milena in order to engage with her, I asked the parents to sit in one corner of my office to observe.

Milena was attracted to wooden blocks. We sat together on the floor and Milena started to take all the blocks and cubes out of the basket in which they were kept. She was very quick at doing this and, as soon as the cubes were all out of the basket, she was then attracted to the wooden animals on the shelf. I decided to give some direction and observe how she responded. I asked Milena to hand me a block and another one, and I started to build a tower. I noticed that Milena could be involved in a simple activity and she was able to interact with me for a short period. As I instructed Milena to continue building the tower, I carefully observed her fine motor skills and eye-hand coordination. I asked Milena what color block she needed next with her building and she mentioned red; when I handed her the red, she accepted it without difficulty. Now I learned that Milena could understand the concept of color. Next, I asked for the names of the other colors she needed. One time, I deliberately handed her the wrong color. She did not notice this. This did not necessarily mean that she did not recognize the color, but it indicated to me that I had to test this in another context to be sure.

After about 5 minutes, I felt sufficiently engaged with Milena. I had the impression that she was a child who lives very much in her own world and, given that I was a stranger, she should have been somewhat reluctant to engage with me at this stage. She wanted to touch and pull out all the things she saw around her. I sat back with her parents and, while we talked, I noticed that Milena was not aware of the adults in the room, that she could easily spend her time moving from one object to another without engaging with objects by playing with them.

I learned from the parents that Milena was the second daughter and the pregnancy and birth were normal. However, after birth, pediatricians determined that she had a heart defect and she went through open-heart surgery at age 2. Even before this surgery the parents noticed that Milena did not develop normally as did their first daughter and recognized that something was amiss. The parents wanted to find out what was wrong with Milena and find an appropriate school for her.

After a short thinking break, I complimented the parents on their good observation skills and told them that the timing of their request for an assessment was excellent. I asked their permission to observe and assess Milena's strengths and needs in two to three more sessions. During these sessions I would meet with Milena alone.

During the next two sessions, one hour each, the following assessment was made:

1. *I offered Milena three books and asked her to pick one. She was able to make a choice. We climbed on the bed and I handed her the book she chose. She did not look at the book, which indicated to me that she needed more direction and guidance. I started to read the story, which gave me the opportunity to learn about the level of her understanding of language. The book also gave her an opportunity to count to ten, which I learned that she could do but that she had not quite developed an understanding of quantity.*

2. *I also wanted to find out whether she could distinguish colors in a different context. She did reasonably well with colors.*

3. *We got involved in a drawing game and I observed how she held a pencil and the shape or forms she could draw. Next I cut a paper necklace, placed it around her neck, and asked her to cut it with scissors, which she had difficulty handling.*

4. *We put puzzles together. Watching her work on them gave me information about her form perception and recognition.*

5. *We played with a ball and I asked her to mimic me. I was looking for clues as to whether she was able to take turns, imitate certain motions, and develop ideas to further the play. For example, when we next played*

"shopping" she understood the activity but she was not able to develop her own ideas about what came next.

6. *I was also looking for whether she had strong visual and/or auditory skills that could be used to compensate for the lack in other areas.*

7. *I needed to learn: whether she liked to be touched and, if so, what kind of tactile activity would hold her interest the most; whether her attention span grew longer as she became older; and which activities would be most useful and helpful to her.*

After the first session with Milena, I wrote down all my observations and then I wrote down what further information I needed to get a larger, more rounded picture of her abilities and needs. My overall assessment was the following:

Milena certainly liked to be active, and her visual perception was strong while her auditory capacity needed strengthening. For parents and teachers, this means that in order to reach Milena or get her to do something, they have to show Milena what they want her to do much more often than telling her. She also needed to be shielded from too much stimulation because she became distracted easily and touching the arm or shoulders was more useful for her. In addition, she needed some help in increasing her attention span by getting her involved in activities that clearly held her interest, such as being physically active in a closely managed and guided manner. Her pleasant personality was clearly her strength and a very useful resource of which her parents and teachers need to be reminded frequently.

When I compared Milena with other 5-year-old children, it was clear that she was developmentally delayed by about two years.

The fourth session was conducted with the parents only. Before they arrived, I had prepared my approach to delivering "bad" news to parents, and rehearsed ways to provide them with answers to questions they had raised during the first meeting. I prepared a glass half-full of blue-colored water. Using simple language I explained to Milena's parents that she had to be considered mentally retarded, and I pointed out everything I had observed—all the activities that Milena and I had done together and the details of my observations, both what she was able to do and what she was not able to. Then I showed them the glass half-full of blue water and pointed to the two parts: the full, blue part and the empty part. Being mentally retarded indicates the empty part. The blue part symbolizes what Milena already had (resources such as her pleasant personality, her strong visual ability, her high energy level, and her liking to be touched). I asked the parent's permission to speak about the blue part and how, with the help of this blue part, Milena could improve her skills by developing her existing abilities. By concentrating on the blue part, they and the therapist could help her lead a good life.

Discussion. I (IKB) particularly like this balanced way of presenting "bad" news to parents about their child. While most parents need and want to know what the reality is, we could offer more hopeful information about what is possible, rather than simply what the limitations are. Besides, we really do not know what kind of new information might emerge within a rather short time. Parents' ability to take in new information about their child varies widely, depending on their readiness to hear the news and a therapist's sensitivity to these individual variations is very important.

ASSESSMENT AS INTERVENTION

Assessment of a problem is commonly believed to be a precursor to getting treatment—that is, unless one is assessed (or diagnosed) one cannot begin the treatment process. We think otherwise. It is impossible not to influence the client's perception by the kind of questions we ask within the context of learning why the parents are talking to you about their child. Every question we raise, including asking a parent, "How old are you?", is meaningful within the context of why the parent or the child is talking to a therapist. This benign question can hold a host of different meanings for the client. For example, the client may hear this question as suggesting the mother's age may have some relationship to the child's problem. Therefore, it is important to gain an understanding of the larger situation—what are the problems, what were the parents told, what are their expectations from therapy, and so on—by asking some of the following questions as part of your assessment:

- Could you explain to me how this (e.g., ADHD, PTSD, personality disorder, trauma, depression, attachment disorder) is a problem for you and your child?
- What is your understanding of why your child has this problem?
- How do you explain this problem to yourself, to your child, or to others?
- What have you been told (read, learned, etc.) about problems like this?
- Suppose your child can tell me what happened or what caused this problem, how would that be helpful for your child?
- Knowing your child as well as you do, what will tell you that things are getting a little bit better for your child?
- What difference would it make between you and your child when things get a little bit better? Between your child and other children? In school? With teachers? With other adults?

By placing the parents at the center of the treatment of the child's problems, we not only are respectful of the parents' wishes but also give recognition that they are the experts on their child. Our time with the child generally tends to be short-term, whereas the parent-child relationship has been there long before we came upon the scene and will last long after our influence is over. Again, it is helpful to compliment the parents' observational skills, what they have tried to do, and how much they are willing to do. At the end of the conversation, it is also helpful to summarize what the parents wanted for their child, and to indicate that we heard their wishes and desires.

FREQUENTLY ASKED QUESTIONS

In order to respond to the many questions we have been asked about specific cases of children with uncommon needs, we will follow a modified question and answer format.

Do You Recommend Medication for Children?

Although SFBT is primarily based on the useful dialogue that elicits the resources within and around the client, medications are useful in certain situations. Our primary goal is finding "what works." We generally prefer to think of medication *not* as the first solution, but there certainly are situations where medications are called for and would improve the quality of life for the child and parents. With the solution-focused approach, we prefer to look at the big picture of the child's functioning first and consider how medication might fit into the overall picture. In other words, we think of medication as *fitting into* the overall solution rather than as being THE solution. This means close and frequent monitoring and adjustments of medication dosage and usage. It also requires paying attention to what the child, parent, teachers, or others are doing that is helpful.

Even though we come across this infrequently, we are concerned that some teachers, parents, and children may believe the medicine has some magic properties and all the child has to do is take the medicine; they have no role to play in its effectiveness or their general improvement. What we witness more frequently, however, are situations where the parents or caretakers have strong feelings against medicating their child for life, again, believing that somehow the medicine changes the child's personality. For example, one mother was adamantly opposed to the school's demand that she put her son, Jason, on Ritalin so that he could learn better; she would hear none of this because she was convinced that once Jason "is drugged, he will no longer be Jason!" Many parents and some adolescents are fearful that taking medications sets them apart from other children, making them "different"—meaning they are "weird" or "mental." As a result, often they are very reluctant to begin taking medications. We are sympathetic to this concern and recognize that parents want to do what is best for their children. Respectfully asking what is their understanding of how medication affects the child, particularly what kind of experiences they have had with any kind of medication, is a gentle way to begin the conversation about their fears regarding medication. It is important to clarify the sense of the "relationship" the child or the parent has with the medication because this attitude will shape what kind of relationship the child or the parent will have toward the use of the medications.

We prefer to emphasize the attitude that clients are in charge of what the medication will do *for* them, rather than being passive recipients of what medicine will do to them. When we first address the topic of medication with parents we usually begin with resource-finding questions such as the following:

- Has anybody (pediatrician, nurse, teacher, neighbor, family member) suggested to you that medication might be useful to... (achieve the client's goal)?
- What is your understanding of how medications such as this (named earlier) might work for your child?
- Has your child ever been on medication of any kind that's been helpful? Not helpful?

When the parent or teacher asks for the medication, the following exploration may be useful:

- What are some of your thoughts about how medication will be helpful to your child?
- Suppose this medication worked for your child, what changes would you see in your child that will tell you that it is working for him or her?
- Tell me about the times when he is a little bit closer to what you want him to be like?
- What are some of your ideas of what you would do to help the medication work for your child?
- What will you see in your child that will tell you that he or she may no longer need to be on medications?

How Do We Discuss Medication with Our Child?

You can discuss the necessity of medication with children, but it has to make sense to them. One of my (TS) favorite and practical ways to discuss medication with a young child is to use the metaphor of a car, something about which all children know.

I begin by bringing up the topic of what is needed to make a car run smoothly, so that the car will get you from here to there. We start with the most obvious things a car needs to run: wheels and tires, engine, steering wheel, windshield, fuel, oil, and so on. I follow the child's lead and then encourage the child to think about the smaller things—turn signals, oil changes, windshield wipers, and so on—and then discuss what happens to the car when these things do not work properly or are lacking. The child usually learns that the car can run for a while but eventually there is a problem—perhaps the car will lose power, does not go as fast as it once did, or stop running altogether. At this point I make the connection between medication and the child's functioning at his or her peak. Ritalin, for example, is like the oil in an engine that makes the car run smoothly and keeps it going at full power. But of course, I add, for any car the most important thing is the attentive driver who knows where to go and which road to take in order to reach the desired destination.

The translation into the child's life is that Ritalin can help the child to have fewer fights with other children, be more attentive in class, and to handle things with more care. But, still, everything depends on the child's decision and interactions with his or her environment. The child is asked to sit in the driver's seat! When we help the child to find a very individual and personal way to think about the medication, the child is much more likely to cooperate and become involved in self-care. Once the child accepts the use of medication, then our role is to hand over control to the child. The next step is to listen carefully to the child so that we will get useful information about how to be a little bit more helpful to his or her attempt to be in control. We want to discuss the case of Henry to show you how these collaborations with the child can be achieved.

CASE EXAMPLE: RITALIN AND A SOFT VOICE

Twelve-year-old Henry had been on Ritalin for one year when I (TS) first met him. His mother had recently realized that things were going badly at school and home: lots of fights with his siblings and friends at school, and, in particular, trouble during math class. His mother found out that Henry had not been taking his Ritalin, which contributed to his current problems.

Frustrated and angry, the very upset mother called me and asked me to see Henry as soon as possible. The last session I had with Henry had been 4 months before.

Henry had been taking one Ritalin SR pill in the morning and one at noon. Initially he was reluctant to talk when we met without his mother (an arrangement of his request) because he was still angry with his mother for making him come and see me. When I asked him what was happening, I also told him I presumed he must have "good reasons" for not taking Ritalin anymore. He mentioned that he was really tired of being reminded every morning that he is different from other kids. In addition, he had "fallen in love" with a girl and was convinced that the new girlfriend would be interested in him only if he was "normal." Furthermore, he realized that Ritalin was not helping him anymore, especially not in math class where he was convinced that he needed it the most. He explained that he pretended to swallow the Ritalin, but that he spit it out later.

His explanation certainly made sense and seemed reasonable. So, I asked Henry some questions about the new girlfriend—a very important person in Henry's life at the time. What did she like about his personality? Why did she think he was different from other boys? What did he like best about her?

Then I engaged Henry in a discussion of Ritalin SR, which is a slow-acting form of medication that he takes in the morning. The physiological reaction of Ritalin SR is that it is slower acting than the regular form but lasts longer. Then I asked about school and learned that recently his math class was changed from 11:00 a.m. to 9:00 a.m. It occurred to me that if Henry took the pill shortly before going to school, the full effect of the Ritalin SR would not be in his system yet. Thus, taking his complaints seriously, I complimented Henry on his good observations and asked him to start in the morning with normal Ritalin and take the Ritalin SR at lunch.

A week later Henry called and was very pleased with how things were going. He was convinced that Ritalin was of some help, although the girl he was interested in still did not want to date him. But he became aware that he could impress girls with his soft voice and he was quite proud of this fact.

How Do You Work with Children Who Are Abused?

Whenever we are asked questions on working with abused children, we hear the following concerns: (1) We want to make sure that all abused children are protected and not allowed to fall between the cracks and suffer further abuse; (2) How can I be helpful when a child refuses to talk about the abuse for whatever reason?; (3) Is there a special way to talk to these children without inflicting more pain on them?; (4) Do I have the responsibility to protect the child immediately when an abuse is disclosed?; (5) What do I need to do with the adult or the parent who has abused the child?

Many beginning and even experienced professionals who work with children frequently ask these and other questions because they want to make sure that they are not making things more difficult for the child. We want to remind you that these children are not so fragile and frail that you need to walk on eggshells. Unless it is an extremely cruel and unusually severe form of abuse—which usually requires immediate action such as taking them into protective custody or to an emergency medical care—outwardly you will not be able to tell these "abused" children apart from other children who were not abused. For most children, it is more helpful to work with them respectfully, taking into consideration their wishes and ideas for what they need and want, as well as their individual characteristics. Avoid grouping them into a category. In this regard, use the same approach as you would with any other children, that is, always listening for what they want and looking for successful mastery of skills and knowledge.

By now, perhaps you are aware of how strongly biased we are in this regard. We feel that

(1)   Even abused children, no matter how badly they have been abused, still have areas that are functioning well;
(2)   You should begin with the healthy part of the child first;
(3)   You should ask the children about what is their idea of how they want their life/situation to be different so that life is a little bit better for them; sometimes they, too, like all children, have an idea of what they want their life to be like, to make things a little bit easier, happier, or a little more safe.

As we have shown throughout this book and elsewhere (Berg & Kelly, 2000), even a small child has some idea of what will make his or her life a little bit easier, such as "I want to have more friends," "not be afraid of other children," "I want to live with my dad," or "have my mother be proud of me," and "I want to see my mom." Being respectful of a child means taking these small children's wishes seriously and addressing their concerns immediately. When you are not able to give information immediately—for example, when it is not clear whether the abuse has occurred or whether there was an accidental injury and it will take time to determine what actually happened—the best thing to do would be to explain the situation as honestly as possible.

We are concerned that when a child is described as "abused," somehow our perception of the child immediately is changed and we begin to see the child as a helpless "victim" who needs to be constantly protected. We see them as fragile, thus making it easier for us to completely take over their care. Certainly all children need adults to make decisions for them, but the steps in making important decisions that will affect the future of the child also need to be explained to the child in an understandable language.

Even if an adult has brought the child to your attention in the wake of recent abuse—when the child comes to day care or school with bruises or black and blue patches on their arm or legs, and scratch marks or broken skin across the back, and so on—while you are treating the child, you can still connect with the child by asking about favorite activities or favorite cartoon characters. This response brings out the healthier, "normal" side of the child even while taking care of the child's imediate need for water, food, clean clothes, feeling safe, and feeling comforted. We want to convey to such children that despite of their serious problems, a big portion of their lives is still similar to other children's. We also want the child to understand that he or she is unique, and we are interested in what makes this child a unique person. Thus, in the middle of learning about the child's unique circumstances, living arrangements, what the child is proud of, what the child is successful at, and so on, you will collect information about immediate concerns the child has for him- or herself. Addressing these concerns is the most respectful way that we know of to interact with the child. Again, we would like to remind you that we could address several different concerns at the same time, but always seeing the child first, then the abuse, rather than the other way around.

Removing the child from the abusive situation is not something that anyone can do; such a decision can only be made with a court order after a careful review of a child's best interests. Berg and Kelly (2000) have provided a detailed description of how to work with abused children as well as their parents from a strengths-focused approach that is respectful of the child's needs and wishes.

CASE EXAMPLE: "GOOD REASON FOR RUNNING AWAY FROM HOME"

When I (IKB) first met Denise, a 13-year-old student in middle (secondary) school, I could hardly see her face because she bent her head down so low and her long, unruly hair made it difficult to notice her pretty features. She was polite enough to answer all of my questions, but in a mumbled voice, so I had to lean over toward her so that I could hear without asking her to repeat her answers. The school social worker who requested a consultation for Denise was very concerned about her repeated episodes running away from home. Every time she was on the run—usually lasting 2–3 days—Denise did not come to school. One thing the social worker noticed was that her mother never contacted the school either to report her missing or to inquire whether Denise made it to school or not. Even though the teachers saw a spark of intelligence in Denise, her general demeanor was uncertain and hesitant, and she would repeatedly comment about how "dumb" she was. All this combined to make Denise seem not such a bright child. As long as she did not create problems when she was back in school, the school was not terribly concerned about her. The one exception was the social worker, who stayed in contact with Denise whenever she returned from her runaway episodes.

Denise did not respond well when I tried to get to know her more; she was very hesitant to tell me about herself, saying that she was "dumb," that she didn't know much about school work, and that her goal was to graduate from high school so that she could become a hairdresser. When asked how she decided to become a hairdresser, she haltingly indicated that doing others' hair was the only thing she was good at. How did she find out she was good at styling other people's hair? Her friends ask her to do their hair, she responded, and that she was always told that she did a good job by her friends. She added that even her friends' mothers asked her to come over and do their hair, and sometimes they paid her a small amount of money in return. In addition, she loved working on people's hair — grown ups as well as her friends—because of the positive responses she always received.

Sensing her reluctance to talk about herself, I told her that I could see that her social worker was very concerned about her running away and skipping school and whether I could ask her some questions about that. Her head went immediately down lower and her back hunched over. Realizing that this was a very difficult topic for her, yet having to address this serious issue, I wanted to put this in as positive a framework as possible. The resource-finding approach was preferable to another lecture about "why you should not run away from home and also miss school." So, we had the following dialogue:

Therapist (Th):   I'm sure you have a very good reason for running away from home and missing school.

Denise's eyes immediately filled with tears and she cried quietly for few minutes. I realized that somehow I had touched on a sensitive spot for her but did not know exactly what. I began to think about safety issues for her first; my first concern was that she might get picked up by some men who might offer to help her and she could be forced into prostitution or being a courier for drug dealers. I had to act quickly to address this safety issue.

Th: I understand that you've been running away from home for some time and you seem like the kind of person who would not do something like this without a good reason. Could you tell me what some of the "good reason" might be?

Denise (D):   I have to run away from home because of my brother.

I immediately thought that perhaps she was being abused sexually by her brother and waited for her to add more information to this. But she was silent for quite a long time.

Th: I don't understand. Tell me again, what does this have to do with your brother?

D: The main reason I run away from home is because my brother beats me up and I run away until he calms down, and then I come back home.

Th: I see. So, you do have a good reason to run away, to stay safe and not get beat up?!

D: Yes.

Th: It makes sense that you have to run away to keep safe. So what does your mother do when your brother beats you up?

D: She doesn't do anything and doesn't say anything to my brother either.

Th: You mean, your mother knows all about your brother beating you but she does not stop him?

D: No, and I think she is afraid of him, too.

Th: So, what does your father do when this is going on?

D: My father died two years ago and so my brother says he is the boss of the house.

Recognizing that indeed she had a good reason to run away, I focused next on her safety while on the streets.

Th: So, tell me how you have managed to stay safe in the street. What do you do so that you have been safe so far? Lots of bad things can happen to girls who run away from home.

D: I know, I hear that, too. What we do is, the other girls and me, we pool our money together and we rent a motel room and we all stay there together during the night. There are some nice girls who take care of me and make sure I have things to eat, stuff like that. We usually stay together and go places together during the day.

Th: So, how do you decide it is safe for you to come home?

D: Sometimes, I come home when I know my brother is not home because he goes to school or I talk to my mother and she tells me when to come home.

So, it became clear to me that to keep talking to Denise about not running away was not effective. The really effective intervention could only be made at the level of helping the mother become strong enough to take care of her children in the way they needed to be taken care of, including her brother. Allowing a 17-year-old son to terrorize his sister and his mother certainly was not doing him any good and he needed to learn to behave like most 17-

year-olds, worrying about what most 17-year-olds worry about, and feeling competent at mastering new skills and knowledge that most teenagers should learn. What the brother needed, as much as Denise, was a strong parenting person who would be able to give him directions, to set limits, as well as to nurture him when needed so that he could prepare himself to be a successful adult, and not feel competent by physically abusing his mother and his sister.

The school social worker recognized that she needed to expand her view of the child's problems to take into account Denise's social context. Recognizing this helped the social worker to realize how narrow her focus on the problem has been. Denise could not solve the problem on her own without her mother's intervention. The child protective service was contacted, they visited the mother for the first time, and they engaged her in becoming the kind of mother that her two children needed her to become.

The mother was not aware that failing to protect the younger child from the abuse of the older child was against the law. She was shocked to learn that her preoccupation with her grief at the loss of her husband was damaging her children. In addition, there was a threat of being prosecuted for failing to protect the younger child. She sprang into action when it was pointed out to the mother that she could lose custody of Denise. It was revealed that she herself had lived in a very physically abusive marriage for 18 years and she was very fearful of the world outside the home because she became very isolated socially, and even from her own family during the marriage. The social worker began working with the mother and Denise stopped running away soon after.

What Do You Do When a Child Is Sexually Abused?

Of course all children need to grow up in a safe and loving environment and meeting these needs comes before anything else is considered. Not only is abuse of minors against the law, but most societies around the world have cultural, ethical, moral, and legal prohibitions against these behaviors toward children. It is easy to take the moral high ground with the offenders and immediately conclude that these horrible people must be punished or put away in prison for life. At least it might make us feel better, when we consider what kind of suffering these people imposed on a helpless little child. However, these situations are much more complex. For many of these children who are abused have several layers of relationships with the offending parent or family members. Alternative options available for these children are not always that clear, nor readily accessible. Whether the child is physically or sexually abused, we would like to emphasize that all children have mixed feelings about the abusive adults, especially if the offender is a family member or a parent. Except for those extremely cruel and heinous cases, most abusive relationships we come across in our practice are very complex, and no simple or easy solutions exist for these situations.

We would all like to believe that removing mistreated children from abusive situations is the quickest way to solve problems. However, for the child who has to face the trauma of dramatic rescue from an abusive situation, removal is not the end of the story; in fact, they are often exchanging one problem with another. Getting away from physical abuse is not necessarily always the best solution for the child because no easy life awaits the child on the other side of the door. Frequently the abusive parents are the only nurturing people the child has known, however meager, inadequate, and harmful the nurturing has been. So being abruptly taken away from friends, neighbors, and teachers is equally, if not more, traumatic for the child.

In our desire to show our sympathy for the child, and in response to the crisis situations that we often encounter, it is easy to forget that children also have some ideas about what is best for them. Again, we believe that asking the child's opinion is the most respectful way to deal with children whose opinions have not been respected by the abuser(s); taking their wishes into consideration is the most loving behavior we can show them. In the following case example, we want to show how these attitudes can be expressed with those children who have been sexually abused or maltreated.

CASE EXAMPLE: HEALING IN HER WAY

Christa, 16 years old, was brought to see me (TS) by her mother because she was sexually abused by a young man at a summer camp. The family was so upset about this disclosure that her older brother in the military even took a leave of absence and came home immediately to be with her and the rest of the family. The family had experienced a string of problems—such as illness, job loss, and financial problems—and this incidence was one more burden added to the family.

Christa, an attractive and bright girl, was eager to explain that she knew how to defend herself. Even though she had not been able prevent the incident, she said, she knew how to deal with the problem herself and kept saying that she was proud of how she acted to defend herself. Christa repeatedly said "I didn't know how strong and clever I was." Even though she was more afraid to go out of the house on her own after the incident, Christa felt OK and complained of her family, especially her mother, being overly protective of her. At the end of the first session she came up with a plan to discuss this concern with her mother. Otherwise, she seemed to be doing fine. But the mother was not convinced that Christa was doing fine and insisted that Christa did not know how traumatized she really was. So her mother asked for more sessions.

During the second and third sessions, Christa and I discussed how her studies were going, what she was doing to make herself continue to be strong and clever, and the various ways that she was getting back to being her old self. She explained that she was going back to being a class clown and she liked that about herself. Toward the end of the third session, Christa mentioned that she wanted to tell me something that she had not told anybody and asked me not to tell her mother. I asked her "How are you hoping telling me this secret is going to be helpful to you? Suppose you tell me about this, what difference would it make for you?" Then she finally revealed what seems like a flashback of "smell memory" from the abuse incident because the young man had been sweating and whenever she smelled sweat, she was flooded by the traumatic memory. This was especially so for the smell of semen. In such situations she did not feel in control of her breathing and got very scared about losing control.

I demonstrated for her some breathing and focusing techniques to help her to be more in control. (She thought about them and then decided which would be most helpful to her.) She finally decided that it would be good for her to protect herself by attending women's self-defense classes. In the meantime, she had to testify against the young man who assaulted her and it was a grueling four hours of testimony examined by a judge about the details of the assault. She did not have a clear memory of the details of exactly what she did, but she managed it quite well. She came away from the hearing with the impression that the judge did not believe her story entirely, but she felt OK about it. She was more worried about how difficult the trial was for her mother. In the following two sessions we talked at length about her fear and courage, and how important these two sides were for her, that they could stay side by side, and which side was helpful in what situations. Christa chose a hedgehog puppet to represent fear and a dog as courage and played out situations with puppets when each side would know when to come out and help Christa. With a family session in which they discussed closeness and independence, Christa decided that she did not need further sessions.

Two and a half years later, I received a phone call from her mother, saying that Christa had eating problems now, but a comprehensive medical exam indicated that she had no physical problems. Her mother was convinced that her eating problem and her depressed demeanor indicated Christa's low self-esteem, which must somehow be related to her sexual abuse two years before. Christa came in alone and discussed her goal to be a day care teacher and how much she likes working with small children. It was obvious that she really liked her work and apparently she was good at it. She thought her "eating problem" was nothing more than some kind of stomach flu she had recently come down with, from which she was sure she was recovering nicely.

Then she mentioned that recently, she had a boyfriend for some months and her mother had pressed her to tell him about her sexual abuse at age 16, although she herself thought it was not wise to tell him about it. Since then, the boy has asked for a time out in the relationship and he has become much more distant in his dealing with her.

Her answer to the miracle question (see Chapter 3) was: "I will do my best in my job as a day care teacher and my mom would be less involved in my private life and I would be able to tell my mother that I desire this without offending her." We discussed how she would know her mother was less involved in her personal life, and what she could do to help her mother to feel comfortable, thus giving her more room to be herself and be less worried. She had a variety of ideas, including how to handle her mother's detailed questions about her personal time away from home and her plan to move out when she finishes her education and starts to earn her own money.

I met with Christa's mother alone for two sessions, during which she expressed two concerns about her daughter: Does Christa need therapy for her eating disorder that may be connected to the trauma of sexual abuse?; and Should I talk to her boyfriend and give him some help on how to deal with his girlfriend who had been sexually abused? At the end of two sessions, the mother had an idea how to handle Christa's asking for advice (a fact Christa never mentioned). She really wanted her daughter to be an independent, confident young woman. Through the miracle questions, the mother came to the conclusion that she also needed to be thinking more about herself and her other child who was still in the military.

How Do You Work with Parents Who Abuse Their Children?

We want to make it clear that the safety of any child is a necessary condition for their positive development in any cultural, social, or economic conditions. Even a single case of child abuse or maltreatment—whether verbal, physical, psychological, or sexual—is too many and should not be tolerated in any society.

Yet it is important to note that the popular media portrayal of extremely brutal child abuse does not occur as frequently as sensational media coverage seems to imply (Berg & Kelly, 2000). There is also a great deal of misunderstanding, among professionals and the general public alike, about parents who abuse their children. We all tend to think that parents who abuse their child(ren) enjoy doing so, that they are horrible and evil people who enjoy torturing helpless children, and that they deserve to be punished and do not deserve to be parents. Of course, there are such parents now and then, but they are, thankfully, not the majority.

Our experience of working with parents who abuse their children is that they are overwhelmed with very difficult lives, often very isolated, unable to cope with many stressors in their lives, and have very little financial, emotional, and social support. In addition, many of these parents suffer debilitating emotional, psychiatric, and physical disabilities, are substance abusers, and have other difficulties. An overwhelming majority of them have themselves suffered physical, verbal, sexual, and emotional abuses as a child, and, for many, it has become a way of life. These circumstances certainly do not excuse them for mistreating, neglecting, and abusing children. But unless they receive help first, the ability of these parents to nurture their children is limited.

We want to make some distinction between *abuse* and *neglect*. Both are legal terms. Many professionals believe that neglect cases are more difficult to treat since a lack of emotional involvement with the child is much more insidious than violent physical involvement, which is easier to recognize and treat. It is much more damaging and confusing to a child when the parent behaves as though the child does not exist, with no emotional expression and interaction with the child seriously eroding the child's ability to trust his or her own emotional reactions, perceptions, and judgment. This is very similar to a child who grows up with no sensory, intellectual, or emotional stimulation. But such forms of abuse are not as noticeable to those outside the family. Therefore, these conditions can, and usually do, go on much longer before the case can be detected and something can be done about the neglect. Many parents, raised in families where the standard of what is "healthy" was a luxury rather than a necessity, may not be aware of the potential for a better life. Other parents view the "healthy" lifestyle they see in media as beyond their reach and may not even entertain the notion that it is possible for them to have the "good life" for themselves and their children. Use of the miracle question and its adaptations have proven to be useful in a clinical setting when you meet children who seem to have given up hope for the better things in life.

When there is physical or verbal abuse, at least there is an intense emotional involvement with the child that can be considered from more than one perspective. Looking at these emotional involvements as the parent's resources give us some ideas on what to do first. Abusive parents respond to strong feelings that the child elicits in themselves, which can be sorted out because the evidence is there to begin the process of change unlike in cases of neglect where such evidence is left hidden behind closed doors. Strong hatred for a child can be viewed as the parent's "misdirected energy" and they can receive help to redirect, but clients with no energy or passion are too difficult to work with.

Use of *coping* questions is helpful in finding out the parent's resources and successful strategies that prevented the parent from doing more harm to the child than already has been done. Coping questions elicit invisible strengths, commitments, and abilities to "stick to it even though it would be easier to give up," thus, acknowledging the client's ability to accomplish the smallest possible success such as "managing to get out of bed this morning."

Relationship questions teach parents to look at their relationships from the child's perspective. (Notice the difference in parent's responses between "What would your daughter say she likes the best about your being sober?" from "What would your daughter say she hates the most about your being drunk?") Be sympathetic about the parent's frustration and engage the parent in what he or she wants to have different in his or her life and with the child. It is also helpful to respectfully find out how the parent wants you to be helpful to them. It is always useful to engage with them by giving them credit for how he or she manages to keep going, in the face of enormous obstacles to attaining the necessary conditions for successful parenting.

It is much more productive to pay attention to exceptions to abuse, that is, the times when the parent could have hit the child but for some reason managed to control those impulses and walked out the door (or, as one mother reported, managed to lock herself in the bathroom to keep from hitting her child). Once parents realize that you are not interested in reprimanding or scolding them for their abusive behaviors but, instead, are interested in finding ways to successfully manage potentially dangerous situations, they become much more open and volunteer information willingly. This openness is usually followed by statement of concerns and requests for help. Once a parent expresses interest in getting help, then you can proceed with your plan to ask for more information on exceptions and how he or she managed to avoid being abusive and what it would take for him or her to repeat this small success.

How Do You Work with Parents Who Are Extremely Critical of Their Children?

During teaching, training, consultations, and supervision sessions we encounter situations where parents and other caregivers are described as extremely negative toward children. Sometimes parents are even described as "sabotaging" the child's therapy. Various motives for these behaviors are attributed to such parents, and much guesswork and hypothesizing are made about the adults' problems. It certainly makes us feel uncomfortable to encounter parents who are extremely negative about their children and we often want to scold them for their negativity. However, we realize that fighting negativity with negativity is not the solution and, if anything, may create a worse situation for the child. When parents feel insulted or demeaned, they may feel like lashing out at the child instead of confronting the person who is insulting them. It certainly does not motivate them to look at themselves.

In addition, we suggest that guessing about someone else's motivation is not terribly useful since the longer such attribution continues, the more we professionals look for ways to validate our perception and, before we realize it, we begin to behave as if these unspoken attributions are all true. They are in fact nothing more than our guesses or hunches, and it is always better to check with the parent about hunches. We suggest the following:

- When parents are extremely critical of the child, you need to quickly recognize that what the parents feel is a sense of failure as parents. Therefore, you need to make sure that you have sufficiently engaged with the parents' vision for themselves and their child. Of course nobody likes to hear some parent say to a child, "I wish you weren't born," "You ruined my life!" or even "You are an evil child!" Train yourself to listen to these tirades with a different set of ears. In other words, it is an indication that you need to engage with a parent by first seeing everything from the parent's perspective, not the child's only, and definitely not yours.
- Try asking, "What tells you that . . . ?" Find small things that you can honestly compliment the parent on, such as, "you must still be hopeful about the child even after years of disappointment." You are addressing the parent's negativity as his or her "wishful thinking" or a wish unfulfilled. It is much more useful to turn this around and formulate questions so that we get more useful information from the parent by saying, "You seem to have the idea that your child can do much more than he (she) thinks he can. What do you know about your child that tells you that he can do all the things that you want him to do?"
- Look for the hidden motives behind the parent's anger and frustration. What intentions could possibly be behind these words that perhaps even the parent does not recognize?
- Reframe the issues: Beauty is in the eye of the beholder. Every description lends itself to two or more ways of interpretation and so do human traits and characteristics. When you hear the first negative characterizations of a child, find another way to look at

the same traits. For example, "lazy" can be viewed as "laid back," "knows how to pace oneself," or even "stopping to smell the roses." The reason "reframing" is so useful is that these different perspectives offer another way to respond, thus giving parents more control and options from which to choose. Whenever parents feel they have more control, they are less likely to feel pinned down or with no options.

What Do You Do with Children Who Have Suffered Trauma?

We recognize that the experience of trauma is subjective and individual. The death of a loved one or a pet, personal injury, a natural disaster or human-made horror, and other events that cause us suffering—all are experienced in different ways by each child and each adult. What is an unbearable traumatic experience for one person may not be similar in the intensity of devastation for another person. The path in which one finds healing is also very individual. Therefore, the challenge for us is to know how to be respectful of clients' personal need to heal at their own speed and via their own methods, while being sensitive to their pain and suffering.

Relying on our principles of connecting with people no matter what their problems might be—beginning with who the person is, what their passion is, what they value, and most of all, what are their ideas on how we can assist them—is what guides our work. There is no uniform, prepackaged, one-size-fits-all formula we have prepared before meeting the client. As the following cases show, even though the family of four experienced the same traumatic death of the father and a husband, each family member expressed his or her fears, anxiety, and concerns differently. Therefore, we believe the most useful thing we clinicians can do is to listen to their ideas carefully and meet their needs as they arise, rather than planning or anticipating certain predictable reactions.

Contrary to the general view about the timing of the grieving process, we find that when someone is ready to "deal with" trauma is also very individual, even the children. Thus, the most difficult aspect of working with people who suffered trauma is determining how to be helpful without becoming intrusive and imposing our ideas. People know when they are ready to talk, and respecting this intuitive sense of knowing oneself should be accepted and respected. There is no timeline that fits every person; sometimes, it may mean waiting for months or years. We also find that while the trauma continues, the person in the traumatic situation may have no emotional capacity to deal with the meaning of the event and it may take time, sometimes even years, to gain that emotional capacity.

We believe that each traumatic event forever changes one's life and that we will never "go back" to whatever we were before the event, just as each day and each task we perform changes us in small ways. Therefore, concepts like "working through" a trauma imply that one must somehow get through this life-changing event and get back to "normal." Our job is to help clients accept the event and still keep going by reorganizing and reshaping their lives in such a way that clients can still be productive, find meaning in their lives, and experience both the joy and sadness of the changed life.

CASE EXAMPLE: DEATH ON THE HIKING TRAIL

A mother of three children (ages, 9, 7, and 5) called to make an appointment because her husband died while the family was hiking in the mountains. The circumstances had been especially traumatic and dramatic for the entire family because the mother had to leave to call for help while the three children were left on their own watching over their father who had suffered a heart attack. The father died on the way to the hospital. Afterward, the mother had been told by various professionals that her entire family, including herself, needed psychological help to cope with the trauma of this event. We want to describe the treatment process in detail, including parts of dialogues, in order to give you a better feel for how a dramatic and traumatic situation such as this family experienced has moved along to termination.

Therapist (Th):   What needs to happen during this meeting today so that you can say it's been useful?

Mother (M):   I was told to get professional help for my children but I decided that I want to talk to you first and that's why I came alone today. But I want to tell you what has happened.

Th: OK . . . in order to listen to your story in the most helpful way, tell me what would be helpful about telling me your story.

M: (Begins to cry) You know I was told that my children should talk about what they have seen, they should be helped to express their feelings. By telling you what has happened, I hope you can decide whether this therapy is necessary or not because none of my children want to talk about it, and they don't want to come and see you either.

Th: I realize you take seriously what you've been told and at the same time, you are also sensitive to the children's wishes. Before you tell me what has happened, since you know your children best, what difference would it make for them if they come and talk about what has happened to them?

M: I'm afraid that they will go through this all over again and won't sleep anymore again. They are just beginning to get some sleep at night, but until recently none of my children slept more than two hours straight and this was very difficult to cope with.

Th: So it sounds like there has been a little bit of improvement with their sleep. What do you think made this improvement possible?

M: We all started to sleep in the same room together, even though I was told not to let this happen too often. And I started something we all do together: We all tell an amusing or pleasant story, a joke, something nice we have seen during the day; something pleasant, and things like that.

Th: Amazing! And it works?

M: They don't sleep like before, but it sure has improved.

Th: How did you find out that this could be helpful?

M: You know, I consider myself an intuitive person and I sometimes have bizarre ideas but they always seem to have worked out. I've always been like that.

Th: I'm impressed; it seems your intuition once more turns out to be valuable. What else would be helpful with the children if they came to talk to me?

M: Well, it could be helpful for my youngest and the oldest, but I'm not sure for the one in the middle.

Th: So how could it be helpful for the two you mentioned?

M: I don't know, but the oldest one worries a lot since her father died and is very afraid; I think she is afraid that I could die suddenly, too. She has become very serious and I would like to see her laugh again.

Th: I understand. So when you see your daughter laugh again, this would be a sign to you that things are getting better. Tell me, are there times when she laughs?

M: Yes, recently we started to walk farther away from our house. For some time, we had not left the house, but after we started to take a short walk in our neighborhood, she seems happier and even smiles.

Th: It sounds like when positive things happen, this gives your children reassurance and makes things a little better. What about your youngest child?

M: Since this happened, he seems to forget everything. He can't remember the way to his kindergarten. He starts to cry quickly and gets very angry sometimes. He has very bad dreams at night and screams. I think he needs the help the most. I mean, what happened was really terrible for him.

The mother began to cry again and told me the details of the event. I was very touched listening to her harrowing story, and I felt a great deal of respect for this mother who had done quite well in such a difficult situation of taking care of a dying husband and three children who were helpless. Yet, I still *needed further clarification from her about what she was hoping to accomplish by bringing her two children to see me.*

Th: Suppose you were to come along with your youngest child, what differ-
      ence would that make to you?
M: I would be sure that my children are doing well. Having to make so
      many decisions alone is new and I don't want to miss anything about my
      children if there is something I can do to help them.

After a short thinking break, I complimented the mother on her keen intuitive sense and the courage to trust her own feelings in the middle of so much turmoil and change. I told her that in my understanding there was no single right way to deal with this kind of tragic situation and that it seemed to me perfectly all right to go step-by-step as she had done. It seemed like the youngest child could benefit from my meeting with him and the mother was welcome to come along with the boy. She could always make appointments for the other two children if the need arose. The mother agreed to this.

During the first meeting with the boy and mother, I began by asking the little boy what he liked to do, what he was good at, and so on. Then we visualized all the helpful things he and his mother had found to make "his heart a little bit lighter" (mother's wish) and then made a list of things he found helpful to achieve this goal. His mother was amazed at the list of things the child mentioned because she did not realize that the things the boy mentioned were helpful. We also talked about what he liked best to do with his father and we played a little picture drawing game together.

After the thinking break, I complimented the boy on his ability to draw, normalized the wishes he expressed about his father and how he sometimes wished he was dead because then he would not have to think about the terrible things that had happened. I told both the mother and the child that I was impressed by all the helpful things they had found out on their own. She was pleased to hear that lots of things she tried were helpful to her son, and took satisfaction in my impression that she was on the right track.

During the second session, we talked more about the helpful things they were doing to get "a lighter heart." I met with the mother alone during the next session. By taking a closer look at her coping strategies, the mother realized that on those days that were going well, she regularly had taken some time out for herself to give herself a chance to slow down and take a break. She also realized that she was trying too hard to make up for the children not having a father and, in the process, she was exhausting herself. She came to the conclusion that she had to find a way not to burden herself with the added responsibility and came to the decision that two questions she asked periodically helped her a great deal: "What expectations do I have to fulfill and which do I want to fulfill?"

The third session alone with the mother took place three months later, to see whether she was on track. Her biggest question was whether she should wait for signals from her children that they are ready to improve their everyday life or if it was up to her to move one step further and allow the children to catch up with her by doing something new. For example, she wondered whether she should wait for a signal from the children that it was OK for her to go out of the house in the evening alone for one hour once a week, or should the children let her know that they can cope with her absence in the evening. She eventually decided that she had to take the first step and then children will learn to accept it.

Five months after the father's death, the mother called to set up an appointment for the 9-year-old daughter, Maryanne, the oldest of the three children. Two weeks prior to the phone call to set up this meeting, the mother had become very ill and Maryanne became very frightened that her mother would die as her father had done.

I met with Maryanne for six sessions. For most of the sessions, the mother joined us during the ending phase of the session. During the first session, Maryanne's answer to the miracle question was that her father would be alive, that she would stand up to people with her own ideas, and she would feel less angry at the world.

During her second session, Maryanne described the process of "standing up" for her own ideas as follows: She would change from a turtle into a pig. I talked with the pig and the turtle hand puppets as well as with Maryanne. During the conversation Maryanne described how she would change when she finally turned into a pig. She ended the session by painting a huge angry face with her hands. During the third session, Maryanne reported that she fought more with her brother and she painted the face of her art teacher, whom she had been very angry at, and she started to express some very strong angry words about people in general.

During the fourth session we competed for who could say the most naughty words while making faces in the mirror, both angry and sad. She started to talk about her sad feelings and her fears. I decided to read a picture storybook in which a lady who is worried about everything under the sun teaches a young frightened bird to fly. The essence of the story was that the lady who worried about everything and was fearful of trying anything new or strange even learns to fly herself.

During the fifth session Maryanne drew a picture of her fear monster that jumps on her once in a while. She piled up tin cans and placed this picture of a fear monster in front of the pile of tin cans. With a tennis ball, she aimed at the fear monster picture and with strong force threw the tennis ball at the pile of tin cans. She repeated this several times. During the sixth session, she reported that she has been playing a game of hide-and-seek with other girls near the woods in her neighborhood. While she looked for a place to hide in a tall grass area, she saw an old man lying unconscious and she had to find an adult to organize a rescue operation with an ambulance. Even during this terrible situation, the fear monster did not jump on her shoulder! I suggested that she write a note in her diary about her having stood up for her own ideas. She was pleased about what she had already learned and was hopeful to do well in the future. This was the last session.

As usual, every session began with my question of "What is better?" since the last session and making a list of the answers (as we have described in Chapter 3). This took place during the last 10 minutes of each session while her mother joined us.

The following case example shows that sometimes, parents are not aware of how much they have done on their own before the first meeting. In such situations, our task is to validate, support, and encourage them to stay the course, even though the symptoms or the events that preceded the phone call may indicate the need for a much more extensive treatment.

CASE EXAMPLE: ACCIDENTAL GUNSHOT WOUND

Ms. Campbell called on a Monday morning in an urgent voice, insisting that I (IKB) must see her the same day, saying that her 11-year-old boy was in "bad shape." Because of her urgency, along with her use of the phrase "gunshot wound," I decided to give up my lunch hour and meet with Ms. Campbell. I didn't catch everything she said because her speech was so rushed on the phone, but she agreed to come at noon. When she showed up, about two hours after her phone call, she indeed looked frantic and it was clear that she had suffered some terrible experience. I had to ask her to slow down a bit so that I could comprehend her pressured speech and find the subtle details of her story.

The story was that about 4 days before, her 11-year-old son Corey was playing down the street with his best friend, 14-year-old Curtis, who was like an older brother to Corey. While the mothers of both boys worked, the two friends played in the basement family room at Curtis's house two doors down from Corey's. It was quite normal for these two boys to play together after school while they both waited for their mothers to come home from work.

Ms. Campbell's understanding of what happened was the following: While they were playing "cops and robbers," the boys found a gun that belonged to Curtis's uncle, who had a license to keep the gun in the house. Without realizing the gun was loaded, they picked it up and "fooled around" with the gun, playing cops and robbers and cowboys and Indians. Corey held the gun in front of Curtis and pretended to shoot. The shock was that the gun fired and grazed Curtis's right ear. Curtis fell to the floor. At first Corey thought Curtis was exaggerating, and then realized that there was blood running down the side of his head. Corey called 911 and got the paramedic to come and take Curtis to the hospital. As of this first meeting, Ms. Campbell told me that the police were still trying to determine whether this was a felony, misdemeanor, or an accidental case, as they waited for the outcome of Curtis's treatment.

Ms. Campbell told the most remarkable story next. She explained that Curtis's mother, Beverly, and she have been friends for many years, almost like sisters. The two woman had a meeting at the hospital. They decided that no matter what the police concluded—whether a felony, misdemeanor, or an accident—they would remain friends and the two families would remain friends no matter what the outcome because two mothers knew in their hearts that it was an accident.

Ms. Campbell described how Corey had been affected by the episode: He was unable to sleep, clung to her, was afraid to go outside the house, and had not gone to school that day. He was generally very frightened, jumped up when the phone rang, and of course had not been able to eat. In addition, she described that when her son went outside the house, other children in the neighborhood had already began to call Corey a "killer" and ran away from him. This has been equally traumatic for the child.

In admiration for her courage, I asked Ms. Campbell how she had been coping with this during the last 4 days. She explained that it really got her worried and she was very concerned about her son. She noticed that Corey was convinced that Curtis was "dead" because he has not seen his friend since the accident and because the rumor has spread that he was a "killer." So Ms. Campbell got the idea that perhaps if Corey actually saw for himself that Curtis was in the hospital and that he was not dead, it would help her son with his nightmares and fears, and he would be able to go back to school. The day before the appointment, Ms. Campbell decided to take action to show Corey that he did not kill his friend as other children in the neighborhood accused him of doing.

When she took Corey into the hospital holding onto his hand, she was met with hospital staff who told her that children were not allowed on the ward and that she would have to wait for the visiting hours. She disregarded their words and gestures. (One staff member tried to block her way to Curtis's room.) She grabbed Corey's hand and forced their way into the room. Curtis and his mother were indeed surprised to see them both, and with a shocked but smiling expression on his face Curtis said, "Yo, man, how'ya doin?" Corey's mother reported this was the first time in days she saw her son smile. Corey answered back to Curtis, "Yo, man, how'ya doing?" Both boys were so glad to see each other. Although Corey only stayed a few minutes, he left with a promise for return visits.

Ms. Campbell reported that Corey slept a little bit better that night and seemed to be in a better mood. I was speechless, amazed at this mother's intuitive sense about what her child needed, her courage to know and do what was required. All I could do was admire her and I told her so. When I asked Ms. Campbell what her child needed as the next small step, she replied that he needed to go back to school and be a "normal child" again. Then she got up and said she will call me if she needs to talk to me again. I got a phone call from the mother few days later saying that she didn't need to come in and she thanked me for talking to her on such short notice. By the way, I never got a call from Ms. Campbell again.

Although this example is not typical, neither is it so unusual to meet clients who need only a brief contact (as little as a single session) to put their lives back together. It is also not so unusual to treat a child, never having met the child. When we listen carefully to the adults' clues and listen attentively to what their child needs as well as what they want for their child, we are able to help the parents to be parents, thus making it possible for them to continue to take care of their child. There is no set, one-size-fits-all formula that applies to children with traumatic experiences, and their parents. Individualizing treatment is very important. Years later Corey may or may not need treatment related to this event, and, even if he does, there would be a long list of positive things he and his mother did in the intervening years to manage their lives in spite of such a shocking event. The long list would be the foundation on which to build what he would need as the next step.

How Do You Work with Children Who Have ADHD (Attention Deficit Hyperactivity Disorder)?

This is such a controversial topic, and there seems to be so much confusion and misunderstanding about this "disorder." There are many different theories about what makes a child "hyperactive." Some experts believe that a child's hyperactivity is an effort to compensate for the deficit in attention, and that the child is trying to make sense by working hard to focus his or her attention, while others view hyperactivity as falling under the wider umbrella of autism. Still others view children with this diagnosis as lacking the ability to focus their attention, but they argue it might be more helpful to view these children as being too sensitive to the stimulus from the environment. Some children with an ADHD diagnosis seem to do better when the adults are calmer, are slow to get aroused or stimulated, and also when adults give ample warning about what is to come next when changes in location, procedures, and sequences are necessary. Some ADHD children seem to have more difficulty when abrupt changes in plan or spontaneous changes are frequent. The questions we hear most commonly from parents and professionals are listed here, and we want to offer our observations on these questions.

- Does my child have ADHD?
- Is this a handicap my child has to live with for the rest of his life?
- Is Ritalin always necessary? Is Ritalin addictive? Will he become a drug addict later in life if we put him on this medication?
- Does Ritalin increase the risk of becoming drug dependent or addicted?
- Besides medication, what other therapies are helpful?
- What does our child's ADHD say about us as parents? What do we have to do? What might help?
- Does the school have the right to exclude our child or insist on medicating him or her?
- How can we have a constructive dialogue between the parent and the school?

The diagnosis of ADHD or ADD normally includes the following: normal or average intelligence (an IQ of 90 or higher); reduced attention span; reduced ability to be patient; tends to become tired easily; and perceptual, visual, or auditory difficulties in assessing proportions and form recognition. In addition, there often are distortions in acoustic or auditory perception and recognition; some difficulties in hand-eye coordination; and difficulties in keeping the physical balance are frequently observed. Sometimes there are also distortions in interpersonal perceptions, which explains the standard observation that the child has difficulties in getting along with others.

It is generally accepted that the diagnosis must be made before the child reaches age 9, and at least five or more of these difficulties need to be identified for this diagnosis to become established. Of course we believe such a diagnosis must be made very carefully, because it is easy to give the impression that something is wrong with the child, which in turn influences the behavior of the child and others around the child.

This diagnosis is most common among male children. One can say there is a degree of handicap involved, because some effort and steps are needed to compensate for and correct problems such as perceptual and movement coordination difficulties. Therefore, most children with this diagnosis can benefit from sensory integration therapy, speech therapy, music therapy, and special auditory training. Ritalin can produce some startling and remarkable changes in a child. But with some children it is not effective, and therefore it is difficult to generalize about whether Ritalan will be helpful or not. We suggest therapy as the first step. If nothing else, therapy will help clarify what parents and teachers are expecting the medications to do for the child, and whether these goals can be achieved to a manageable level without medications. Our experience is that many children respond quite well to our typical SFBT approach to looking for small successes, looking for exceptions carefully, and trying to replicate the successful strategies until they reach the level of success they are comfortable with.

Ritalin is not known to be addictive, although some children describe a period of lethargy after they stop taking it. Some parents have the children off the medication during the weekend, extended school holidays, or even summer vacation periods without ill effects. ADHD and ADD children are not short-term therapy cases, but it does not mean that you need to see them frequently either. After an initial assessment, which may be quite intensive, during the maintenance period you may only need to stay in touch 2–3 times a year. Again, when and if there is an unusual problem at school, the contact may become more frequent until the child's behavior is stabilized.

CASE EXAMPLE: NO MORE SUSPENSION

Nine-year-old Robert was referred by the family doctor two weeks prior to his ninth birthday with the question of whether he had ADHD. This referral was triggered by a fight he had with the teacher during which he attacked the teacher as well as his classmates. Robert had a history of being excluded from school somewhere between a half-day to a whole day every week because of his behavior problems. The parents described him as having a great many problems: short attention span, explosive temper, and clumsiness. He also frequently needed a great deal of sleep in order to regroup himself. Other problems included Robert's inability to write within the lines, indicating perceptual difficulties.

His answers to the miracle question were: I could stay in school without suspension for a while, get along better with other children, be able to control my bad temper, write faster, and other people would know that I am not only aggressive but that I am smart. The parents' miracles were: Robert would be treated fairly in school instead of being sent home all the time, the school teachers will find a respectful way to discipline Robert so he does not have to be ashamed and embarrassed so much in front of other children in class. He would listen to the us better, follow our suggestions, but most of all, he would be happier.

I (TS) met with Robert three times in order to find out his resources, his skills, and his needs. I also had to conduct some tests to give information to the insurance company. From testing and observations and the description the parents provided, I agreed that the child did have ADHD. The parents could easily accept the diagnosis because they had felt for a long time that Robert was different from other children. They decided to follow my suggestion to work with the insurance company to get special services such as the computer that would make his learning easier. I also met with the teacher since her information about Robert was important. I learned that the parents and the teacher did not get along well and they blamed each other for Robert's problematic behavior. I decided that by observing Robert in his classroom I would be able to begin the change process with the teacher immediately. The teacher and I decided on a time when I should come to the classroom. By observing Robert in the classroom, it was not difficult to agree with the teacher that indeed Robert was a difficult student to have in class, and I complimented and supported the teacher for all the good things she was doing with Robert.

After this visit, the teacher was in a much better frame of mind to look for some useful ideas. One of Robert's miracles was that he would be able to write on a computer instead of writing by hand. She agreed that this would be acceptable if the parents provided one for him. In spite of all the progress that had been made, the most difficult situation for the teacher was in music, art, and crafts. We looked for exceptions to these difficult situations and made plans to allow Robert a time-out when the teachers noticed early signs that he was becoming frustrated. This worked out reasonably well and the teacher and I agreed to set up a regular monthly phone contact to discuss Robert's progress. In addition, I asked the teacher to remind Robert, just before he came to his monthly appointment with me, of all the things she thought he was doing better. These little successes became building blocks of his success tower (see Chapter 6).

I continued to meet once a month with Robert and his parents, during which meetings we discussed what was going better. His parents began reading up on ADHD and they often came to the session with lots of questions. During this phase of therapy, parents need to be empowered to make careful observations and then make their own decision on which remedies they might want to try out from the things they were reading. The questions I asked frequently during this phase were: "From what you have observed in your boy lately, what tells you that this could be helpful?"

Things went well for about six months. Then there was an episode where Robert became aggressive toward his teacher. It was shortly before his class was going to get a new teacher and it was upsetting him a great deal. I find it not uncommon for children with ADHD to become anxious about big changes. Robert's parents were rightly very concerned and the school administration also was involved in discussing what to do. Even though the parents thought they might want to try Ritalin, Robert refused in a very strongly worded, emotional outburst.

I was asked to be actively involved again following this episode of aggressive behavior toward the teacher. I discussed with the school and the parents what might be helpful. The parents decided that meeting with the future teacher, in spite of the fact that the school objected to it, would be helpful for Robert. The new teacher took a chance in agreeing to meet with Robert although she knew it was against school policy. The parents trusted their own intuition and arranged a meeting with the new teacher. It turned out to be a big relief for Robert, and the key for him to be able to enjoy the summer vacation.

The parents also listened to their son's opinion that this was not the time to start medication. Robert felt that because he had done so well, he wanted to try without it—even with a new teacher, which was a big change for him. Around this time, I spent most of one session with Robert finding out what would tell him that medication could be helpful and how he would know it was the right time to start the medication. He had a very clear idea: "After the summer vacation I will be learning new and more difficult subjects, and getting to know new kids that I don't know yet. The signs of needing medication will be that when I get angry as fast as before I came to see you the first time, then it will be the time to try Ritalin." Robert started his new school year well, but it was evident that all the changes coming at the same time were very exhausting for him. On weekends he did not want to go out and he was very tense and unhappy most of the time.

The first session after school started, Robert was very proud that he maintained his cool without aggressive outbursts. I complimented him and we had a lengthy conversation about how he achieved this. Robert finally said at the end, "I know now I can do it, but it takes just too much energy and just too long," indicating that he was willing to try Ritalin now.

His willingness to follow the routine of the medication was very good, even though he had to fight the side effect of an appetite problem, and he was convinced that Ritalin did some good. As he was making a good adjustment to the new environment, he reminded me that his real wish was that his miracle would really come true, that he will stay in school all day, have more friends, control his temper, write faster, and other people would realize that he was really smart.

Because Robert did extremely well, he was promoted to the advanced level math class called "top shots" made up of gifted and talented math students. He finally felt that he was recognized for being smart. During the past year, I met with Robert and his parents only three times. Because he made so much progress, he stopped the motor skills therapy sessions. In one year's time, he would face another change in his school because he will be moving on to high school. There he would have to face as many as 12 different teachers during the school year. But with good networking and coordination with many interested professionals, including their listening carefully to his ideas

*on what would be helpful to him, I am confident that he will continue to make
progress.*

The key to a successful outcome in working with a child like Robert,
I believe, is that we respect what the child says and ask the right
questions at the right time. More than any other uncommon needs of
children, I believe coordinating and working collaboratively with other
professionals and parents of children with ADHD is very critical to
successful management.

How Do You Handle School Phobia (School Refusal)?

Common questions and concerns that we are asked about children
who have difficulties going to school seem to cluster around:

1.   Should the children be forced to go to school?
2.   Do you think changing the school would be helpful?
3.   Does school phobia indicate some sort of difficulty in the family
     system, and therefore, family therapy should be indicated?

Again, these kinds of questions imply that there are common denomina-
tors among children or parents and these cases should be treated as a
separate entity. As far as we can tell, the only common denominator
among children with school phobia is that they do not want to go to
school. Other than this one element, we believe each child is an individual and different from every other. However, the refusal to go to school
seems to be based on a child's fears, whether perceived or real, mild
or severe. In some cases, not going to school may be a coping strategy
to a difficult situation. If not going to school is based on fear, then it
certainly would be better to see the child as soon as possible, the same
day or the day after you receive the referral; the longer the child avoids
school, the harder it is for him or her to return to school. The goal is
always to help the child find coping strategies so that he or she can
fit in at the school.

We believe that changing schools may help in certain unusual situations, but it rarely is the only solution. When a clinician explores with
the child and his or her parents "what difference" it would make to
change the school, the answers usually center around avoiding a certain
bully, a certain aggressive child on the way to school, and so on. These
problems are related to developing better social skills or an ability to
manage difficult relationships with teachers, school officials, or other
children. Again, rather than looking for large solutions to an urgent

problem of school phobia, it is always most helpful to look for the smallest, easiest step to take and from there work toward a desired goal.

Whether it is related to problems in the family or not, the solution-building approach is not interested in finding the causes of the problem; we are interested in finding out what can be done to get the child and the parents to get the smallest possible solutions started and keep moving toward their goals. Perhaps a detailed description of another case may explain things more clearly here.

CASE EXAMPLE: FROM DINOSAURS TO PIZZA

Mrs. Blume called about her 10-year-old son, Bobby, at the suggestion of his school because he had refused to go to school for the past three days, saying he felt that his classmates were laughing at him. Bobby had problems going to school on and off, and every time both parents and school were mystified by the problem. Bobby was not a problem for the parents in other ways. Mrs. Blume related that what was different about this time was that the school was strongly suggesting that she force Bobby to come to school, even if she had to drag him physically. She felt, however, that he was too strong for her to handle alone. The father worked out of town during the week and only came home on weekends.

I saw Bobby and his mother the following day, and Mrs. Blume explained how difficult it was for her to bring him into the office. He started to cry immediately and had to be stopped by his mother from running away. I told Bobby that it seemed to me that this is a very difficult situation and I thought he must have good reasons for not wanting to come and see me.

Bobby (Bob):   Of course, because you want me to go back to school and I will never do it in my life.
Therapist (Th):   What would you like to do instead?
Bob: I want to go away, right now.
Th: And do what? Let's say in 10 years' time, what would you like to be?
Bob: (Looking at his mother) I don't know.
Mother (M):   He wants to become a paleontologist.
Th: Is that right? How did you find out this was what you want to become?
Bob: I don't know. I want to go now.
Th: Of course, I just wondered, I have never a met boy who has this kind of interest. It is amazing. (To mother) It is really amazing; what an interesting boy you have!
M: Well, he reads a lot and of course knows everything about dinosaurs. I think that made him think he wanted to become a paleontologist. He has seen Jurassic Park 1 *and* 2 *and of course recognizes which animals are well made and which are only poor imitations.*

Th: Lots of children are interested in dinosaurs, but they usually don't have
      such a deep knowledge as Bobby seems to have.

I suggested we go into the office and sit down.

Th: As I realized what a clever boy you are, I would like to ask you a
      question that needs some imagination.
Bobby's immediate answer to the miracle question was that he would be all
grown up and he would work as a paleontologist and as a specialist. He would
go around and find traces and dinosaur footprints all over the world. He
would become famous and other people would listen to him because he was a
very good observer and made clever conclusions from his observations. In
addition, he would not have to go to any gym and music classes anymore,
children would not laugh at him anymore, and there would be no fights on
the way to school. The mother's answer to the miracle question was that she
would see Bobby as happy as he just was when he was talking about dinosaurs,
he would get up quickly in the morning, maybe even sing in the shower, and
of course go to school without any fuss. Bobby guessed that his father would
find out the miracle happened if he was interested in football.
    I summarized Bobby's answers as: other children would listen to him and
he would play more with other boys. When asked about the most recent time
when this had happened already, he replied that when he was in the fourth
grade his friends were interested in dinosaurs. They were no longer interested
in dinosaurs, Bobby said, and now nobody wanted to talk to him.

Th: Tell me, Bobby, suppose you were to surprise other kids, I mean a really
      big surprise, what would you have to talk about?
Bob: I don't know . . . (long pause) Maybe if I made pizza for the whole
      class. I don't think they know I am a good cook.
Th: Wow, what else?
Bob: I don't know.

*I spread out the basket of animal puppets and asked Bobby to select a puppet
that matches the situation now and one for the day after the miracle. He
selected a turtle for the current situation and a dolphin for the miracle. (I had
no dinosaur puppet.) I talked to the turtle first about how nice to be under
the shell that protected him but it is hard to hear what others are saying.
Next I talked to the dolphin, which is very flexible and has lots of fun in a
group with other dolphins. The topic of conversation eventually turned to
how both animals exhibit both of these aspects or interests and therefore it
would be nice to be protected and also have lots of fun in a group; both sides
were needed because one could not just be protected without fun and you
could not just have fun all the time because one has to be alone sometimes.*

His answer to the scaling question before the thinking break was that he was at 2 today (0 stood for "no way I can go back to school," 10 stood for "nothing to it"). When asked what brought it all the way up to 2, Bobby answered that it was talking about his dinosaurs. His idea was that he needed about three or four kids to talk to regularly in order for him to go back to school. When asked to name the children who would most likely talk to him, he came up with three names.

After a thinking break, I complimented Bobby on his serious interest in dinosaurs and how well he described the difficult situations with the other children in school. I thought it certainly made sense that he did not want to go to school because everybody wants to have somebody to talk to and have fun, but I was really impressed with his idea about making pizza for the class and wondered what number on the scale he would be when I saw him next time. I complimented the mother on bringing Bobby to therapy and the firm way she handled Bobby's not wanting to come to the session; it was obvious that she had a very loving and close relationship with Bobby.

I asked Bobby's mother to talk to the father and find out what they as parents have been doing in the past that helped Bobby to show his strong side to other children. I suggested that she talk to the teacher and inform her that they have started therapy. Bobby's mother could tell the teacher about the scale and how the family is working to raise the number on the scale. The teacher was welcome to call me if she needed more information about Bobby.

The teacher indeed called and she was very open and ready to do anything to help Bobby. The teacher added her assessment that Bobby was a very intelligent boy, but was very shy, with limited social skills, and too attached to his mother. I told the teacher about the scale and also informed her of the three names Bobby mentioned. The teacher immediately had an idea that she could group the four children together because she frequently made the children work in groups.

Second Session. *Bobby reported very proudly that he had baked pizzas for his class with the help of Jack, one of the boys he had named. His mother helped to arrange the event and he thought it was a big help that mother made the phone calls because he would not have had the courage to call Jack. Bobby's mother also called the teacher to make arrangements for the best time to deliver the pizza to the class. Even though mother played a big role, she managed not to come into the classroom and the teacher arranged for other boys to help bring the pizza into the classroom during the last hour of the day. Bobby managed to stay in school this last hour.*

The teacher informed Bobby of the plans for the last hour of the next day's class and Bobby thought it was something he could do. A plan was made for Bobby to come to the class again during the last hour only. Between the first and second sessions Bobby had been to school three times altogether, a huge success for him. Of course I was curious about the details of what was helpful to think about as he entered the school building, what did he do during the class that helped him to sit through the class as pre-arranged. Bobby explained that he brought two plastic animals, a turtle and a dolphin, in his pocket and he squeezed the dolphin in his right pocket, saying to himself, "You are going to be a flexible dolphin" as he entered the school building. As he entered his classroom he squeezed the turtle, saying, "I can be like a turtle if it becomes too hard." But as soon as he entered his classroom, he had to look for Jack; Jack's presence made him feel calm. He forgot all about the turtle once he got into the classroom. On the scale of how easy it was to stay calm, he said it was at 4.

When I asked what would tell him he was at 5, Bobby replied that he would go to school for 4 hours straight. When we discussed what would help his number to go up to 5, he said he would dare to look around and would know what to say to other kids in his class, but he had no idea how he would learn to do this. When I asked him how willing he was to learn these skills, his immediate response was that he was at 10. As I explained this to his mother, she recognized that she had to "let go of him a little bit," explaining that Bobby has always been a special child, unlike her two older children, especially since her husband started to work in different towns during the weekdays and she had a lot of time on her hands. But she realized that he needed more social skills to relate to other children and not just to her. I agreed with her.

After a short thinking break, I complimented Bobby on all the steps he had taken since our last meeting and how impressed I was that he wanted to learn new things to do with other kids in class. When asked how many sessions he thought he would need to learn new things, Bobby replied at least four more, so we agreed that I meet with Bobby alone for four more times. I suggested an observation task, and told Bobby to observe carefully, since he was a good observer, to listen carefully to what and how the other kids talked to each other, and to note what kind of topics held their interest. I also complimented the mother on how she helped Bobby just the right amount—that is, she made arrangements for Bobby but she also knew how to stay out of his way just the right way because she wanted him to grow up and have all the social skills he needed.

Bobby decided to come to the four sessions on his own. Our primary focus was on self-perception. One exercise involved my taking video pictures as Bobby acted out different moods, such as joy, sadness, anger, hesitation, and different characters (movie star, professor, thief, captain of a football team). In using this technique, it is important that the therapist also join in, creating different feelings and characters as well. Of course, reviewing the tapes we made was great fun and we shared many good laughs. We also played several games of "Simon Says" which Bobby liked very much; it became our ritual to end each session with this game.

The topic of aggression came up frequently and we simulated boxing; Bobby needed to learn to look at his opponent while boxing. He decided to sign up for a karate class. We also played scribble games several times and we always ended the scribble game by making up a little story using one of Bobby's scribbles. The content of these stories became more and more bold, and he became much more comfortable with his own sense of assertiveness. During each session we scaled his progress and looked for signs of improvements. Observing other children's behavior also became a routine pattern for him, and I was really impressed with his observation skills and how good he was at selecting what he wanted to adapt and what he did not want to.

During our sessions the name of Andy kept coming into the conversation and I learned that Bobby spent more time with Andy than any of the other children. Whenever I asked about other children's perception of him, Bobby usually had difficulty; questions about Andy's perception were no exception. Bobby finally mentioned one day, "Why not ask Andy to come to a session with me?" After having discussed what would be interesting to Andy and what kind of things Bobby wanted to ask him, Andy finally arrived to the session with Bobby. I began with asking Andy what he thought Bobby was good at, what kind of further improvement he thought Bobby needed to make yet. This was the last session with Bobby.

There were two sessions with the parents alone, mostly discussing what the parents could do to reinforce the changes Bobby was making. I learned that father and son made a deal that they would go biking together at least twice a month; father and son had already gone to see a Jurassic Park *movie together and there were plans for more activities. For the first time the father was able to express his feelings of being pushed out of his relationship with Bobby because whatever he said about Bobby, the mother always defended the child. Bobby's mother also expressed the feeling that the father was too harsh with Bobby. Both came up with ideas on how to change their ways to cooperate together as parents.*

We now want to describe another case that could lead even an experienced therapist to wonder whether one is doing the right thing or not, both ethically and professionally.

CASE EXAMPLE: MOTHER'S DIFFICULT DECISION

Mrs. Carpenter called to set up an appointment at the insistence of the school because her 11-year-old son, Rick, was having a great deal of trouble in school. Of particular concern was Rick's extremely aggressive behavior. The school believed that Rick needed to be sent away to an institution and that they were only willing to take Rick back in the school after the summer holiday when he learned to manage his temper better. This referral was made at the beginning of summer vacation. Rick was the middle child of three: one brother Jon was 14 and a sister, Becky was 7 years old.

The family already had more than their share of problems; the father had been on the waiting list for a liver transplant for several months already. Mr. Carpenter's life had been threatened several times because he suffered from severe stomach bleeding and he was very weak. Mrs. Carpenter had to go to work to support the family and the father had been looking after the children, but with his current physical condition, his parenting ability was quite limited.

In the first session I learned that Rick was good at math, liked drawing, and had a good sense of handling animals. He had no friends and spent his time mainly alone. The relationship with his sister was just OK, but he felt his older brother, Tom, was taking over the role of the father and Rick resented it. The father was appreciative of Tom's efforts, however, and felt relieved. Rick would often express his resentment toward his brother, saying, "He can't tell me what to do; he is not my father."

Rick's answer to the miracle question was that he would get along better in school, father would get a new liver, and people would leave him alone and worry about their own business. The father's miracle was that he would be considered not as the main problem for the family but be thought to be a valuable person for the family. The mother's answer was: "I can not think of any miracles."

The rest of the first session was spent finding out the family's ideas of a good summer for Rick, and they agreed what would be most helpful for everybody was for Rick to have a good time playing with other children and that other children not be afraid of him any longer. We arranged for Rick to have an appointment with a school psychologist after the vacation to find out whether Rick needed some private tutoring or some special education programs, because he seemed motivated to earn good grades.

At the end of the session, I complimented the family on their strengths and wishes to make things better for everybody, and told them that many things are going on in the family that would make any family's life very difficult. I told them that it seemed like it would be very useful to look at their situation and Rick's problems with a fresh eye and search for solutions from a different perspective. I also complimented Rick on his desire to be a good student and on his interests in learning.

Second Session: Five weeks later. Rick successfully completed a sports camp without an outburst. He even made a friend and they began writing to each other and sending e-mails. Yet, he was not able to give any answer to my question about how he has been able to do so well at the camp where many children have to spend time together day and night and they are all strangers to each other. Rick kept answering, "I have no idea." Even when I decided to use more visual and tactile media, and suggested that we talk using puppets, it still made no difference. Rick even refused to play a scribble game.

Rather than trying to force him to talk, I suggested that Rick wait in the waiting room and I asked to speak to the parents. Mrs. Carpenter thought that Rick was a depressed child, and because all the children begged her to get a dog, she went out during the summer vacation and bought two little puppies that were not even housebroken yet. The father was not wildly enthusiastic about the puppies, but he said he had to accept it. The mother, however, found walking the two dogs with Jon to be very helpful somehow.

Even though it was beyond my imagination to bring two little puppies into the house with so many problems, and I certainly would not have done what Mrs. Carpenter had done, I accepted that clients are the experts of their lives and mother found having puppies around the house helpful. I complimented Rick on his successful sports camp and asked him to observe carefully what he did when he gets along well with other children, as he has done at the camp.

<u>Third Session.</u> *Rick was brought to the session by force against his wishes by his mother, and he refused to speak but threatened to break up the furniture in my office. I told him I thought that he must have a very good reason for feeling like this, but he refused to talk and it was pretty clear that no dialogue was possible. So I told Rick that it was fine with me not to talk if he prefers to be quiet. Instead I talked to his parents and discussed what had gone well since the last session. Rick had been to a class camp and it had gone well. Again, he managed without a temper outburst. Mother reported that he even seemed happy when coming home from the camp. He had also made some new friends.*

I spent quite a bit of time finding out more details about these periods when Rick was able to control his temper at home and how the teachers could see that he was managing his school work and getting his temper under control. Mrs. Carpenter reported that Rick was even doing better with his writing. There were a few times when he was sent home from school because of his inability to manage his temper, but they were still minor compared to what it was like before the summer. It was difficult to decide whether it was good or bad that he was sent home from school because Rick refused to participate in talking and he simply stood by the door.

The only comment I heard from Rick during this session was that people did not treat him fairly. The parents elaborated on this, saying that there was a girl in his class who had been sexually abused and that she was getting on Rick's nerves because everybody was making such a fuss about her. Recently, Rick had hidden her gym shoes and then got punished for this when he was found out. "People should go home and have a close look at what happens there rather than talk about our family. We don't have any problem. Rick will soon learn to control his bad temper and nowadays schools don't know how to deal with children!" the Father said, very upset, defending his son.

I remembered what the father said during our first meeting, that the miracle would be that he (father) would not be blamed as the reason for all the troubles his family had. So, I decided to stick to all the positive steps Rick has taken to manage his temper and all the little and big things the parents had done to help Rick with his school work. As we got to talking more about their successes so far, the father suddenly began to say that not everything was going well in the family. In fact, it was very difficult, he said, because "I'm afraid of dying before I can get a new liver."

Mrs. Carpenter said that whatever it took, she wanted to stay independent and would work day and night to keep the family together and not go on welfare. The session ended with my complimenting the parents on noticing all the little and big things Rick was doing to make progress, and I was very moved by their determination to stay together as a family in their own way, even though it may be very difficult to do. The parents asked me to contact the school and gave me permission to have a meeting with the teachers to discuss different options on how to deal with Rick.

Before I could set up a time for a meeting with the school, Rick attacked another child and he was immediately sent home from school. From that moment on, Rick absolutely refused to budge on going back to school.

Mrs. Carpenter called and said she wanted to come in to talk to me alone. I had a sense that she needed a longer time to talk, so I scheduled her at the end of the day so that I would not be pressured to limit my time with her. When she came in, I offered her a cup of coffee and let her know that we had lots of time. Mrs. Carpenter immediately started to cry, saying that she was at the end of her rope, that she just could not cope with the stresses anymore and she decided that Rick would have to go away from the family if everybody in the family was to survive. She added that Rick was a very sensitive child and he had suffered a great deal about his father's impending death, and she was convinced that this was the only way she could think of helping him. She knew that the father would not like it, but she decided that this was the best all around and she had already started looking into some residential schools that would be a good match for Rick. She also mentioned that she was looking for another job, where she would have a more stable income and better working hours so that the family could move away from the suburbs they've been living in and have a new chance at a new life. I was stunned.

Mrs. Carpenter asked me for two favors: The first was to get in touch with the school and talk to them about her decision for Rick, the second was to write a letter to the local child welfare office to make an arrangement to have Rick placed outside of the home and in an institution. For my own information and to make sure that she had thought things through and she was not doing this on an impulse, I asked many different questions such as: What told her that this was the helpful step for Rick and the family?; What would it mean for Rick to be separated from the family?; How would she include the father in her plan?; What would tell her that she had made a good decision for herself as well as for Rick and the family?

I was very torn and wondered about my own perceptions and feelings during the thinking break. Obviously the mother was a very strong lady and she seemed to have come to a decision in what seemed like a short time, but I realized that she had been struggling with this and many other issues for a much longer time than I had known her. I ended with supporting her decision and complimented her on her courage and her love for Rick that helped her to decide on what was best for everybody, but especially for Rick.

I had four more phone contacts with Mrs. Campbell. Some time later I got a message from the local child welfare office that the family had moved away and now Rick was in a special school that the mother had helped select.

Discussion. *This is one of those difficult cases, not because the problem was very complex or difficult to solve but because the decision and the outcome the mother, as the head of the household, arrived at could easily be looked upon as not a "positive" outcome or not the solution we would have chosen as best for the family or the child. There were many difficult points where many practitioners may have veered away from the family's goals: the father's imminent death; Rick's struggle with need for more structure and help from his father, who was unable to give it; the school's demand that Rick be transferred out of the school immediately because he was just too "violent and aggressive" to handle; and the mother's resistance to Rick's transfer. One could easily be appalled and question the mother's judgment in deciding to get two untrained puppies, or to ask the child welfare office to place Rick in an institution at a time when Rick seemed to be making some inroads to making friends and improving his school work. The mother's decisions seemed to have come from nowhere and so suddenly. However, the movie of the struggles of the family and the school had been running for a long time before I came upon the scene. It was therefore easy to forget that we, as therapists, usually are asked to walk into a movie theatre long after the plot has become quite complex, making solution-building difficult. And we are expected to help shape the ending of the "movie" as if we had seen it from the beginning.*

Even though I was somewhat stunned at the mother's final decision to place Rick out of the home, it was also clear that this decision was not easily arrived at, judging from the mother's demeanor, timing, and the way she asked to see the therapist alone. We liked the way the mother declared that it was her decision; she was the only person in the family who must carry the burden of raising two other children who needed just as much parenting as Rick. Now that the husband was dying, it was even more poignant that she recognized that she must make all the important decisions—pertaining to her job, where they will live, and which child will be given what kind of help, and so on. Mrs. Carpenter faced these challenges alone and apparently made the right decision for her family, based on what she knew about herself and her children, and her family.

Having been practicing solution-focused therapy for many years, we have been accused of being too optimistic, refusing to see the problems. It may also have been true in the therapist's work with this family when we look at the positive changes Rick had made even with a couple of sessions: he successfully completed the sports camp during the summer, even became friends with a boy. At home there was no violence or aggressiveness toward his siblings or his parents that we heard of. These were many hopeful signs that showed us that change was possible, even for a child like Rick. Yet, we really had no way to know all that was happening in the family and realizing this keeps us humble. The only option we are left with at times is the steadfast belief in "leading from one step behind" and a strong trust that, whatever the rationale, Mrs. Carpenter must have had "very good reasons" to make the decision that she finally did.

Even with the same outcome of Rick going away to live in a different environment, HOW this decision was made makes a big difference to Mrs. Carpenter and to Rick. Had this decision been made sooner, by the school, the therapist, court, or other people in authority, the responses of Rick and his parents would have been very different. We think there is a great deal of difference when parents decide what is best for their family, in contrast to when an institution or professionals make such important decisions for them, sometimes before the family is ready to face them.

What Do We Do About
Enuresis Nocturna Primaria?

The most common questions from parents and professionals about bed wetting could be grouped as follows:

- Is it a sign of much deeper psychological troubles in a child?
- Is this a genetically-inherited problem?
- Is there a certain age when a child should get psychological help?
- Is medication useful? Is a mechanical apparatus helpful?

It is commonly believed that children who wet their beds must have deep psychological problems and in fact have been treated with psychotherapy for a long time. But there are no data to convince us that this is so. A large study involving hundreds of children has shown that their ability to control their bladders occurs between the ages of 2 to 4. Of course, this study also shows a wide variation among children in their ability to do so for a variety of reasons. There seems to be some genetic component in enuresis, but it cannot be said that there is a direct causal relationship—that is, there may be a predisposition to a late onset of being dry. Many children also seem to outgrow the problem when they reach adolescence.

Psychological treatment, if offered, must be related to how badly the child wishes to control his or her bladder. In other words, successful control of the bladder is related to the child's determination and motivation to do so; and, of course, it is always helpful for the child to know that the parents are supportive of their effort and willing to provide any help, when needed. As the second of the two following case examples shows, the parent's belief in looking for a small change in the child is important. But most of all, we believe that the child's motivation plays a significant role in a successful outcome. Many children begin to control their bladder when they reach the age at which they love to sleep over at friend's houses, or when they become interested in girls or boys. Some children want to change their interaction around the wet or dry bed, as one boy explained. "I hate my father controlling my bed every morning, not saying anything, but just looking at me with his terrible expression on his face!"

If the child responds to medication (such as Minurin) it can be useful, but relying on medication alone does not seem to be enough.

CASE EXAMPLE: ELIZA'S ROAD TO A DRY BED

Eliza's pediatrician referred her to therapy for enuresis, after finding no physiological disorders by means of a thorough checkup, including the concentration capacity of the urine. At age 6½, Eliza was the oldest of four children and was attending the kindergarten. She was very shy and timid, was afraid of the aggressive boys, and therefore liked to draw pictures or play by herself.

During the first session it became obvious that the parents were not so much worried about her wetting the bed, but only followed through on the evaluation of the family doctor and the teacher, both of whom told them that Eliza needed psychotherapy.

Eliza's answer to the miracle question was: I want to be as courageous as a tiger so that I can tell off my brother and not be afraid of other kids on the way to school. The parents' miracle picture was that Eliza would speak up for herself, have little fights once in a while, and be more open to experience new food, new things, and new situations. The miracle of neither child nor parents was related to her dry bed. The parents were more concerned about increasing Eliza's self-esteem so that she would be more confident of herself, especially now that she will face the first grade in the coming year. If by any chance she learned to be dry, this would be fine, but we all agreed that the enuresis was not a problem and therefore, it needed no solution.

I had a few sessions with Eliza alone, visited her in kindergarten, had some sessions with Eliza and her mother, and with her mother alone, for a total of

12 sessions. We stopped meeting when Eliza made a good start in first grade.

Two years later the mother called again because she and her husband were discussing divorce and wanted help to make sure that the children were not harmed by it. Eliza was very upset and sad about the parents' separation and came up with the idea that she could be helpful to her mother if she learned to have a dry bed. She decided that she wanted to try the alarm, an alarm clock that rings and wakes up the child as soon as the pants get wet. Eliza also wanted to try medication in order to help with sleepovers at her friend's house. Her parents' separation and her wet bed was the first time she thought about what might be helpful with her bed wetting, not because she wanted to become dry but because she decided that her mother's life would become a little bit easier during this difficult time.

This time I saw Eliza a total of 6 sessions, once a month for 6 months. She made improvements in her ability to control her bladder by use of the alarm and several times she woke up with a full bladder in the morning. But overall, the bed was often still wet, although not as wet as it had been. I complimented her on her success and during the last session, we made a "most wanted person" picture. As a special adaptation she wrote down special things about herself that take a long time to learn, such as writing, reading, playing the piano, and getting dry. She had a lot of hope that she could reach the goal of staying dry. She stopped using the alarm clock and used medication only on special occasions.

One year after these 6 sessions, Eliza was now wildly determined to have a dry bed and this time she wanted to become dry for her own sake. I learned that during the past year, she had maintained the level she reached before—that is, there were some dry nights but she really did not improve. This time, the miracle would be that she would become dry without working so hard. I asked her how likely she thought it was this could happen. She said, "I know I have to do something and I want to work on it, and that is why I am here. This time I will make it!" She wanted to know from me all the different methods I knew that could be helpful. She was very interested in the "mental training" and the "intensive night," two methods from behavioral psychology with medication as an additional help.

For the mental training, a child and his or her parents choose one evening as the day of training and they all must be prepared to lose sleep. Before going to bed, Eliza had to imagine being asleep, with her bladder full. The child counts to 50 and imagines waking up. Then she gets up, goes to the toilet and tries to urinate. She goes to bed again, and repeats the same procedure 10 times. The intensive night starts with the mental training. Between 9:00 p.m. and 2:00 a.m. the child is woken up by the parent. The child goes to the toilet. If the child thinks she cannot urinate, the child gets a drink. If the child thinks she can urinate, she is asked whether she could hold the urine one more hour. If the answer is yes, the child is sent to bed without using the toilet. Every time the child goes to bed, the child touches the dry bed and tries to hold onto the sensation of a dry bed. If the bed turns out to be wet, after having changed the sheet, the child goes through the mental training 10 times again.

It took Eliza four months to become and stay dry. We had six more sessions during this period, including the celebration session when we drank non-alcoholic, children's champagne. Eliza found the mental training most helpful, and although it took a great deal of time and she had to give up some of her playing time in the evening, she decided it was a good choice for herself. During the third session, she painted herself a silver medal because she had been dry for 7 days consecutively. In the fourth session she was still doing her mental training, but reduced the repetition to 5 times. We discussed with her mother what Eliza wanted as a reward for her success, and Eliza arrived at the decision that she and her mother would learn the "stomach speech" and she would get a puppet. During the fourth session Eliza showed me the result of the previous month. She has been dry 23 times and only 12 times wet. She had medication for only 10 more days, but she was convinced that she would succeed in making herself fully dry even without pills.

During the fifth session Eliza reported 24 dry nights and 10 wet, without the help of medication. She was determined to make it a complete success and she wished to play games during most of the session. Eliza showed up for her sixth and last session with a surprise. She had been dry except for two nights at the beginning of the month. We drank children's champagne, and she played with her mother and her new puppet.

Discussion. This remarkable little girl showed such determination and will to do what she wanted for herself; when the time was right for her, she was willing to work hard to achieve her goal. This reminds all of us that personal investment and motivation are what was needed to overcome a difficult problem. It again shows how even young children take pride in the mastery of a difficult task and the successes from their own achievement. Unfortunately, it is rare to meet such wise parents as Eliza's. Many parents easily get into a battle with their children over matters that only the child has control over.

Contrary to the physiological limitations central to Eliza's situation, other cases of enuresis and encopresis may be helped with looking into parents' attitudes and expectations of a child. When parents lower their expectations of their children, the children usually accommodate the parents' perceptions, as the following case indicates.

CASE EXAMPLE: FROM NAPKINS TO THE TOILET

Six-year-old Gina, an intellectually challenged child, seemed to have no control over her bladder or her bowels. The parents reported that she had never been toilet trained, nor had she ever used her potty or toilet. She usually relieved herself using a pile of newspaper or napkins on the floor, usually under the table. I learned that Gina attended a children's group three times a week and amazingly she was always clean there.

The parents' wish for Gina was that she would control her bodily functions, especially now that she would be going to kindergarten soon. But the parents were convinced that Gina had no ability to take this next step and become toilet trained; they always excused her lack of toilet manner as a part of her retardation. When I asked the details about her current toilet habit of using napkins under the table, her behavior indicated a considerably different story. Whenever it was time to urinate or move her bowels, Gina would stop whatever she was doing and then go under the table and stay there until she finished. When I asked in detail about how long she stayed with the children's group, what they did about going to the toilet, and other details of the group's activities, the parents became very thoughtful and began to wonder about my curiosity. They recognized that perhaps they had undermined Gina's ability and realized that it was important for them to make clear their expectations of the child and acknowledge the progress she has made. They needed to trust that Gina could make even more progress toward a complete toilet training.

The parents first began placing Gina on a toilet seat and then they told her that she would get her napkins only after she finished using the toilet. She was not forced to use the toilet but the goal was to help her become familiar with the idea of sitting on the toilet. After sitting on the toilet for a period of time, Gina was rewarded with the napkins, therefore, she learned the connection between her napkins and sitting on the toilet. The next step was to reward her with napkins only at night time and not during the day. The parents' concerns were that she might use the napkin and might smear her feces all over the place, but their fears did not materialize. What the parents eventually learned was that Gina was afraid of anything coming out of her body and her solution was to hold her bowels for too long until she could not wait any longer. She could hold her bowels a long time and then her feces would force itself out in a dramatic manner. With the help of her parents, Gina was able to celebrate her success the following week. Eventually Gina learned to control her bowels day and night.

How Do We Treat Autism?

We would like to address the treatment of autism by describing a case example in an out-patient setting. Again, learning about the child first, and then his or her difficulties, and then finding ways to reach the child and communicating through unusual and creative means is the best way to proceed. As you can see, the family's active role in figuring out what works best for each child is very important.

CASE EXAMPLE: AUTISM

I (TS) first met Glen when he was 15 and attending a special school for seriously challenged children. As is usually the situation, there were serious difficulties at home, in addition to Glen's own uncommon needs. This complicated the work with Glen. He frequently had aggressive outbursts, usually when he felt he was too close to other children and had no way to get out of such situations. As one can imagine, this situation further complicated Glen's progress because other children avoided any contact with him. Mrs. Burns, Glen's mother, called to set up an appointment, indicating she had many concerns about Glen. Her worries included a serious and long-standing disagreement she had with her husband about how to be helpful to Glen and how to understand what was wrong with him. She also indicated on the phone that her husband would not come to "professionals" because he believed that only God could help Glen's problems.

First Session. Mrs. Burns came alone, saying that her husband refused to participate in this meeting about Glen, and of course Glen did not want to come either. This underscored Mrs. Burns's account of the long-term disagreements over Glen's problems and what might be the solution to them. Mrs. Burns, a Methodist, was trained as a nurse and believed in medical help and special education for Glen, while her husband was a farmer and a very conservative Catholic. According to the mother, the father's position was that nature would take its course and that only God knows what is in Glen's future. The father took Glen to mass regularly, taught him to pray the rosary, and was opposed to the special education program Glen was attending. In response to my initial question of what needs to happen to make this visit worthwhile, Mrs. Burns began to sob, indicating the tremendous burden she has been carrying. After composing herself, she began to speak of her worries about Glen's sleeping habits and his social isolation. Glen had no friends because of his "odd" behavior and his temper outbursts; he slept only 4–5 hours a night and spends most of his time in his room, even isolating himself from the family. She thought it was time that two brothers, ages 11 and 13, learned about the handicap that caused Glen's "peculiar" behaviors, because sometimes they became very confused and upset about strange things Glen did. They no longer believed their father's explanation that Glen would become fine someday. The brothers were upset that Glen was often laughed at by other children. They felt embarrassed about Glen, while at the same time resented the special way the parents treated Glen, especially their father. They were also resentful of the way the parents allowed Glen to stay in his room and not participate in chores. In addition, Mrs. Burns thought that it might be helpful for Glen to get some medication to help him sleep.

As a result of the father's attitude, it was always Mrs. Burns who organized and made arrangements for special classes, medical checkups, and contacts with the school. Torn between two parents with such opposite views, Glen came to believe that his problems were caused by his mother and the best solution was to stay away from her. He hardly spoke to her anymore and Mrs. Burns was very anxious about her loss of influence on Glen.

After a brief thinking break, I complimented the mother on her patience and persistence. I told her that having a child with a diagnosis of autism is very difficult to live with, day after day, especially because the diagnosis is hard to make and her family situation made it even more difficult because she had to make important decisions all by herself for such a long time. I told her that, as she might already have known from her medical training, there was no single special treatment that works for every child with this diagnosis, but her attempts to give her son a special education and a structure was in the right direction. The mother was confident that she could bring Glen next time so that I could meet him. I agreed to see Glen next time, but only after the father was informed.

I felt overwhelmed by the complexity and enormity of the problem Glen and his family faced. I had to take some time to remind myself that I needed to take one small step at a time in a step-by-step fashion, always remembering what the client wants. I thought that if Glen refuses to come next time, I can always talk to the mother. But I trusted that she must have a good reason to believe that Glen would come to the next session.

<u>Second Session.</u> *The mother brought Glen and the three of us started the session together. When asked whether the father was informed about the day's meeting, the mother replied yes, and that he did not object. In trying to learn more about Glen, I immediately realized that it was quite difficult to communicate with him. He did not look at me and even though we were sitting side by side, he was clearly uncomfortable. I tried to engage him in simple conversation by asking about his name, grade, teachers, his classes, and so on, but his typical answer was, "I don't want to speak now." At last I learned that he liked to play a commonly known game, Eile mit Weile, and he wanted to become a farmer when he grew up.*

About 15 minutes after we began, I took a break and returned with compliments for Glen on having come today, even though it was obvious that he would have preferred to do something else. At this he smiled for the first time. I told him that I was glad to hear that he wanted to go into farming when he grew up and it was helpful to have a goal in life. I also mentioned that it seemed that his mother was trying very hard to be helpful to him. I asked him whether he wanted to play the game Eile mit Weile with me, while his mother could go home and come back to pick him up later. At this moment Glen looked at me for the first time and nodded. We played our game, which went very well.

Before the end of the session I asked him whether I might ask him a question to which he answered yes. I asked him about his sleeping habits. He explained in clear sentences that it normally took him a long time to fall asleep, except when he had been working on the farm. But to him this was no problem and there was no reason to worry about it. I complimented him on his very clear answers and told him that I was impressed by the way he coped with his sleeping rhythm. When asked whether we should make another appointment, he answered, "Why not?"

Third Session. Since the second session, Glen had a temper outburst at school. The teacher had contacted me and told me that he had Glen write down his ideas about this incident. When I met Glen, the first thing he did was to hand over what he had written. I thanked him and asked what had been better since last time we met. He did not answer. Then I told Glen I wanted to talk to him about the last session, about what impressed me. I told Glen that I had the impression there were times when he could answer questions easily and that other times it was harder. I also told him that I had been thinking about that, and he was not the only person I knew who did this, and that it was perfectly fine with me.

I suggested that we try something new this session. I had prepared a little old cigar box that had a sliding cover which made it possible to slide the cover back and forth, to open the box just a little, halfway, or wide open. In fact, you could decide how much or little to open the box as you wished. I asked Glen to draw a heart on a piece of paper, write down his name on it, and then cut it out. I took his heart and put it into the wooden cigar box, then showed him how I experienced him last session. I had the box almost closed to represent the beginning of the session, I opened the box a little bit the time we played the game, and to represent the end of the session I represented how I experienced by opening the box even a little bit further. I told him, "Well, I've been thinking that you could indicate to me with this box how things are with you each time you come. You know, I would like to respect the different situations you are in and don't want to ask you questions when it is not the proper time for it. But for that, I need your help and would like to ask you whether you would be kind enough to let me know." Glen agreed. He took the box and closed it shut.

We played Eile mit Weile and he did not say anything at all. He won the game. "School is shit," was the only comment he made before setting up the next appointment.

Fourth Session. When I handed him the box at the beginning of the session, he opened it only a tiny little bit. "OK," I answered, "I'm not going to ask you what is better today. Is there anything you want to tell me?" Glen talked about his hope that everything would become different next summer so that he could change schools. I told him I was interested in the school he attended at the moment as well as the school he will be attending next summer. I also told him that his teacher had invited me to visit him at school and I wanted to know whether this was OK with him. He said it was OK with him.

Fifth Session. I visited Glen's school between sessions 4 and 5. I observed a singing class where all the children of the school were together, and two other lessons in his classroom. During the singing it was obvious that Glen needed a lot of effort to stay in the room and he obviously looked very uncomfortable being in the crowd; he did not participate, but just stared at the floor. During the next two classes, however, I was amazed at the math skills he demonstrated. The teacher told Glen to show me what he was doing and he was calculating correctly, but it seemed not to have any meaning for him. Glen did not interact with other children at all and it seemed like they had given up on him also; none of the other children even made a gesture of trying to get his attention. But when he was alone with his teacher, he was much more at ease and he even smiled.

When I said hello to Glen at the beginning of session 5 (after the visit to his school), he smiled at me and shook my hand as if we had known each other a long time. I handed over the box and he opened it halfway. I asked him whether he could show me with the box where and with whom he could open the box widely, with whom it was better to close the box. It was amazing how he could visualize with this little cigar box and communicate which situation was OK to have the box open and in which situation it was better to close it. He even explained that his singing class was one of those situations where it was best to close it. I complimented Glen on his ability to have figured out where it helped him to have the box closed and where it was useful to have it open. I showed interest in getting to know more about his opening and closing plan in subsequent sessions.

While we played the board game again, I told Glen that I would meet with his parents next time and asked whether it would be OK with him if I showed them his cigar box. He agreed it would be OK.

Sixth Session. This was the first time I met Mr. Burns. He immediately declared that one should not say Glen has handicaps and using the word autism was a sin; for him, Glen was just different. Mrs. Burns countered her husband by saying that it was important to name this difference and that it had helped her a lot to know the diagnosis because then she did not feel guilty anymore, and the doctors had told her that it had nothing to do with the family or their failure as parents. When I asked what should happen in this session in order to be helpful, the father stated that he would get an idea of how much the mother had suffered, but for him it was only God who could help Glen. He thought it might be useful if the family could come together to this meeting once as a family, because he realized that their two younger boys were quite tense and upset.

I showed them Glen's box and suggested that with this box it might be possible to show special ways to communicate with Glen and understand his special ways of dealing with the world. They both agreed and the mother added that this could be at least the first step.

Seventh Session. Glen came alone. It was after Christmas and the box was closed today. I suggested that we play the board game and another game he did not know yet. I informed Glen about the family session and asked him about the conditions he needed to have the box as open as possible. "I will be here for 20 minutes" was his answer. I told him that I would use the box during the session with the family.

Eighth Session. Glen attended the family session for the promised 20 minutes. I started the session by asking everybody to go around in my office and look for an item that each would choose as a symbol to represent themselves. I had wanted to emphasize through visualization that everyone was different in this family. The family members started to talk about different characteristics they attributed to each other and Glen mostly sat and listened. The brothers agreed that Glen always acted like he was the big brother but they did not want to say much more than this, except they both agreed that he was stubborn.

This gave me an opportunity to talk about children like Glen who have different ways of communicating, and I showed them the box. After this, Glen left. I added some more information: the difference in perception, in ability to sort out auditory and visual information, the ability to get the meaning of the word, and so on. The brothers were listening carefully but also took the opportunity to express their anger about the situation with Glen and that they felt they were treated unfairly by their parents.

After the thinking break, I complimented the two boys for having participated in such an attentive manner. I normalized their angry feelings, especially when Glen was different from other children's siblings. I added that it was more difficult for them because the difference between Glen and them was not immediately apparent to people like it would be if Glen were sitting in a wheelchair, for example.

Follow-up. I had 10 more sessions with Glen in different intervals. The box was not in use anymore and instead Glen told me when it is time to ask questions and when not. Occasionally we played games during the entire session and other times he brought up an amazing variety of topics such as what is pedophilia and what to do to protect oneself from such people. It seemed that he had such an experience but could not sort it out adequately. He talked about his religious experiences with his father and that he prayed the rosary in secret. He wanted to know my opinion about purgatory and told me that he had lots of fears whenever he thought about it. In later sessions he talked about girls, how he imagined what his girlfriend would be like, and where would be good places to get to know girls.

Mrs. Burns requested two sessions for herself to discuss different options for the ways to take care of Glen. Mr. Burns also came to see me twice, and each person knows about the other's visits with me. They both think it is better for each to come alone and rejected the suggestion of having sessions together.

Discussion: As of this writing, I (TS) still meet with Glen and his mother periodically, on an as-needed basis. I expect to continue to follow his progress for many more years and this will be one of those situations where Glen may need periodic help as he goes through monumental challenges of various developmental stages. Glen is also a client who defies classical diagnostic categories. Working with children such as Glen feels like walking along a cliff: one mistaken step and one can easily fall off the edge. Therefore, it requires delicate balance. If we only looked at Glen's problems isolated from his social and family context, he could be easily categorized as an autistic case. However, when we look at the family situation in which Glen must live, it also becomes much more complicated and complex. Such profound and long-standing disagreements and a lack of goodwill between parents certainly influences Glen's progress, especially as he is someone who cannot articulate himself as clearly as others.

For therapists, the notion of looking at and working with Glen isolated from his family is unthinkable because no matter what happens to him individually, his family can and will be a valuable resource on one hand. On the other hand, one can imagine the tremendous pressure a child such as Glen must deal with, caught in the middle of the tension between Mr. and Mrs. Burns, particularly when the child has no other resources such as friends or a social network such as a caring uncle, grandfather, or even a neighbor who would nurture and support him. Therefore, either social service programs, counselors, volunteers, or therapists become his extended family. We come to recognize the crucial value of volunteer services and other options made available throughout the life of someone such as Glen. Most of us take these informal support systems for granted, but one can easily imagine how desperate and bleak a life can be for someone like Glen without this support.

Glen's parents eventually divorced. Mrs. Burns still comes to see me periodically and Glen has moved into an institution where he is well taken care of. Over time, he eventually was able to talk, in bits and pieces, about his having been sexually abused by a priest, and he seems to have put it in perspective. A situation like Glen's could be considered as a brief therapy case, although he would need some level of supportive services for many years to come, because the basic philosophical position a therapist takes is the same— with the exception that therapy is offered only as needed and when the client finds it useful.

Do You Work With Children Who Lie and Steal?

Here we address the type of problem that baffles and confuses many adults. As a result, parents can come to view the child's behavior as either a willful defiance of their wishes or a character flaw that the child inherited from relatives who did not turn out to be a success. These two problems of a child lying and stealing seem to be the most upsetting to parents and teachers. We believe that neither willful defiance nor a character flaw is an adequate explanation; neither leads us to satisfactory solutions because the focus is solely on changing the child, while ignoring the context in which these problems may occur. Therefore, it is frequently more helpful to widen the lens to look at these problems in the context of society and family. This makes it a bit easier to look for solutions, as the following case examples show.

Almost all parents and teachers become very upset and concerned about these two problems, and for very good reasons: Their task is to educate and teach the children to become contributing members of society; and certainly the children would likely end up in a great deal of trouble in the community with these bad habits. Frequently many thoughtful parents and teachers feel they have failed in their jobs if children exhibit these behaviors.

By the time these problems come to our attention, most parents and teachers say they have tried everything they can think of to correct the problem: lectured the child; screamed, punished, bribed the child; tried to overlook the problem; some parents even tried to scare the child by taking the child to the police or a priest. Everything they could imagine might help, they have tried.

This situation calls for Doing Something Different (see Chapter 6 on useful tools). This approach begins with asking the parents or teachers, who are usually more upset than the child about stealing or lying, "What would be the most surprising thing your child (student) would expect you to do with him or her when you discover this problem again with your child?" Many parents and teachers have a difficult time imagining what the child might say they would do. You may help them by offering some hints, such as "What would your child say would be the least expected thing you would do if your child is found to lie or steal again?" If they list several answers, once again ask the parents, "Which would your child say would be the biggest surprise to him or her?"

Many parents come up with answers that are in the nature of "tit for tat"—they would steal or lie to the child in return to "give him a taste of his own medicine." This kind of retaliatory response is very similar to knee-jerk responses out of anger at the child or venting frustration at the child. Similar to the responses to the miracle questions, answers to these questions require some reflection on the part of the parent or the teacher. A good guideline is to remind the parents what they are hoping to accomplish with the child. Most parents answer that their earnest wish is for the child to gain control over his or her stealing or lying behavior and to do what parents or teachers say, even though he or she might not feel like doing it. Doing what is least expected (and most surprising) to the child is designed to interrupt the familiar, but tiresome and repetitive, patterns that everybody knows do not work.

What Does the Child Need to Know?

We believe it is important that adults clearly communicate to the child in the following manner.

1. The child needs to understand exactly what is expected of him or her. We find that many parents tell the child what *not* to do, instead of what to do. Most children understand very quickly what is expected of them and therefore we believe it is not helpful for the adult to repeat the rules once they have been made clear. Most children do not need help on the cognitive level, but only on the implementation of what they already know.

2. Whenever the child breaks a rule, that behavior has to become a problem for the child as well, not for the parents alone. You are likely to meet parents who become extremely upset with the child or themselves about a problem. Using scaling questions, when we ask parents how badly they think their child is upset about the problem in comparison to how upset the parents are, the typical answer is that their own number is much higher than their child's. This is not a very good incentive for the child to change, because the pressure to change the child is all on the parents and not on the child. Shifting this burden of change from the parent to the child is much more useful. That way the parents feel they are guiding the child in the proper direction, rather than trying to force the child.

   You can negotiate with the parents about ways to shift the burden of finding a solution by asking such questions as: "Knowing your child as well as you do, what consequences would be most helpful to your child to learn to follow the rules?"; "Of all the things you have tried with your child, what did you find was most successful in convincing your child that he must change?"

3. We find that stealing or lying is seldom the child's goal. Because children cannot explain to adults what they are trying to accomplish by stealing, for example, so parents or teachers need to help sort out what problem the child is trying to solve by stealing or lying.

We find that the following questions are useful in figuring out what the child is trying to achieve by stealing. These questions can be easily adapted to cases of lying or any other rule breaking behavior.

- You must have "good reasons" to steal. Can you tell me what they are?
- How is stealing helpful to you?
- Can you explain what difference it makes when you steal?
- Make sure you do not ask the child "why" he or she steals. Most children do not know the answer, particularly when the question is asked under pressure and under threat. Such questions only lead to more frustration on the part of the parent, which further deteriorates the relationship with the child.

Frequent answers we hear from children in response to these types of questions are: "I will have more friends," "I want to feel important," or "I want other kids to pay attention to me." Once the parents discover these "good reasons," it is much easier to sort out how to help the child to achieve these meaningful goals by other, more acceptable means.

CASE EXAMPLE: GOOD REASON

Michela, a 12-year-old girl, was brought to therapy because she had been stealing a considerable amount of money (several hundred dollars). She had been stealing only at school. This had been going on for several months and her mother, Mrs. Morris, decided not to make a fuss about it because it was too embarrassing for her. When Michela got into trouble in school because of the missing money, her mother would pay the money back in order to make things easier for Michela, out of a belief that Michela had poor self-esteem and she did not want her daughter to be in trouble with the police.

When I (TS) asked how much this stealing was a problem for the mother on a scale of 1 to 10 (10 being the most upsetting and 1 being of least concern), Mrs. Morris replied that it was 8 for herself but 3 for her daughter. She added that she knew exactly what consequences Michela needed to change her habit. Surprised to hear this, I asked, "Perhaps I didn't hear you correctly, could you explain this again?" Mrs. Morris answered, "Well, if I didn't give the money to pay back the theft, I knew the police would have to be involved and that would be very hard for Michela." Of course Mrs. Morris and I had a lengthy conversation about how her actions were not helping her daughter and how she saw a troublesome outcome for her daughter was looming unless something changed.

In the end, Mrs. Morris decided that she must do what was best for her daughter in the long run and told her daughter in front of me that in the future she was not going to pay back the money she steals and the police will be called to report her. The mother laid out what the consequences for Michela would be when she stole money again. Of course, it was easier said than done because, if the police were involved, Mrs. Morris would have to face the fact that it will become public information and she would have to face shame and embarrassment for herself as well. To her credit, Mrs. Morris was willing to face these consequences.

During the following five sessions with Michela and her mother, I learned from Michela that her "good reason" was that she was having a considerable amount of problems in school because she had no friends, and other children teased her about her being overweight. In an effort to buy friends, Michela bought CDs, candies, make-up, and movie tickets for the other children. We looked into many different ways to make friends. During the scribble games, in which we created pictures and then made up stories related to the scribble, I learned that Michela was quite talented in writing poetry and rhymes. In addition, her sparkling sense of humor peeked through. I contacted the teacher and discussed possible ways to turn this talent into a resource for making friends. The teacher decided to stage a "poetry" competition in the class and invited all the students to present as many rhymes and limericks as they could compose. Michela was a big success, and her mother enrolled her in a special program for overweight children.

There were five sessions with Michela, one session where she came with her mother, and one session her with mother alone. There was no need to call the police. Who would have expected that a solution to stealing was to make up rhymes and limericks, and begin a weight reduction program!

How Do You Work with Children Who Are Violent?

It is understandable that clinicians and laymen alike talk about children who are violent and explosive with much concern, for the welfare of other children as well as for their own safety. Before we get into a detailed discussion on how to help these children and their parents, we would first like to assert our view that there are serious misconceptions about these children's problems.

For the sake of convenience, children who exhibit symptoms of violence are often described, often without much thought, as "violent children." What was initially designed to be a short-hand term—thus avoiding a long-winded description of certain characteristics of some children—has become a label for these children. Thus, we are often asked, "What would you suggest I do with violent children?"

or "Do you think the solution-focused approach works with violent children?"

These questions imply that violent children are all alike, or that children who are violent are that way all the time. These questions also convey the misperception that "violence" is a unitary phenomenon and there has to be one solution to all children so labeled. Similarly, many parents and practitioners often describe the "violence" in children as if some mysterious forces are operating within these children and their violence erupts anywhere and anytime. Our clinical experience indicates that when children who are described as violent are helped to communicate, frequently we find that they have some reasonable explanations for their behavior. (We may not, however, agree with their logic or conclusions they draw from their perceptions and interpretations of events.) Being clinicians, we want to focus on what to DO, how to talk to these children, rather than figuring out "why" they are violent.

Over the years, we met many children who were described as violent, yet almost all of them exhibited an ability, under many circumstances, to not be violent at all and even to be gentle and quite loving. Other children could or normally would have become violent in their usual circumstances but somehow they had managed to control themselves. In other words, all children show violent behaviors from time to time, and they certainly are selective about when to be violent and when not to. Even children labelled as "violent" show some indications that they are able to control their own behaviors.

Another common misperception is that these children are "out of control." We disagree with this assertion and contend that all "violent" children have control over themselves, although there is no predictable pattern to their violent outbursts, these outbursts are usually in response to the social situation. All violent behavior occurs as a response to something the children have experienced; therefore, it is important to discuss the social context in which children become violent. What is needed is to observe more closely and look for small differences that show us they are able to control themselves, and then, of course, to nurture these small abilities. It is also very important to look at their violence within the context of where, when, with whom, and how they come to behave in a violent manner. Therefore, the context of the violence must be understood before we proceed to give advice or suggestions on what the individual child should do.

For example, once I (IKB) met with a mother who literally packed her child's suitcase for a hospital stay because she was convinced her 11-year-old son needed to be hospitalized immediately because "he went after his brother with a knife." Initially shocked and in disbelief, this mother has been advised by her friends and neighbors that a "child like that needs to go to a mental hospital," and the mother was asking me to make the necessary arrangements to hospitalize her son. I calmly asked the mother about the details around the violent episode, and then about how her 11-year-old got along with other children at school and in the neighborhood, the history of "going after somebody with a knife," and so on. It turned out that this son had no particular behavioral problems in school and he has many friends he gets along with fairly well. By asking about these details, the mother realized, to her relief, that the fights were limited to sibling rivalry and that her one son was not a "violent" child after all, but that she needed to monitor his brother's quiet ways to provoke "violent" responses.

Children's violence is a complex phenomenon and needs much closer study of what the child or adolescent is trying to achieve by violence. Doing so is not always easy because most children are not able to articulate their reasons or feelings. Lacking an adequate explanation, it is easy to conclude that the child is violent. As the following case shows, sometimes there are no connections between the problem and the solutions. But wherever a possible solution exists, a creative therapist can create solutions out of a seemingly unconnected source.

CASE EXAMPLE: A STOLEN COAT AND A TURNING POINT
Akisha, a 16-year-old, tall, attractive young girl, was brought to therapy by her foster mother, Mrs. Evans, who said she "has had it up to here," gesturing to her neck with one hand. This was the third time Akisha was "thrown out" of the foster home because Mrs. Evans could not cope with the troubles Akisha caused since she came to live with her three years ago: Akisha was violent in school ("she went after another girl with a brick"), snuck out of the house in the middle of the night to meet older boys, was violent with other foster children in the home to the point that Mrs. Evans had to worry about the safety of three other children in her home. Akisha would attack them, grab their hair, and once even threw another child down the stairway. The foster mother had demanded that the social service remove Akisha from her home three times already, but Akisha somehow "worms her way" back into the house and the foster mother relents and takes her back. I spent some time finding out about Akisha's ability to "worm her way" back into the good graces of Mrs. Evans, who readily agreed that indeed not only was Akisha charming but she was bright, smart, and knew how to behave herself when she decided that it was in her best interest to do so.

Akisha had been homeless on and off several times and each time she decided that being on her own and doing whatever she felt like doing was not really good for herself. Unfortunately, there was no family to speak of and nobody in her biological family who was interested in looking after her since her biological mother disappeared some years ago. Her father lived in a nursing home and there was no option of living with him, she reported.

The appointment for therapy was part of the condition for being allowed to stay at the foster home this time. Akisha also had to refrain from reprimanding or disciplining other children at the foster home, but instead was to report any problem to the foster mother. In addition, there were not to be any more reports of fights either from school or the police, she was not sneak out at night, and she was to obey all the house rules.

The session began as usual: What are her successes?; What is the reason Akisha keeps returning to the same foster mother (but no mention of her being being thrown out)?; What motivates the foster mother to repeatedly take her back (and again, not about why she "throws her out")? Mrs. Evans readily agreed that Akisha was attentive, concerned, and was more than willing to nurture and take care of the foster mother whenever she was ill. Even though Akisha was very clear that she wanted to live with the foster mother, Mrs. Evans was not sure she wanted to keep Akisha; Mrs. Evans was also responsible for the safety of the other children in the home and she was concerned about the harm that Akisha could inflict. After a thinking break at the end of the session, I complimented the foster mother on her ability to see lots of potential for success in Akisha, and for spelling out the rules and conditions very clearly this time instead of just allowing Akisha to "come and go." Akisha was complimented on her good judgment to recognize that living with Mrs. Evans was good for her and her future at an age when most teenagers might think otherwise.

The second session began with "What is better, even a little bit?" and Akisha listed how she was following rules, going to school on time, not sneaking out at night, and even doing school work on her own without being reminded by Mrs. Evans. When asked about how she managed to respond differently to other girls who wanted to pick fights with her, Akisha explained that she was able to "just walk away" by reminding herself that she was not going to allow the other girls who wanted to pick fights with her ruin her future. I also spent a considerable amount of time learning about her decision not to do drugs. (Her biological mother was reported to be a long-time drug user.) I was impressed by the degree of insight into what was important to her and how she wanted a "better life" for herself.

Between sessions 2 and 3, another foster girl who "got on Akisha's nerves" ran away with Akisha's overcoat, among the other things she took with her. Akisha would normally have been extremely upset and become violent when her own things disappeared, including smaller items such as a shirt, sweater, or even a comb. Her usual approach was to pursue the guilty person even if it meant chasing the other person "to the end of the earth" and "beat the s_____ out of her," according to the foster mother. But somehow this time *she managed to report the missing coat and the girl to Mrs. Evans and did not pursue her on her own, skip school, or spread the threat to kill her among friends in school. When I heard about this, I was astonished at her decision to follow the house rules instead of deciding to "take the matter into her own hands" as usual.*

This episode of exception to her usual behavior was thoroughly examined, along with other small but, significant successes, such as having followed the house rules for a month, not having been punished for an entire month (something of a record for Akisha), and not making phone calls from school. The other important difference that contributed to Akisha's change was the very clear rules and conditions that Mrs. Evans had laid out for Akisha in no uncertain terms. Unlike in the past, Mrs. Evans explained that she realized how important it was for Akisha to have a mother who will set the rules and tell her the consequences of not following them. Through the "stolen coat" episode, Mrs. Evans explained how she relied on "promises" and "heart to heart" talks with Akisha. What was different this time? Mrs. Evans explained that unlike in the past, she is coming to the sessions with Akisha and she is learning about how important she has been to Akisha, and how much Akisha needed a mother and not just a foster mother. Because of her seeming maturity and street smarts, Mrs. Evans did not recognize that Akisha needed much more firmness from her. Akisha and her foster mother decided they no longer needed therapy after 4 sessions in 5 months and their levels of confidence to maintain the gain they made were quite high—7 for the foster mother and 9 for Akisha.

Chapter 8

Making a Difference with Teenagers

I (IKB) WAS RETURNING HOME ON A LATE FLIGHT FROM THE EAST COAST and I got into my seat on a plane, hoping to catch up on some sleep and feeling dead tired from standing up and conducting a seminar all day. I really looked forward to some quiet time alone, before arriving home. When I saw a good-looking young boy come on board, I hoped against hope that he would not sit next to me because I felt the last thing I needed was a young person bouncing up and down next to me with his earphones plugged into his tape player. Of course, he did sit next to me, this 16 year-old boy who was bouncing up and down in his seat without his tape player, so excited about going home after a semester at an art and music school for gifted students on scholarship. The young boy could not contain his excitement about going home after a semester of being away from his family for the first time in his life, he explained. What caught my attention was how he kept looking at his watch and would blurt out, "I think my dad just pulled out of our driveway so that he can pick me up at the airport." "They must be passing through Highway 43 near the town of Belgium." "I can't wait to see my dad and my kid brother." And "I think they are now at the airport parking lot." He announced his family's driving route from their house to the terminal. Amazed to hear how he was anxious to see his dad and his younger brother, and hearing his openness about how much he missed his family, I almost forgot how tired I was.

I imagined an emotional embrace between father and son, so happy to see each other, older and younger brother hugging each other, big and welcoming embraces for a long time as they smiled and told each other how much they missed one another. Wanting to catch this homecoming scene, I managed to walk off the plane behind him and hung around to see his long-anticipated reunion with his family.

As we walked out of the jetway and into a waiting crowd at the gate, the same young boy was the picture of cool itself! He waved his hand toward an older man who was standing and waiting for him, and waved toward his young brother and said, "Hi, yeah" and walked ahead of them toward the baggage pick up. In sheer disappointment, I stood there for a few minutes and debated with myself whether I should catch up with his dad, and tell him how much his son missed him and ask whether he knew how important his family was to his young boy? Of course I realized I was not the therapist in that context and I walked out into a cold winter air, thinking about what I just had witnessed and what it must feel like to be his parents, and how much they must have missed him.

A GLIMPSE INTO ADOLESCENCE

This experience taught me how important families are to all adolescents, but also how important it is to stay "cool" and to behave "differently" from them. It reminded me how infrequently parents of teenagers are given any overt sign of affection and how they have to learn to live with such a need to be cool and detached looking. I also remembered how difficult it was to raise a teenager myself. How difficult all these must be for the young man himself!

We debated the relevance of addressing adolescence. We also solicited feedback from our colleagues about whether it makes sense to create a special section on working with adolescents in a book that deals with working with children and their parents. We could not agree on this topic, nor could many of the colleagues we asked. Our original idea was that, unlike younger children, adolescents are able to express themselves well enough verbally, so that there are not much difference between working with adolescents and with adults. Yet some of our colleagues advised us that teenagers present a whole different configuration of problems in therapy and we ought to write a separate book that deals with adolescents from a solution-focused approach. This point did not contradict our sense that, because teenagers can express themselves verbally, the many differences between adults and teenagers do not substantially affect the SFBT model. Yet, many of our trainees and colleagues lump "children and adolescents" into a single group. Therapists also express many frustrations about not knowing how to work with adolescents who present unique clinical problems.

Therefore, we decided to include a chapter on working with adolescents but place it at the end of the book rather than in the middle. Therefore, you have a choice of looking at this chapter for your own reference or ignoring it entirely if you do not work with adolescents.

DIFFERENCES BETWEEN CHILDHOOD
AND ADOLESCENCE

We began to look into the differences between children and adolescents that give adolescents the reputation as a challenging population to work with. Even parents agree that when a child reaches adolescence, somehow, something happens to him or her that sets the new adolescent apart from children. These differences go beyond hormonal changes. Teenagers are often described as "impossible" to understand, unwilling to listen, and so changeable and moody that it is difficult for adults to keep up. Many friends and colleagues warn about the impending danger period when one's child reaches the magic 13th birthday; and lots of jokes are told about how to survive a child's teen years.

Transition From Childhood
to Adolescence

What is it about adolescence that makes teenagers so baffling, mysterious, infuriating, and so utterly delightful? Whether you are a parent, a therapist, or just an uninvolved observer, nobody has a bland reaction to them: either you love them or you can't stand them. And those feelings can fluctuate almost daily or hourly. What is it about their stage of development that elicits such strong reactions from those around them? Why do parents clash with them so much and we hear so many complaints about screaming matches between the parents and adolescents? What happened to a once-delightful child?

If the difficult character of adolescents were owing solely to rapid developmental change, we might ask why don't the parents of infants complain so much about how difficult it is to raise a baby? An infant goes through more changes in a short time span than an adolescent. We believe the difference between raising an infant and an adolescents lies in what is asked of the parent as a caregiver. Raising a small child means everything depends on the parent—to provide as much protection as possible, to create an environment that is sufficiently safe and yet challenging as the child's developmental needs change over time. Initially the basic needs are quite obvious: food, shelter, affection, attention, physical and intellectual stimulation, as well as various necessary skills to survive and become self-sufficient. Meeting the child's basic needs is largely left up to the parents' good will toward the child, as well as their intuition, discretion, common sense, and creativity. The emotional rewards parents derive are generally plentiful and parents are usually successful. As a result, it is relatively easy to feel competent at parenting a child.

When the same child turns into an adolescent, the parents' task changes drastically. There may still be the need to provide food and shelter, but what about the guidance and direction from the parents that were so important before? Adolescents have this great need to be DIFFERENT from their parents. This is often expressed in a confusing, puzzling, and, at times, bizarre manner. The intense search to be "different" is not uniform in all children and is not consistent over time; it is expressed differently with every adolescent, and the timing can be confusing to parents. Some children begin quite early, while others wait until they are a bit more grown up. While one child is extremely outspoken about his or her search for "Who am I?" or "What do I want to be?," other adolescents are more quiet and orderly about achieving such goals. Some go through fits and starts, while others are more even-keeled.

The mystery for parents is how to decipher the secret code of the adolescent. It is terribly baffling to see a child so articulate and eloquent at one moment, be so bumbling, confused, and confusing the next.

One of the most frustrating aspects of living with adolescents is their interminable ambivalence toward their task of growing up and becoming independent and self-sufficient adults. This can be very confusing to all of us. An important point to remember, is that a teenager is still a child and all the assumptions we discussed in Chapter 2 still apply to adolescents—that is, they want to please their parents, and want to have their parents be proud of them. Clearly this desire is expressed in a much more covert manner than how it is manifested by a young child. Adolescents need to feel "grown up," and are unable to express their desire to be praised or nurtured as they did when they were children.

The Parents

The parents' task in following the adolescents through this tumultuous time of "differentiating" from their parents, as well as from their peers, is confusing enough; this task is made even more confusing because it is easy to expect more from a teenager than he or she can deliver in a consistent manner. Many parents are baffled by their teenager: How can their smart, bright, articulate adolescent do such dumb things? How can a teenager be so vulnerable one day and turn so defiant the next (as if he or she will never need a parent's help ever again)?

Unlike a younger child's needs for consistent guidance and his or her willingness to accept such help, teenagers are less clear about what they want from their parents and give mixed signals. Thus, the parents' role becomes less clear. In other words, the parents need to become much more low key and detached, yet they must do this at a time when the adolescent's potential for making serious mistakes seems to be the greatest. No wonder parents are ready to pull the hair out and often make moves that lead their relationship into troubles. Parents are regularly asked to turn a deaf ear or blind eye to apparent problems. They must often mute their voices and hold their breaths instead of offering advice.

Adolescence is a period where maturing children need to find out what their abilities and limits are. They need to know where their body ends and where the next person's begins. They need to discover that they are not invincible, but they need to learn this without seriously risking their well-being and safety. They need to learn where their parents' values end and where their's begin. They need to understand how they are both different from and the same as their parents, their peers, and others.

For such an immature and inexperienced being as an adolescent, all of this forms a daunting task. No wonder parents are so confused and confusing most of the time. What is most difficult for parents is that they must teach all these important lessons without "lecturing" or "repeat yourself over and over again," as one 15-year old girl spat out at her father. Parents often describe their experience of raising an adolescent as being asked to "set their life-long knowledge and experience of life aside and let go of their set of values and common sense and intuition of what will work and what will not," as one baffled father explained. No doubt this is confusing but that's exactly what parents need to do: allow adolescents room to experiment with how different they can be so, finally, that they can also choose to be similar to their parents.

Working with Parents of Adolescents

For most parents, adolescence is a serious time to challenge their parenting abilities, even for those parents who have successfully raised the child up to that point. We meet parents who have successfully raised their other children into young adulthood, and yet still begin to doubt their ability as parents when one of their teenagers face more difficulties than other young people at the same age.

One of the most difficult aspects of working with adolescents is knowing how to relate to the parents who are frequently more upset, anxious, and worried about the adolescent's behaviors than the teenagers are themselves. When parents are very alarmed, concerned, and anxious about the child's future, the adolescent's response seems to move in the opposite direction; that is, the more adolescents display a behavior of "couldn't care less," the more alarmed the parents become. Alarmed parents, in turn, alarm and pressure therapists to act on their behalf. Knowing how to deal with this pressure to do "something immediately" and channel it in a productive and useful direction is one of the most difficult aspects of working with adolescents.

We find that the house and furniture metaphor is helpful to calm some parents. We will explain this metaphor in a moment. You may already have your own stories or metaphors that work equally well for you. Whatever you do, the best information the parents need to hear is that they have done the best they could and nobody could expect them to do otherwise. This position conveys to the parents our assumptions and attitude about them: with few exceptions, they want what is best for their child and they need to know that they have given their child everything the child needs to know. When and how to use this knowledge is up to the adolescent.

The house and furniture metaphor goes something like this. When a child is born, he or she is like a house without any furniture. The parents, being loving and caring people, have carefully furnished the house by paying a great deal of attention to various details: where to place the couch, chair, bed, desk, and so on; what color to paint the walls; and what color matches which chair, curtains, and so on. Now when their child becomes a teenager, the teenager takes over the house and in order to make it his or her own house, the teenager will move all the furniture out. Sometimes, they may not put back one single piece of furniture at first. As time passes, however, the parents can see that the new owner has put almost every pieces of furniture back in the house. Maybe the items will not be exactly in the same spots as before but the house and furniture will look familiar. Perhaps the new owner may have a color scheme, wallpaper, or pictures on the wall that are different, but they will be certainly recognizable to parents. It is important for parents to remember that the teenager, as a new owner of this house, is not changing things around to be spiteful, but to make it their own.

Compliments, Compliments,
and More Compliments

We find that the more parents are reassured that they have done a good job of raising their child, the easier it is for them to calm their anxiety and uncertainty about whether they have done their best as parents. The more parents recognize their own successes as parents, the easier it is for them to have hope—not only about themselves as parents, but about their child—and the easier it is for them to patient. When parents are confident of their own successes, it is easier for them to be calm and also see humor and fun in allowing their teenager to struggle with becoming an adult. We find that it is the parents who are unsure about whether they have done a good job of teaching their child, who "nitpick," "badger," and "argue" with their teenagers endlessly, thinking somehow they may still improve on the job. Compliments and acknowledgments of their child's successful mastery of skills also help parents to calm down and allow their adolescents to make mistakes and learn from their mistakes. These compliments are not flattery, but are based on factual information that you heard from the parents during the session, while some compliments derive from your reframing of the parents' perspectives. Perhaps it is best to illustrate what we have in mind with a case example.

CASE EXAMPLE: SUGAR IN THE CEREAL

A father and a stepmother of two sets of children—his children and her children from their two previous marriages—requested an urgent appointment and insisted that it must be that same day. Because Mr. and Mrs. Cooper sounded so upset I (IKB) agreed to see them immediately. The couple and their respective sets of children moved into a house together less than two years before and it had been nothing but turmoil with constant battles among the children, especially between the father's two teenage boys and the stepmother. They reported that the relationship between the stepfather and the mother's two younger daughters was much smoother, but there was ongoing tension between the stepmother and the father's two boys. Both parents had believed that they would be able to conquer the difficulties eventually with steadfast love and kindness, but now they were finding that love is not enough.

Mrs. Cooper was anxious to describe the event that erupted that very morning, but explained that the tension has been simmering for a long time, almost immediately after the couple got married and the two families merged. She declared that unless the issue between her and his teenage boys (particularly between her and 15-year-old David), was resolved, she was walking out of the marriage.

Because of her pressured speech and the request of an emergency session, I was interested in listening to the mother's account of the morning's event. Apparently Mrs. Cooper was always very careful to pay attention to the children's eating habits and nutrition (for example, she always reminded the children not to use too much sugar in corn flakes in the morning). David, on the other hand, was used to eating whatever he pleased and lived on junk food before the stepmother came. So of course he could not comprehend what the big fuss was about. It had become a morning ritual where Mrs. Cooper reminded David about his overly-generous use of sugar and, "just to spite me," Mrs. Cooper explained, he kept scooping sugar into his corn flakes, with a look of defiance on his face. When that morning Mrs. Cooper once again reminded him, David stood up from the table and threw his cereal bowl at the kitchen wall. Corn flakes, milk, and sugar were splatterd all over the kitchen wall, on the counter, over the sink, and on the floor. The bowl was shattered into small pieces. Yelling and screaming followed, and David stormed out the door and went off to school.

Listening to her relate this painful exchange, I kept thinking how much Mrs. Cooper had worked to make this family blend together and how hard she was still working, with very few signs of succcess, little appreciation from the children, or support from her husband. As I began to think about ways to let her know that indeed she had given it her best shot and how important the boys were to her, I blurted out, "Boy, you really care about David, don't you?"

Mrs. Cooper was stunned for a moment, then she continued to explain how she felt she had done everything humanly possible to try to be a good mother to David and his brother Keith, but she had had it (her hand slashing across her throat). She demanded that the therapist help them arrive at some sort of solution today, or else their marriage was over.

Mr. Cooper tried to be sympathetic to his wife but he also tried to downplay how bad a child David was by pointing out how kind and loving David can be with his stepsisters. There were times David even offered to help clean up the kitchen, that he was generally a quite well-behaved child outside the home. This infuriated Mrs. Cooper even further, and she became more agitated and insisted that the therapist see David because there was such a devious side of him. Mrs. Cooper stated that this was because David's own mother, who abandoned her two boys and ran off with another man, had failed to raise him properly. Mr. Cooper was always trying to make up for his ex-wife's failure as a parent, Mrs. Cooper went on, feeling guilty for raising the boys without a mother. It was becoming clear that the more the father supported and protected David and his biological mother, the angrier and more agitated Mrs. Cooper became.

I recognized that Mrs. Cooper needed more support and validation for having been a good mother and I turned the conversation toward a consideration of how she decided to take on such an enormous responsibility of raising two teenage boys, when most women in her situation would have chosen to either live separately and keep dating Mr. Cooper until the children became old enough to live on their own, or even would have left the boys to their own devices, and not really cared how they turned out as adults. I became curious about what made her so committed to raising the boys properly and doing a good job with them, even though they were not her own children. Mrs. Cooper became tearful at this point and said that she certainly did not walk into this situation with her eyes closed or blinded by her love for her husband, but she had thought very seriously about how much she wanted to be the mother the boys deserved to have. Then she turned to her husband and said how much she loved him and actually wanted to make their two families become one real family.

We cannot emphasize strongly enough the value of complimenting the parents, of reassuring the parents that they have given the children all the necessary foundation to build their own life, and of noting how they worked hard to teach the children what is right and wrong. Only when the parents are reassured that they have done a competent job of raising the teenagers are they able to sit back, look at their accomplishments, and look for solutions. Then they are able to back off and give the teenagers room to do their job of experimenting and testing to find out what kind of person they want to become as an adult.

Discussion. One can easily misunderstand Mrs. Cooper as a stepmother who wants to control the boys, force them into her own image of good children, and rule the roost. We are not denying that such a view has its validity. However, we believe that viewing her as a "control freak," for example, does not offer a viable alternative to the way she has been looking at herself—that is, she sees herself as a tireless mother who wants to help the children see what is good for them. When we view a client as a "control freak," the next logical step is to try to control the control freak so that she no longer controls the children. Such logic unfortunately does not work very well with human beings, even though it might with machines. Nobody likes to be controlled, even those who are labeled as "control freaks."

Alternatively, viewing her effort as an "act of love" and as an expression of her commitment to the boys makes it possible for her to let go of this controlling method of showing her love. This opens up the possibility of her looking for more workable, less frustrating ways to show her love for David.

In addition, since every behavior has more than one consequence, purpose, and outcome, we prefer to attribute a positive motivation to the mother's behavior. This makes it easier for her to find more workable and cooperative ways to work with David, so that both would ultimately achieve their goals. When the mother feels she is respected by the therapist who works within her frame of reference, it is easier for her to respect and work with David. An unforseen consequence of our session was that the father became much more active in disciplining the boys. It thus became easier for David to see that it was not just the "stepmother" who was out to make his life miserable, but that his own father also believed that good nutrition was important.

BEGINNING THERAPY
WITH ADOLESCENTS

We want to describe some common positions that teenagers take in therapeutic encounters and offer some alternative strategies to becoming frustrated.

"I don't know . . . " or "Whatever . . . "

Many parents, as well as beginning therapists, become very frustrated when adolescents respond with the expressions "I don't know . . . " or "Whatever . . . ." These expressions are usually accompanied with a shrug of shoulders, a slouched posture, eyes rolled up to the ceiling, or other indifferent attitudes and words. When the topic of training pertains to adolescents, the question of how to respond to these attitudes invariably comes up. Rather than think about immediate, fast answers, we would like to suggest that you need to think about the following points before adolescents will trust you enough to talk to you.

1. Whatever they do, do not take it personally and do not feel offended by adolescent behaviors or a lack of proper manners.
2. Do not mention the reason for the referral, but learn as much as you can about the adolescent. Try questions such as: "So, what would your best friend tell me you are good at?"; "How did you get to be so good at _____?"; "What would your favorite teacher say you excel in that you are too shy to tell me about?"; "What would your girlfriend say is the best reason why she is attracted to you?"; "What would your best friend say makes you a good friend?" These questions allow adolescents to talk about themselves without admitting that they are doing so—and these questions provide a wonderful opportunity to indirectly compliment themselves, thus presenting a different kind of information than the type of discussion the teen dreaded.
3. The liberal use of relationship questions works very well with adolescents because they are not asked to express themselves but to present someone else's perception of themselves. They are free to agree or disagree with someone else's opinion of them, thus making it safer for them to risk saying things about themselves.
4. Ask about someone else's opinion to negotiate the goal. For example, you can inquire, "So, what gave your mother the idea that

your coming and talking to me would be useful for you or for her?"

5. Because most adolescents tend to be involuntary or mandated clients, make sure that you have a clear idea of what the adolescent wants from the contact with you. Teens may not be able to articulate what led them to even bother showing up, so you would need to normalize their reluctance, for example, "I can imagine you have better things to do that come and talk to shrink types like me. I'm sure this is no fun and you have much more fun things to do than talk about stuff. So, what could come out of this that would be useful for you, even a little bit?"

6. Talking about termination criteria reassures adolescents that there is an end to this.

Goal Negotiation Between Parents and Adolescents

When working with any clinical population, SFBT begins with goal negotiation because it defines what kind of conversations we will have and for what purpose. Children as young as 5 years old may be able to provide some information about how they would like to have things change, as we described in Chapter 4. This ability to express their wishes and stick to the core issues of what they want increases as children become older because they develop more sophisticated language skills and have clearer ideas of how a situation could be different and what they want. However, to be able to negotiate a goal, children need cognitive ability to reason things out and make connections with previous experiences and future possibilities. Furthermore, they need the ability to assert their own opinions and the linguistic and intellectual ability to state their wishes but also to negotiate what to give up and what to insist upon.

Therefore, goal negotiation is primarily possible with adolescents and adults. When we work with parents and adolescents, our task is to structure the sessions in such a way that this back and forth—giving up and gaining something, without feeling one is losing ground—is important. The use of scaling questions, for example, makes it possible to look at both sides of the conflicting views simultaneously: What is the likelihood that one or the other side can move up or down on the scale?; How both sides can move one step closer to each other? We, as therapists, are very much in charge of the structure of this conversation. After all, we are the keepers of the structure and procedures of the conversation. The clients are in charge of the content—of what and how much to give away, what to gain and how long to wait, and other details.

Heart-to-Heart Talks

Many parents have been encouraged by media such as newspapers, TV talk shows, popular psychology magazines, and books to "talk to your child," and parents have taken this advice to heart. The only trouble with this advice is that it usually comes without instructions on exactly how to do it. As a result, many parents believe that "talking" to their children means giving them lots of lectures or telling them what to do, "until blue in the face," as one mother put it. We have also met many parents who carry on lengthy "heart-to-heart" talks, believing at the conclusion of the talk that the child has agreed with them and has seen his or her behaviors as the parent sees them. Thus, parents expect their adolescent to follow the parents' wishes and change his or her attitudes, give up "bad friends," and drop other undesirable flaws. Parents become disappointed when these changes are not model and they can easily feel hopeless about their children and decide that only a professional can help them. When faced with such situations, it is helpful for therapists to gently ask the parents how the teenagers saw the same event of talking to their parents. Useful questions to parents are:

- Suppose I talk to your daughter about this, what would she say about how useful (or helpful) this talk was for her?
- What would she say you can do to make this a little bit more useful?
- What would your son say about how much you trusted his judgment after the talk?
- What would your daughter say was helpful about shaving her hair off?

As you can see, these questions force the parents to see things from their child's perspective, not just from their own. This sensitizes the parents to listen to their child, instead of just lecturing or trying to teach them. Using clichés or asking rhetorical questions is the most direct way to alienate teenagers because they often feel demeaned or talked down to. Contrary to the popular notion that parents must "talk to your children," we believe it would be more useful to "listen to your children respectfully." Listening to someone, even one's own children, respectfully, means not making judgments about what they say but trying to find out what kinds of meaning a teenager attributes to an act or an event.

SIMPLE RULES FOR PARENTS

There are some basic rules that help us to stay a steady course.

Do More of What Works

The first rule is to find out what works, even for a little while or only in small areas. For example, if a young person is not going to school but goes to his job at a fast-food restaurant, it is an indication that the child is still disciplined enough to show up for work on time, has an ability to follow rules and instructions, and must know how to do what he is paid to do.

Sixteen-year-old Fred, who was suspected of having ADHD still went to his "boring" job as a salesperson in a shoe department of a large discount store. Of course his parents were concerned about his failing grades and his inability to accomplish his school work. Further discussion revealed that his parents were very anxious to have him not end up in prison as his two older brothers had done. When the astonished therapist asked how he decided to be different from his two older brothers, Fred explained that he wanted to finish high school, go to college, and get a good job. He was determined not to be like his brothers, especially now that his father is dying and on a long waiting list for a liver transplant. His parents never heard him talk about his ambitions. Even though they knew that his job was boring, they never heard Fred talk about all the little tricks he used on himself to stay focused at work. In addition to doing what he was already doing, just discovering these small but successful strategies made the parents feel more hopeful and it was easy to add on some new and different ideas to help Fred focus better on his school work.

As soon as it is possible to do so without disrupting the engagement with the parents and adolescents—whether individually or as a group—find out about the *exceptions* to the problems or accounts of behaviors when they were not as troublesome as they were at the time of the session. Asking the details of past successes also reminds the parents and the child that there was a period in their lives when things were going well. This is also the simplest and easiest way to reassure both the parent the child that there is hope that the child can be a little more successful and that they have actually done quite well, teaching their child everything he or she needed to know to grow up. This reassurance helps the parents to be calmer, more relaxed, thus becoming a bit more detached from their intense concerns about their child and better able to come up with a more workable solution.

"Doing more of what works" also applies to therapists. Whatever you do with young children, adolescents, or parents that works for you, you need to do more of it. This "doing more" includes giving parents the credit for having taught their adolescents everything they need to know.

The following are some techniques we found that work well with adolescents. These are certainly candidates for "doing more" with adolescents.

1. A shorter session is better than a longer one because adolescents have shorter attention spans, and they become bored very easily. Sometimes a session as short as 15 or 20 minutes to 30 or 40 minutes is quite adequate for most adolescents.
2. Flexibility also requires your willingness to conduct the session outside the usual office setting and sitting across from each other, face to face. Activities, such as "walk and talk," hiking in the woods, shooting baskets, driving together in a car to go shopping or to a hardware store, or other physical activities often make it easier to open up a dialogue. It always works better when it appears that the "talking" part occurred spontaneously or by accident, while you are doing physical activities together. Many experienced leaders of outdoor group activities know that even the most "difficult" adolescents do remarkably well when they are in the wilderness camping or participating in new activities.
3. Make available some objects to fiddle with. We find that, while they talk, many adolescents like to fiddle with small objects in their hands, "doodle" with paper and pencil, or find something useful to do with their hands. (Some adults, especially male adults, also find fiddling with their hands helpful instead of trying to maintain eye contact.)
4. Ask open-ended questions.
    Listen to the following dialogue that makes many parents feel frustrated with their teenagers:

    Parent: Where have you been?
    Teenager: Out.
    Parent: Where is out?
    Teenager: A place.
    Parent: So, who were you with?
    Teenager: People.

The natural response for the parent is to press for more details and concrete, factual information, but this is not likely to go anywhere. Many intuitive and wise parents who have much experience with teenagers drop the conversation at this point. They, in turn, become increasingly vague until the teenager becomes more curious about the parent instead of persisting in their own elusiveness.

We think this pattern applies equally well between an adolescent and a therapist. It is much more productive to ask a "What is different?" question with adolescents, especially in second or later sessions instead of "What is better?" as you might usually ask adults in the follow-up sessions. We have no explanations to account for this, but somehow it seems to work better. We are told that "What is better?" is heard by teenagers as pressure to do more, do a better job, or even as "you must do more."

5.   Willing to be even more flexible? Invite adolescents to bring a best friend or neighbor, dog or other pet, or even a favorite stuffed animal to the session. We have had some surprising results from such contacts, and solutions can come from a source that we would not have imagined. Some teenagers want to bring their guitars or other musical instruments to show you how accomplished they are in music.

Do Something Different:
Pattern Interruptions

There are times when parents need to do something quite different than what they have been doing for weeks, months, or even years. Good clues to determine what the parents have been doing does not work is when they describe their frustration with their adolescents using such words as: "If I told him once, I've told him thousand times"; "I keep saying the same thing until blue in my face"; "I feel like I'm hitting my head against the brick wall"; "I've tried everything under the sun"; "I just don't know what is going on in his mind"; "We are at the end of our rope." When you hear these statements, with obviously exasperated tones of voice and frustrated expressions on their faces, it means the parents are working far harder to figure out what is going on than is the young person. It is also a good signal to you and to the parents that they need to start thinking outside the box. When you are faced with this kind of situation, the following are some helpful steps you can take:

1.   Keep track of all the small details of interactions between the parent and the teenager. This means: What does the parent do?; What does the teenager do in response?; What comes after this?; What do

you do?; What does she do?; How does this kind of unproductive interaction usually end?; Who ends it?; What happens next?

2. Ask what might be the last thing your child or teenager would expect you to do when this gets repeated next time?

3. Introduce some new element: What is done?; When it is done?; Where does it occur?; Who is involved?

4. Because the parents are the experts on their child, ask the child how he or she is likely to respond when the parents do something unexpected.

5. Find out from the parents how likely they are to try this experiment.

Even if the parents decide not to do something different, just conducting this exercise seems to free the parents by letting them know that they have an option to respond to their teenager differently. At times, just knowing they have a choice of doing something other than their usual response seems to give parents enough confidence to interact with their child more calmly and more rationally, and not overreact out of frustration. When the parent is able to interact with the child from a place of competence and confidence, the quality of the relationship is much more likely to improve.

CASE EXAMPLE: SHE KEEPS RUNNING AWAY

The parents of 14-year-old Diane came in utter frustration and desperate for some solutions. She had run away from home 19 times during the past year. When it first began, the parents discovered that the usual running away occurred every time Diane left for school. Therefore, in order to prevent her from running away, the parents stopped her from going to school. Instead a home school teacher came to the house for two hours, three times a week, and left lots of homework for Diane to do on her own. Unfortunately, only Diane can stop running away and no one can force her to do this. In addition, because she ran way 19 times, it also means that she returned home 19 times. The parents may have some control over when and how she returns home.

Since the running away began, the parents had tried to offer therapy but Diane refused to return after one meeting with a psychologist. They asked for an out-reach in-home treatment team for high-risk children to come to the home, thinking that if she refuses to go to a therapist, then the therapist will come to the home. After an initial meeting, Diane made sure that she was not home whenever the appointed time came. Because she got bored being locked in the house with her parents and a sibling of preschool age, Diane stole her parents' car and got into an auto accident. Out of frustration and anger, the parents reported her to the police and she was placed on probation. One of the conditions of her probation was that Diane was forbidden from running away from home. The parents were responsible for keeping her from running away, and they were to file a missing person's report to the police each time Diane ran away. The surveillance on Diane increased incrementally; she was forced to accompany her parents grocery shopping, to church, and on visits to the doctor, dentist, haircutter, and what have you. The parents curtailed their social life, not going out to eat, not visiting friends, and friends were not invited for fear she might sneak out while they were distracted.

In response to increased pressure from the community (school and the probation officer, and the police) to curtail her running away, now the mother made a list of likely "friends" or classmates who might know where she might stay while on the run. Her mother reported to me (IKB) that she had 70 names on her list of potential friends who might know where Diane was if she was not at home. At the first discovery of her disappearance, the mother would get on the phone and call all 70 people on her list. Of course, none of the 70 friends and classmates knew where Diane might be staying. The mother's next step was to make a list of known "friends" who allowed Diane to stay at their houses while she was on the run. She would jump in the car and visit these places and find out whether Diane was staying there. This was also unproductive because none of her "friends" were willing to be the "stool pigeon." While on the run, her mother reported that Diane would usually call her and just say, "Mom, I'm doing fine, don't worry about me" and then hang up before the mother had a chance to say anything. Of course the mother would become furious, angry, put upon, and, all the while, still worried about her daughter's safety. The effort to stop her from running away increased and Diane became "sneakier."

One time Diane attempted to jump out the second-floor bathroom window and injured herself. The parents shut and locked all the windows in the house in order to keep her inside the house because now they were fearful of suicide, in addition to running away. She still found a way to run, however. So, the parents decided to guard the front and back doors of the house and took turns sleeping to make sure that she did not run away. The parents bitterly complained about how their family life is wrecked and how they felt victimized by this 14-year-old child, saying that they felt like they were "jailed."

When asked what would likely to be different in their life, they said that they wanted to have a "normal life." When I reassured the parents they probably have done more than any parents would have done in their situation, they sighed deeply and started to pour out their frustrations at having their life turned upside down. Because Diane did not want to come but they also could not leave her at home on her own, they brought her along to my office. Diane refused to participate in "useless counseling," as she described it, and chose to wait in the waiting room. I began to consider about the following during the thinking break.

The detailed information about the typical pattern of behavior indicated that the parents did a lot of chasing after Diane. They now feared the police would charge them with child neglect if they did not track her down. Thus, they felt obligated to make every effort to find her, including calling all her friends, driving around, and looking for her everywhere. Next they waited for her phone call which usually came within two days after running away—usually a short, crisp voice saying, "Hi, mom, I'm fine" before the line went dead. This kind of phone call upset the mother, and when Diane eventually "waltzes into the house as if nothing happened," the mother and daughter would scream accusations and counterattacks at one another. The parents were obviously exhausted and wanted some relief from all this, but it was clear that they did not know what else to do. Otherwise, they seem like a very reasonable and loving parents.

When I reassured the parents that they certainly have done more than many parents would have done, they asked if I had any idea what they could do to protect Diane and have her return to the way she was a couple of years before: a sweet, likeable child who was fun to be around. Now, as the parents described her, Diane had turned sullen, unhappy, snarling all the time. She fortunately did not get into any big trouble while on the run; Diane usually stayed with friends and within easy driving or walking distance from her neighborhood. There were no big family troubles or other concerns except her not wanting to stay home when she was told to. Her mother was confident that once Diane got back into school, she would be able to catch up with her schoolwork because she was a bright child.

A gentle way to get the parents to look at their contribution to the predictable, action-reaction pattern is to ask, "What would your _____ (son, daughter) say would be the last thing she or he expects you to do when she or he runs away again next time?" I passed this question to the parents. Even though the parents groaned and dreaded even thinking about it, there was also rational and reasonable side of them that recognized that they were behaving in a very predictable manner. The parents looked at each other and were at a loss as to what Diane might say would be their least likely response to her running away next time. Then they began to describe what friends, family, school counselors, probation officers, and other professionals suggested but they rejected. Some very sensible and reasonable suggestions were rejected because they seemed too simple, punitive, or not punitive enough.

I suggested that they obviously needed some time to think about this difficult task, but what was clear to me was that they certainly needed to Do Something Different. They had exhausted all logical and sensible approaches anybody could suggest. Indeed Diane needed some very different kind of help in order to get back into school because since she is too young to think about these things on her own.

The parents leaned forward and asked in earnest what this "doing something different" involved. I realized that providing a quick and easy answer to parents who had reached this desperate point, and yet rejected all other reasonable suggestions from other thoughtful people, was not likely to be helpful to them. I could be misunderstood by parents such as Diane's and they could think that I did not understand the depth and degree of the problem. It is even more crucial that parents come up with solutions that might work for them and their child because doing so increases the likelihood that they would actually follow their own ideas for solution.

I said to the parents that I did not have a clear idea of what exactly "doing something different" entailed. I suggested that doing something different might include anything that they might consider wacky, off the wall, or downright crazy; but it was clear that the more they repeated the same old behaviors (doing more of the same), the more likely it was that they would get the same results. They agreed to this last point. They suggested that two weeks would give them sufficient time to think about what exactly they might do.

Second meeting. The parents returned in two weeks without Diane and were in a much more relaxed mood, even laughing and joking, which was such a contrast to the first meeting. When I asked "What is better?" they burst out laughing and explained that they had never talked so much as they did since our last meeting because they kept talking about all the things they could do to Diane to "pay back" all the grief she had caused them. They finally settled on a list of ways they could respond to her running away and the manner in which they could respond to her returning home. One of the things on the list was that they would "pretend she never ran away."

Sure enough, Diane ran away again and they decided only to file a missing person report with the police. They then waited and considered which response on the list made sense. The mother also reacted calmly to Diane's phone call. The parents had decided they can only control their own responses and there was nothing more they could do, which they reported was enormously helpful to the rest of the family as well. When Diane finally "waltzed into the house" as usual around dinner time, the mother decided to pretend that she never was missing during the last two days, and without missing a beat, she said to Diane, "Dinner is almost ready. Why don't you set the table?" The mother was very proud that she eliminated the usual shouting and arguing about Diane's running away again. The mother was delighted to report that Diane was shocked at the mother's "no care in the world" attitude. Diane immediately set the table and the family had dinner as usual.

The most surprising thing that happened was that Diane demanded to be sent back to school. She went to school and returned home for the 3 days in a row, and the parents continued to pretend nothing unusual happened. The parents decided that they would call me when the problem recurs, but I have not heard from them since.

All the Credit for the Child's
Successes is Returned to the Parents

Whenever possible, the credit for the child's successes, however small, are always returned to the parents. For example, I (IKB) recently met two teenage sisters, ages 12 and 14, who were described as absolutely uncontrollable because they intimidated their depressed mother—demanding that she drive them to a teenager disco and drop them off, not going to school, studying witchcraft, dressing in black most of the time, and having their bodies pierced everywhere including eyebrows, nose, tongue, and belly buttons. One sister had her hair dyed pink and the other had purple hair. They were labeled as uncontrollable and were told to show up at the juvenile court hearing to find out whether they needed to be placed outside of the home as the mother had requested.

The first turnaround began when the therapist expressed amazement at how the mother managed to get the two girls to come to the court hearing at 10:00 a.m. when they routinely slept until 1:00 or 2:00 p.m.

This tiny success became the sign of other small successes as the "helpless" mother showed to the world and her daughters that they still knew how to listen to their mother. If the therapist had not caught this small but significant success, it would have been lost in the mountain of problems the mother faced. But because it was noted, this success became a small building block on which to start establishing solutions.

At the hearing, all three said that they really did not want to be separated from each other and they wanted to stay together as a family, especially since their alcoholic father had committed suicide a year ago. The court commissioner was astute enough to realize that this family of three wanted to stay together and supported this decision to stay in treatment and with much help, learn to get along. The mother, who felt overwhelmed just coping with life, was enormously relieved to find that she was not such an incompetent mother after all. She felt relieved that somebody recognized her small success in getting her daughters to awake earlier than usual and getting them to dress and arrive at the court hearing on time. When a therapist makes an ordinary event extraordinary, many amazing things can happen.

How Do You Know Your
Child Can Do Better?

This question immediately sets the parents on the right track to talk about their child's successes. This is a particularly useful question when asked in front of the adolescent because they often hear for the first time that their parents think they have some good qualities that the parents approve of, respect, and even feel proud of. Teenagers are not likely to openly express their need and wish to be supported, accepted, and approved of by their parents but this is something we all know that adolescents need and want. Like the 16-old bright, talented, and ambitious young man I met on a flight home, they need to become older before they can accept and acknowledge that they need and appreciate support and approval from their parents.

Helping You to Help the Parents

Keep these three techniques in mind.

Stay Neutral

The most difficult aspect of working with adolescents and their parents is how easy it is to lose neutrality and begin to take sides with one or the other. Adolescents have a way of exaggerating issues and they often behave in such a provocative and outrageous manner that we can easily become upset with them and thus forget that they need our approval. It is also easy for parents to respond in an exaggerated manner, thus adding fuel to the fire. Therefore, defusing the tension between the two sides is very important. Contrary to the popular belief, a therapist can see and agree with both sides of the issue simultaneously without alienating either side.

Normalize the Conflict

The most common issue for adolescents is keeping the curfew, and the battle around this topic is the beginning of the "nag-withdraw-nag-more-withdraw-more" pattern between teenagers and parents. This pattern can easily escalate into more serious relationship problems, and even physical confrontations. Rather than seeing this as problematic, normalizing such conflicts as what both sides must do in order to sort out the differences often helps to cool tempers. Often saying things like: "I know the parent's job is to nag the children, and of course, the children's job is not to listen to their parents" is a nice way to be sympathetic to both sides of the conflict, yet normalize the conflict.

Reframe

Reframing means offering a slightly different perspective to the same event or action. For example, just as one would reframe a mother's constant nagging as her expression of her concern, reframing is done by offering two or three equally credible ways of looking at the same behavioral descriptions. You can do this by placing what the teenager does into a larger context—for example, that it is the adolescent's job to be difficult, provocative, and outrageous because the parents have been such good parents to him and now that he is growing up and separating from his parents, he is experiencing more than the usual number of difficulties of other adolescents in his situation.

INVOLUNTARY CLIENTS

As is true when working with young children, most teenagers are either referred or forced to see a therapist and they are not shy about letting adults know that they are not happy about it. We are glad. We think it is a sign of health for teenagers to reject therapy because being in therapy means they are "abnormal," or a "mental case" and they do not want to stand out as too different from their peers. Just as we do when working with involuntary or mandated adults, always find out the adolescent's concerns first. Keep this in mind and always frame your future focus around the adolescent's important concerns, not what a referring person or therapist believes should be important.

As is true with many involuntary adult clients, adolescents provide many opportunities for therapists to offer them educational or teaching modes. Unless the adolescent asks for information, it would make your job much easier if you resist the temptation to give advice, teach, or lecture them, but remain focused on finding out what their thoughts, ideas, plans, and preferences are. It is always safe to assume that behind even the strangest, most nonsensical, or bizarre behaviors, must be a "good reason," as the following case example shows.

"You must have a good reason for . . . " This is a very useful sentence to utter in many cases, particularly when adolescents are involved in harmful or inappropriate activities and behaviors. Asking this usually leads to general goals or explanations which sound more reasonable than the behaviors seem to indicate. Thus, adults are able to interact with adolescents in a calmer manner and begin to treat them as reasonable people. Again, we remind you that drinking, attempting suicide, doing drugs, and so on, are not their goals, but just teenagers' ways to achieve something else they cannot articulate. Sone of the most common answers we get from adolescents to the "good reason" question are: to have peace, socialize, feel relaxed, have more friends, be popular, and feel strong, all of which are quite reasonable and expected.

CASE EXAMPLE: NO TROUSERS IN CLASS

A colleague of ours is a consultant to several junior high schools in Korea, and she tells this amusing but alarming real-life situation she encountered. One morning she came to a particular junior high school for her usual round of troubleshooting and consulting work, except there was a tension in the air and the staff spoke to each other in hushed voices. What she eventually learned was that a second-year student came to school without trousers—only in underwear showing under his school uniform jacket, and uniform shoes and socks. It is quite normal for students to wear uniforms specified by the school, from head gear all the way down to the shape and color of their shoes, including book bags.

The teaching staff was shocked, numb, and at a loss—they had never encountered a situation like this in their long teaching careers. Everyone started to whisper, as speculation about what might be the problem ran all over the school: The student must have had a breakdown; maybe he needs to be rushed to an emergency psychiatric hospital; maybe the school work was too stressful for the boy. There was also discussion about whether to call the parents, who should call them and if so, what were the correct procedures and policies. Our colleague, Professor Choi, who teaches solution-focused therapy, decided she must step in and help sort out the problem. She finally asked the principal whether anybody talked to the boy directly to ask him the reason for this unusual behavior. The staff all looked at each other and realized that nobody had. They selected a strong, tough, male physical education teacher to go to the class and call the student out into the hallway and ask the reason for such behavior. Choi suggested the male teacher speak to the boy in a soft voice, and begin by asking, "You must have a very good reason for coming to school today without your trousers?" The boy answered, saying, "Yes, of course I do." He began explaining that he felt he was unfairly punished the day before by a science teacher, who mistakenly blamed him for causing a commotion in the class, and the teacher did not want to listen to his explanation about why it was not his fault. So, the boy continued, as a way of protesting the unfair and unjust punishment, this was the only way he could show his disagreement with the teacher. Indeed he did have a "good reason." Thus a potentially difficult situation was nipped in the bud.

We find this question of asking, *"You must have a good reason for . . ."* is a useful way to defuse what could potentially become an explosive situation, and this is good information to pass on to parents as well. We have had many professionals who report back to us about how they found this useful in defusing tension between parents and adolescents, and teachers and students, or teachers and parents. The subtle nuances and assumptions behind this question suggest respect for the other person, even for an adolescent who seems so goofy, immature, unruly, and exasperating at times. Rather than arguing with adolescents over what they are not doing, asking this question is useful in learning about the teenager's motivation behind what seems like bizarre behavior. When we listen to their reasoning, we begin to understand where they are coming from, that is, what are their thoughts behind dyeing their hair blue, piercing their body, smoking pot, or even hanging out with a bad crowd.

Some beginning practitioners worry that implying there is a "good reason" behind doing drugs, drinking, cutting, and other unacceptable behavior is condoning these things. It can certainly be heard as such if the practitioners say it with sarcasm or an insincere tone of voice. However, when asked out of curiosity, sincerely trying to learn how he or she interprets such behaviors and what their understanding is, teenagers become engaged in sustained conversation in such a way that they begin to think differently. It opens up the possibility for further dialogue, instead of closing the door. You must be sure that the adolescent knows that doing drugs is not supported by any reasonable adult, and it would be very unusual teenager to not know this. Listen to the following conversation:

Counselor: I see that you got into trouble with the principal for smoking pot again. This is a lot of hassle for you to put up with, because you have to come to people like me and of course, your parents will find out about this, and you told me last time that they give you a hard time about it. You must have a good reason for smoking pot and getting into lots of trouble.
Kevin: Yeah, of course I do. I like smoking pot and it is not a drug, anyway.

The counselor certainly would not want to get into an argument about whether or not pot is a drug because, first of all, one would not win such a debate with a teenager, and second, it would distract the counselor from his or her primary goal of wanting to find out the meaning the teenager attributes to smoking pot.

Working with Violent Adolescents

We both have worked with many adolescents who are often described as having "burned all their bridges," and their contact with us was viewed as a "last ditch effort." The referring persons often report that the adolescents have not responded positively to a multitude of services that have been provided to them over several years at great cost to the municipalities, state, or county, the community, their families, and, the adolescents themselves. Because young people's problems tend to be long-standing by the time they come to our attention as teenagers, they often tend to be cynical about treatment providers. They have learned how to manipulate the system to get by, and the treatment methods they encounter are from the same problem-solving mindset as most treatment facilities. Many teenagers know how to "comply" with the demands placed on them for a short time so that they can "beat the system." And the system they encounter tends to follow the do-more-of-the-same approach that proved unsuccessful over the years. No wonder adolescents have no respect for a familiar system they know how to manipulate. Unless their problems are of short duration, in most situations, just getting the attention of the teenagers is difficult enough. We do not want the adolescents to just comply while they are under duress; we want them to *change*. This is certainly easier said than done, but this new thinking begins with the professionals rather than with the adolescents. Here we want to describe an unforgettable encounter I (IKB) had some years ago with Marcus, a tough-looking, tall boy with a well-toned body that he obviously worked very hard to build.

CASE EXAMPLE: VIOLENT AND LOVING

I first learned about 16-year-old Marcus through a referral from the juvenile detention facility (a euphemism for juvenile prison), which is the most restrictive setting for hard-core delinquent boys, primarily from the inner city of large urban areas. I had a contract to provide reunification services for these adolescents when they were close to being discharged so that they could return to live with their families (for those teens who had family) and help them to successfully integrate into the community. These young boys had committed violent crimes in the community, which ultimately landed them in such an institution. Marcus was one of these boys who had not lived with his mother for the past four years because he was placed in various institutions, from foster homes, residential treatment centers, group homes, and various long- and short-term facilities. He ran away from these facilities often, lived on the street, got into drug use and gang activities, attended school sporadically, and he was thought to be a poor reader.

Marcus was different from the usual case referrals I received because he was nowhere near being successfully discharged, even though he had been at the facility for 4 months at the time. On the contrary, his behavior problems escalated and I was asked to look into his situation because his violation of various rules increased, he was continuously reprimanded or punished, and what's worse, he recently attacked a female staff member for punishing him. As a result, he was now placed in a "security isolation" unit for the most difficult and dangerous boys. When I agreed to accept the referral, the social worker insisted that she needed to know when I would come so that she could make an arrangement to post a guard outside the interview room. I insisted on not having a guard posted and reassured the social worker that I was confident in my ability to take care of my own safety.

I picked up the boy's mother and we drove to the "school," which was located about 40 miles outside of the city. We spent the driving time getting to know each other, and I learned the heartaches and disappointments Mrs. Washington felt in Marcus when she explained her belief in Marcus and the special qualities she saw in him. I learned that they had not lived together for the past 4 years because Marcus was placed in various institutions and programs, including a psychiatric hospital, and the mother could not count the number of professionals they both had met over the past 4 years.

Mrs. Washington had given up hope on the various treatment programs and had wished the current, most restrictive environment might be the final answer for her son, and that being in this place would finally "wake him up." She felt one more institution had failed to reach him. According to the mother, Marcus's troubles with the law began when he got involved in drugs, alcohol, stealing, and street gang activities which led to numerous fights and arrests. Her memory was that Marcus was a rather quiet, shy, very sensitive child who usually followed other boys, rather than leading them into trouble. She thought that her boy was timid, unsure of himself, but she had a great deal of trouble finding out exactly what was wrong with him.

As I was putting this information together, what became clear was that numerous professionals, all of whom were competent, thoughtful, and caring, had failed to touch Marcus in a helpful manner and therefore, I needed to do something very different from what everyone else had done: talk about his problems, suggest behavioral management approaches such as token system, punishment and reward systems to shape his behavior, including the most restrictive measures any adolescent may face. But I really had no clear idea of what that "something different" might be.

We met Marcus in the small, confined security space that doubled as his living space, classroom, day activity room, and sleeping space. As soon as he saw his mother, Marcus bent down and kissed her on her cheek in the most loving and gentle manner. I was astounded and touched to see this picture of a tall, tough, angry-looking young boy kissing his mother in such a loving way. There was not trace of the angry, hostile, violent, aggressive delinquent criminal that I heard about, and he was a gentle boy hungry for affection from his mother. Of course, Marcus completely ignored me, with no sign of acknowledgment when I introduced myself. Another therapist was the last person he wanted, and I was not interested in repeating the usual approach with him.

Soon the mother and son were engaged in animated conversation about the family, sharing photos from a recent family birthday party the mother brought along. I sat in one corner of the triangle, completely out of the loop of their private conversation, only observing their loving, intimate looks, laughter, smiles, and gestures. About 15 minutes into the session, I spoke up and asked, "Marcus, I am really confused. How come nobody knows you are such a gentle, loving, and caring person?" Marcus behaved as if he could not be bothered with such an absurd question and he grunted, "I dunno," and turned away from me. His mother picked up on the topic and went on describing what a caring, thoughtful, and loving child he was as a young boy. They resumed their private conversation for another 15 minutes, at which point I interrupted again, repeating the same question. Mrs. Washington added more examples and episodes of his gentle and loving character, saying what a special child he was to her and how close they were. During the first session, I repeated the same question four times. On the way home, Mrs. Washington was much more animated and was in better mood.

We met three more times, essentially repeating the first session, with Marcus scarcely participating. The fourth and unplanned session took place when I visited the school to follow up on a referral for another boy. When I walked into the cottage, I saw Marcus hanging out with other boys, smoking cigarettes. Surprised to see him smoke, I blurted out, "Marcus, I didn't know you smoked!" He replied in a low, soft voice so that other boys could not hear, "I don't smoke in front of my mother because it is disrespectful." Not only was this the longest sentence he uttered to me, but this also gave me more areas in which to raise questions with him during the subsequent sessions. During the following sessions, my language alternated between "loving, caring, gentle" and "respectful, thoughtful, obedient" of those in authority, and even to strangers like me. Surprisingly, Marcus began to achieve better grades in classes in a rather short time and his behavior improved to the point that he was allowed to work in the cafeteria, which earned him extra points.

I initiated the discussion of Marcus's furlough on weekends, and the school reacted with caution, concern, and worry that he might run away, get into fights or involved with drugs, and the initial proposal was turned down. Because furlough is a precursor to eventual release, I persisted, but asked for 12 hours instead of the usual 48 hours. Mrs. Washington, with my assistance, made detailed plans to keep Marcus occupied for 12 hours, with the help of uncles, cousins, and church members. He completed a successful first furlough, then 24 hours, and eventually 48 hours, twice. By this time, Marcus made tremendous strides in all areas: academic, social, behavioral, personal, and his rebuilding of relationships with his mother and his family became more solid. He needed to build new peer relationships, which would take time. Marcus was eventually released, first to a halfway house, then to the custody

of his mother. His progress was not always smooth, nor trouble-free, but he
certainly made steady progress toward eventual return home.

Do Something Different

It seems that the easiest and simplest way to avoid creating further resistance from an adolescent such as Marcus, is to limit intervention to commenting on something that is factual and attribute positive motivations to the behavior that nobody had noticed before. By noticing something new nobody before had paid attention to, and commenting on it in the form of questions, one is more likely to draw the adolescent's attention to strengths and resources. Discovering the smallest possible successes that are the opposite of violent or aggressive behaviors, and pointing out and highlighting these small successes, is like putting the spotlight on what we want the adolescent to do more of. A similar approach to treating domestic violence offenders shows remarkable promise of considerably reduced drop-out and recidivism rates in 8 sessions (Lee, Sebold, & Uken, 2002).

Suicide Gestures, Threats, and Attempts

The anxiety level in all of us rises rapidly whenever we hear someone utter the "S" word, and our immediate response to this word is the internal dialogue of, "Oh, no! Please tell me it's not happening." The notion of potential suicide seems to require a certain level of intellectual development and sophistication to even entertain, since we rarely see this phenomenon from younger children. Of course, there are precocious children who may have been exposed to such talk in their environment, but overall, it takes a certain level of cognitive ability to even entertain the notion. We are frequently asked about our strategies and beliefs regarding suicide prevention in general, and we would like to address some of our ideas and thoughts about the type of questions we hear.

The most common questions are:

1. How seriously do we have to take this suicide talk, whether in the form of threats, gestures, and attempts?
2. What is the benefit of a "no-suicide contract" and how do we negotiate it?
3. What do you do when a teenager threatens suicide?
4. When do you decide to hospitalize a teenager?

These questions convey a sense of urgency, and it is certainly easy to respond to a suicide attempt or gesture in a knee-jerk manner with alarm or anxiety. But this is generally is not very helpful.

Any suicidal ideation, threat, gesture, no matter how veiled or frivolous, must be taken seriously, not just by looking in detail into the method contemplated by the adolescent, the triggering episode, past history, or actions planned, but by engaging a teenager in conversation. This means taking the time to listen, respecting the suicide as a potential means of solution to difficult problems, and being curious about their thinking. Engaged conversation also means looking for alternative means to achieve the goals that teenagers might have been seeking, and trying to determine whether such goals might be achieved through some other means as well.

We believe that rushing in with the notion of negotiating the "no-suicide" contract with a teenager is missing the boat. A no-suicide contract is a document essentially designed to protect the professionals from potential liability, and it asks the client to sign a promissory note that he or she will not commit suicide. When we do this, we think it implies to the teenager that an idea of suicide is a done deal and there is no way out of it, except by stopping it in its tracks. In addition to such a notion not being very useful as a goal, it implies that options are limited to only two: either suicide or no suicide. Many adolescents want to feel that they have a choice, not forced into either yes or no choices, a power game that most teenagers know exactly how to defy. When a teenager is helped to see suicide as one of many options open to him or her, then we are increasing the number of possible choices, rather than limiting them. Listen to the following initial conversation with a teenager who was referred to a school counselor because she told a friend about her thought of suicide. The client is also chronically tardy and the counselor begins with a more neutral topic and waits for Gail to volunteer information about the talk of suicide.

Counselor: I understand you are having some difficulty getting to school on time again lately. You must have a good reason for this and I wondered what that might be.

Gail (G):   Of course I have good reasons. I hate living in this foster home, not seeing my mother, and I'm not doing well in school. I'm always ragged on about things at the foster home and I hate other kids there and I've been thinking I'd be better off dead than living like this.

Counselor (C):   It sounds pretty terrible. You have been coping with lots of stuff, sounds like.

G: The reason I'm tardy so many times lately is that I just feel like I'm never good at anything, so why bother? Nobody gives a damn, nobody cares about me anyway.

C: So what is important to you is that you want to do better in school, you want somebody to care about you, and you also want to be good at something, is that right?

G: Yeah, doesn't everybody?

C: Of course, it is natural for you to want these things. Actually everybody does, even grownups.

G: But I will never have those in my life.

C: I'm not sure if I agree with you about that. Suppose . . . just suppose, you have these things, become better at school, find something you are good at, and have somebody who loves and cares about you . . . what would you be doing then that you are not doing right now?

G: I would be coming to school on time, have friends, maybe a nice boyfriend, at least see my mother sometimes, and I would be real good at science. Maybe my mother will tell me that she stopped doing drugs and she will take me home to live with her.

C: So, tell me when was the most recent day that you came to school on time?

G: Yesterday. I really tried to be here on time.

C: How did you make it to school on time yesterday?

This example shows how quickly the conversation can shift to something the teenager wants, rather than how bad her situation is or how serious the problem is. The counselor here quickly turned Gail's problem statements, such as having no friends, not seeing her mother, having no one who cares about her, and not doing well in school, into goals: wanting to do better in school, have friends, have somebody to care about her, and so on. Gail quickly agreed with the counselor that these are acceptable goals and then began to create an alternate picture of what her life would be like. Notice how quickly the talk of suicide was dropped out of the conversation, and the longer the conversation continues, the more Gail will be able to come up with ideas about what she can do to create this alternate, more hopeful, and satisfying life for herself.

If your clinical intuition—or an agency obligation—still tells you that you need to negotiate the no-suicide contract you can bring up the contract as an afterthought, or as a routine, agency policy. Another nice tool to use is the scaling question to make sure that the risk for suicide has been reduced considerably. For example, "I'm going to ask you a slightly different kind of question this time. This is something we routinely do here in this office. Suppose I ask you to imagine on a scale of 1 to 10, where 10 stands for we will have to call for an ambulance to take you to the hospital, and 1 is we don't even have to think about your chance of wanting to harm yourself, where would you put yourself at this moment?" And, "If I were to ask your mother where she thinks you are at on the same scale, where would she tell me she thinks you are?" Then you can discuss ways to attain or maintain the low risk suicide status and what would lower it even more.

Thinking about suicide as one of many options open to an adolescent can be a powerful tool for the teenager to begin to create what she or he wants in life. We find that most teenagers' threats of suicide are usually directed at those people—such as parents, teachers, or therapists—that teenagers depend on, as well as at those they know will value and want to protect them. When the adults view suicide as merely one option, the power of threat no longer works for the teenager. Clarifying and listening carefully to the ideas of desired changes can often bring about more wonderful ideas and dialogue about their advantages and disadvantages, and indeed hospitalization may turn out to be the best possible solution for a short time. Therefore, we do not necessarily see the hospitalization as a failure, because only the results will tell us whether it worked or not.

CASE EXAMPLE: LYDIA'S SOLUTIONS

I (TS) received a phone call from a mother who was very worried about her 16-year-old daughter, Lydia, who attempted suicide with a knife. The mother reported that they had just returned from a session with the school psychologist the same day and she was told her daughter needed psychiatric help, perhaps beyond what the school could offer the girl. The mother raised the question of who should come to this first meeting and as usual, I replied that whoever the mother and Lydia thought would be the most helpful person should come to the first meeting. The appointment was made for two days later. Lydia showed up for her appointment alone.

As usual, I began with Lydia by asking about her favorite pastime, what she was good at, and so on. When the topic turned to what would be the most helpful thing for us to talk about, she mentioned her urge to commit suicide. The following is a part of the dialogue that followed:

Therapist (Th):   In what way would talking about this urge to commit suicide would be helpful to you?

Lydia (L):   I don't know, I had to sign a contract that I will not do it, but I feel so miserable.

Th: I see. Suicide is always an option and it creates a big change, you are
      right. It seems you are in a pretty difficult situation. Tell me what would
      have to change to make things just a little bit better?
L: It's my mother's boyfriend who causes all the problems. I can't physically
      stand him, I get sick if I see him, so mainly I stay in my room. You know
      I take after my father, like habits and interests. My parents divorced two
      years ago. Our family got along pretty well, then my mother started a love
      affair two years ago and my father had to move out. After the divorce, her
      boyfriend moved in. Ever since then I can't talk to my mother any more.
      Her boyfriend tells me off because he can't stand the tone I use when I talk
      to my mother and he acts like my mother is so weak and needs him to
      protect her from me.
Th: It sure sounds pretty tough, what have you done to make things a little
      bit easier?
L: Yes, this week I'm living with my father, but I have to go back to my
      mom's house.
Th: So, staying with your father makes a difference?
L: Yes of course, I don't have to see him [mom's boyfriend], and I can laugh
      more.
Th: Is that some thing you would like to be, a more cheerful person?
L: Yes, I laughed a lot when I was a little girl.
Th: I am going to ask you a very special question, that maybe needs some
      imagination . . .

Her answers to miracle questions were: I would laugh more, and my mother
would do things with me like she did before, like going out to eat, talking a
lot, going to the movies, shopping, just the two of us; I would go out more
and meet my friends again, get better grades in school; I would express my
opinions more often instead of being timid; I would be straightforward and
proud; I would be in the living room watching TV more and maybe, I would
somehow give Jerry a chance.
     I was surprised to hear that and asked her, how she would know that she
had given him a chance. She replied that she had never talked with him on
any topic he raised when she could tell that he tried very hard to get along
with her. She could imagine talking to him about the dog they both liked.
     After the break, I complimented her on how well she could describe her
situation to me and that I was impressed with how thoughtful she was, even
about people she didn't like. I then told her that it was clear that things have
to change in her life and that committing suicide was one way to do it, but
I was very impressed how many different ideas she already had to make
changes in her life. I asked Lydia whether her mother knew how badly she
wanted to spend more time with her, just the two of them. She answered
"no," and I said it might be very important for her mother to know this fact.

Lydia thought that she could tell her mother about this on the way home from her father's at the end of the week because the two of them would be driving back together. I added that to be proud and to laugh went together, and suggested to her to choose just one hour every day between now and the next time we met, and pretend during this one hour that her miracle actually happened.

During the second session one week later, Lydia reported that she had been out with friends more, told her mother her wishes, and even called her mother at her job from a fast food restaurant because it made her feel better. She also cleaned up her room because she decided that a tidy room would go better with the cheerful person she wants to be. She was even planning to spend an evening in the family room with everybody, watching TV. When I asked for the details of how she was going to do this, she described buying her favorite chips, picking out her favorite program, and how she will rent a movie if the family did not like her program of choice. She also described a situation where she would voice her opinion and how she would do it next time Jerry answered for her mother. She even considered the right words to use and how she would say nice things to him for protecting her mother but would tell him that she had a very strong mother she was very proud of, and that her mother could stand up for herself. After a thinking break, I complimented Lydia on all the changes she had made, her courage to go out more, and her skill in planning ahead.

Lydia decided that she did not need any more sessions and told me that she would call if she felt like she was losing track. I have not heard from her for over a year now.

Whatever it takes, it is helpful to stay calm, listen to the full story, and then, again, think about the "good reason" for someone to have entertained such a drastic solution to his or her difficulty. Shifting into a curiosity stance allows us to listen intently to the adolescent who has either issued a threat, made a gesture, or attempted suicide. This is a very helpful way to connect and engage the teenager and the parents into looking for an alternative solution to suicide.

CASE EXAMPLE: PINK HAIR AND INDEPENDENCE

Fifteen-year-old Rhonda was described as rebellious, not doing her school work and running away from home regularly two or three times a month. Recently she told her teacher that she wanted to kill herself. Alarmed by this talk of suicide, the teacher immediately called the therapist (TS). Her family emigrated from a developing country and her parents were struggling to make it financially. When I first met her, Rhonda told me how she was very proud of attending high school because she never considered herself smart enough for high school, as she had to repeat fourth grade. Her explanation was that she made it to high school by sheer will and determination and she worked hard to make it. She likes to draw cartoons and is popular with friends.

Her answer to the miracle question was that she would not have to stay home anymore and put up with her mother's controlling tendencies and overprotection of her. Her parents would talk to her in a normal way, even if she were to color her hair blue, wear very high heels, get drunk, and smoke pot. They would not constantly worry that she was going to end up a prostitute, but would consider her a normal girl. Physical punishment from her parents would stop, and the family would sit together and talk about music, computers, the Internet, and so on. She would get good grades in school and would complete high school, and finally, she would be able to tell her parents how "pissed off" she was at them for wasting their time worrying more about what other people would think of them than paying attention to what they want.

I told Rhonda how impressed I was with her ability to work hard when she wanted to, and that it seemed to me that if she were to have the life she imagined, it would be quite different from what she has now. Of course she was right to try different lifestyles to find out what suited her personality the best, but it was obvious that she was paying a very high price for it. Now that she was on her way to finding out what fits her personality, I suggested that she carefully observe what difference it made to go to school with high heels and lots of makeup.

She came to the second session with a different hair color and explained that she felt strong when she could shock other people with her outfit and outrageous makeup, she felt more self-confident and free. We talked at length about what she does when she feels confident and free, and what she was able to do in such situations that she could not do otherwise. She explained that she has been thinking about becoming a hairdresser and running her own shop, an independent job that would give her more freedom. It was not difficult to point out to her that she was really a determined young woman who wanted to achieve something in life that was different from her parents, and not have to worry about what other people thought, like her mother had done all her life.

In the third session she made a little sculpture in clay called "strong independence." At the end of her fifth session, Rhonda said, "What I like the best about coming here to talk to you is that I always have the feeling that I do an important job, by coloring my hair in all kinds of shocking colors, by dressing up like a punk, by visiting different places that my parents would never go. You were interested in the different ways I did things, always wondering what kind of benefit it had for me. I knew in advance that you would ask me "what is different," and I wanted to have something different to tell you. Your curiosity made me change things quickly. When my parents tell me that they didn't like some of the things I was doing, I wanted to stick to it even more." She was quite articulate for a 15-year-old.

During the five sessions alone with her, Rhonda fluctuated on what she wanted to become, but it was obvious that she calmed down and began doing better in school. As the situation with her parents was still quite tense, I met with the parents alone twice and we had one family session. During the two sessions with parents, it was very important to give the parents all the credit for what they had done for their daughter. The mother suffered a great deal seeing her daughter behave like a "tramp" which was so different from how she grew up in the "old country," where girls did not meet boys without a chaperon, and were generally protected by the family. We commiserated with each other about the different values and ideas different countries had, and I raised the question about how the father could be helpful to the mother during this difficult time during which Rhonda sorted out what kind of person she wanted to be. When I asked about how a father might play a more helpful role for the mother, the father volunteered and readily agreed that his alcohol problems contributed to the family problems, and he was working hard to reach his goal of total abstinence.

During one family session, I kept the focus on how each member of the family was taking steps to make their own life more the way they wished. It was very touching to see how each member of this family described how they tried to be respectful and learned to accept different ways to achieve their goals.

Discussion. You can imagine the changes Rhonda has gone through in her appearance. We are often asked whether we comment and point out the changing appearances of teenagers. Perhaps by relaying what actually transpired, you might get the answer to this question.

Therapist (Th).   Wow, you look different today! What gave you the idea it was the right time to change your hair color?

Rhonda (R):   Well, you know, I like to shock people, especially my parents and the teachers in school, and they had become used to my blue hair, so I decided to dye it in stripes and I thought it would be a good idea.

Th: Do I understand right you right? You wanted to attract attention? Did you succeed in that?

R: Of course I did! My mother told me that she would not sit at the same table with me and have a meal as long as I looked like that!

Th: You attracted attention but also got into some difficulty, the business with the meal.

R: No. I knew my mother wouldn't do it, she likes me too much and besides, she always wants to nag at the dinner table.

Th: So tell me, having attracted attention and found out that your mother loves you very much, what difference does this make for you?

R: (hesitates for a long while) It makes me feel strong and free.

Th: Is that right? Tell me more about situations when you feel strong and
free.

*It can be tempting for a therapist to zero in on the teenager's idea such as
"shocking other people" or "drawing attention to myself," but we believe it
is more productive to learn about the meaning these ideas have for the teenager.
This meaning behind the exaggerated or outlandish behaviors tells us what
the adolescent is not able to articulate, that is, to be strong and free, in
Rhonda's situation. This desire to be "strong and free" is certainly reasonable
and sensible at age 15. Therefore, by further exploring other situations when
she felt "strong and free," we are neither shocked nor tempted to lecture her
about how these outlandish behaviors may backfire on her someday. By learning
about the hidden meanings adolescents attribute to their behavior, we are
learning to guide an adolescent like Rhonda to look for more moderate means
of achieving the same goal.*

*After having explored what she needed to achieve this feeling more often,
what was different about her when she had these feelings, and how she was
coping with her difficult life without these feelings, Rhonda wanted my opinion
of her new hairdo.*

R: I want to ask you a question. What do you think about my new hairdo?
*Th: Well, I'm glad to hear that you got the attention you needed in order
to feel strong and free. I think these two feelings are really helpful to you
and you do amazing things when you think of yourself as a strong and
independent person. I also like to hear that it is important to you that your
mother loves you a lot, and that you kind of count on it and even need it
sometimes. If I look into your face and tell you the truth, I liked the blue
better than the stripes. Actually, in my opinion, the stripes hide your
beautiful dark eyes. I am glad about what you accomplished with your new
hair color, but not the new hair color itself.*

Many adolescents want to know where their parent, teacher, or therapist stands on certain issues, and we believe it is helpful for them to
know our honest opinions. We have met many therapists who believe
that in order to work with adolescents, we need to be well-versed in
all their latest music, fashion, lingo, and hip talk. Many adolescents
can tell whether we are talking straight and honest with them or just
pretending that we understand them. It is important for adolescents
to know where their parents stand on issues such as sex, drugs, dating,
clothing, and music, so that these views can act as reference points for
them. They want to know what our parameters are and where we will
draw lines.

Adolescents and Secrets

What do you, the therapist, do when you are told a secret by a teenager and asked to keep it private from his or her parents? We are frequently asked this question by professionals, and for good reasons. We believe the word "secret" implies some dark, scandalous, or even sinister intentions or behaviors that one is trying to hide. Most therapists are entrusted with information that teenagers want to keep away from their parents, such as whether or not they are having sex, using drugs, or smoking—that their parents would not approve of. Many adolescents have secrets they keep from their parents and frequently parents are very concerned about this, especially concerning the topics of sex and drugs. Parents have good reasons to be very sensitive to the adolescent's desire to keep some matters secret, because most parents know the consequences can be serious and even harmful to their child. We do not, however, believe that there shouldn't be any boundaries between what the parents know and what the children tell them. Also adolescents should not tell every detail of their private life to their parents.

We recently met an 18-year-old young man who would go home after every date and tell his mother every detail of what took place during the evening out with his girlfriend, including how many slices of pizza they had, how much "necking" took place, and where they grabbed each other's body parts. Of course, his girlfriend complained that his mother did not like her coming over and spending too much time with him, she began to question whether he was "man enough" for her, and entertained the notion of breaking up the relationship.

There is a natural tension between keeping secrets and respecting the child's need for privacy, and this should always be negotiated because the question of where the secrecy begins and where the privacy ends is a difficult issue to pin down. It needs constant negotiation between parents and adolescents. We like to think that secrets divide into "good secrets" and "bad secrets," and the outcome of keeping a secret or having privacy is expected to be positive for both sides, especially for adolescents. Again, the important point to remember here is to always return to the meaning the teenager attributes to wanting some information kept from parents. For example, feeling free to keep a secret makes adolescents feel grown up and demonstrates they want to be treated as such. Another teenager might view a need for privacy as betraying his or her parent, who always wants to know the teenager's activities outside of home. Therefore, rather than emphasizing whether an adolescent is having sex or taking drugs, understanding the meaning behind these activities would be more productive. For example, ask questions such as:

- You must have a good reason to want to keep this information from your parents. What are some of your good reasons?
- What does it mean to you that you are having sex with your boy(girl)friend? Taking drugs?
- What do you think it means to your parents that you are using drugs?
- Once they find out you are using drugs (having sex), what are you most concerned might happen as a result?
- Knowing your parents as you do, what do you think is the best way to handle this?
- What do you want your parents to do that they are not doing now as a result of their finding out about you (having sex, shop-lifting, bingeing, etc)?
- What difference would it make between you and your parents when they know (when they do not know)?

In most situations, asking adolescents about the "good reason" for wanting to keep a secret from their parents generally leads to the conversation about what they would like to change in their relationships with parents; thus, the focus shifts into something desirable, not their most dreaded fears. Therefore, the conversation about keeping or not keeping a secret can be a very useful and productive way to take advantage of the issue to produce helpful changes. As you can see, we seldom worry about being caught as the depository of secrets for either parents or adolescents because we are always more concerned about looking for the meaning of the dilemmas, and then for solutions, and not who or what is causing the problems.

However, there are times when a practitioner has a vague feeling that something is missing in a case, what many call a "hunch." This is particularly strong when there is sexual abuse, which certainly would be described as a bad secret. At times, enlarging the picture by speaking with some new family members the practitioner has not yet met, such as grandparents or best friends who are like the members of the family, can be helpful. Another step to take is to reduce the number of people you meet in sessions, or even change the routine of the usual session, that is, change your pattern of interactions with the client. Pressing the family or the adolescent about secrets is not helpful because the child may not be able to tell the difference between good secrets and bad secrets. Rather than thinking of this as "unconscious" denial, or assuming that their inability to tell one kind from another is an attempt at "hiding," it is more useful to think of secrets as something clients are not yet ready to tell you, and trust that when the time comes, the child or the parent will find ways to tell you. While you wait, you may want to think about creating stories that are tailored to fit the client's situations and point out both the positive and negative aspects of keeping a secret, as well as the difference good and bad secrets. This is similar to preparing the soil for flowers to grow and blossom. There is more information on how to create stories in Chapter 6 of this book. The storytelling can be done at the end of the session, following a thinking break and compliments offered to clients, so that there is no discussion about the story.

Unrealistic Expectations
of Adolescents

Clinicians often ask us how to handle a teenager's unrealistic expectations, such as a teenager wishing to find a glamorous job as an executive secretary or a movie actress, or wanting to become a rock music sensation, make lots of money, become famous, or become a star athlete who will be on TV all the time and will be the center of media attention. These expectations are particularly hard to respond to when the teenager is clumsy, lacks social skills, and can hardly initiate or maintain a friendship. Rather than deeming such dreams as unrealistic or a waste of time, we think of these tendencies as quite natural to their current stage of development during which they are preoccupied with themselves (also described as selfish). We would ask questions that would gently help them to come down to earth by assessing the situation with their own ability to observe and assess. Based on these assessments, which change from week to week at times, we believe it is more useful to ask questions that steer the adolescent to increase their skills of self-observation and to become more realistic, without having to acknowledge their own shortcomings. Some examples of useful questions to ask at this stage are:

Therapist (Th): It makes sense that you want to become rich and famous. I think all kids want to be, but you are courageous enough to say it aloud, unlike most other kids. So, what would you be able to do then, I mean, when you become famous, that you are not doing now?

Stacy (S): Well, then I will have lots of friends, lots of fans, go on TV, and things like that.

Th: Let me understand this correctly. So, when you become famous, you will have lots of friends?

S: I will have lots of friends who think I'm cool and want to be with me because I will pay for going to the movies, and we will go shopping, hang out together, and go out to eat and things like that.

Th: So, sounds like what you will really have is lots of friends and
      you will not be alone but will be popular, is that right?'
S: Yeah, of course, that's what I want, to be popular and have lots
      of friends.

TREATING ANOREXIA AND OTHER
EATING DISORDERS

What makes it a challenge to work with young people with eating
disorders is making sure that the many adults, particularly concerned
parents and other medical professionals, do not make you as worried
and anxious as they are about the problem. It is important to view
these people as potential resources who are not trying to meddle in
your work with adolescents. Since most young girls are forced to come
to treatment, it is important to make sure not to focus your conversation
solely on eating issues, as parents frequently do, and allow eating to
become the battleground. It is more productive to take the cues from
the adolescents and work within their frame of reference, rather than
trying to change their perceptions. It is particularly important to pick
the battles well, with the larger goal of winning the war. You might
even need to compromise on the small battles, as the following case
example shows. If possible, separate the medical management of the
eating disorder from the therapeutic task of working with the adolescent. This allows lots of freedom for therapists, as the following case
shows.

CASE EXAMPLE: TO GO TO THE HOSPITAL OR TO EAT
*Cathy was a 17-year-old who began her work-study program as a medical
assistant in a doctor's office. She did well in school, and was involved in
several sports, especially aerobics and some basketball. She had a boyfriend
when she was 16 but it fizzled out. She said that she did not want to be too
close to him because her parents told her not to have sex too soon with a boy,
and that she should concentrate on school work and doing well in the work-
study program. About a year later she found out that all her girlfriends had
boyfriends and they were even having sex. Cathy felt left out of this and felt
as if she had nothing in common with her girlfriends. She reasoned that the
only reason she had no boyfriend was because she was not attractive enough,
and in particular her hips were way too fat.*

*So, she immediately put herself on a diet and increased her aerobics classes.
By the time I (TS) first met Cathy, she had lost 10 pounds in two months
but she still considered herself too fat. Her fights with her parents increased
because they wanted her to eat more, while she secretly purged all the food*

she ate. When the parents discovered this, the arguments around the food increased at home, and when her boss found out about this problem, he laid down a stern warning with an ultimatum: Either you take care of this problem or you cannot work in a doctor's office. Before our first meeting, her boss and her mother called to express their concerns for Cathy. Therefore, Cathy certainly was coming to me under coercion, and it made sense to view her as someone who was mandated to come to therapy.

Cathy (C):   I have no problem, but my parents—especially my mother—and my boss have big problems with me. He can't complain, I do my job and what I do in my private life is none of his business.

Therapist (Th):   Yes, of course, but even though you have every reason to be upset, you still showed up today. What gave you the idea of making this choice?

C: I told you I have no problem, it is my boss and my mother who should be here, but of course they would never do anything like that. They are just too good for that.

Th: Tell me, what made you decide to come and see me today?

C: I want to become a medical assistant, but I know I don't need to come and see you for that. I really don't know what I should discuss with you. Your office is really hard to find, I had to take the bus for more than 40 minutes to get here.

Th: Wow, that sure is a long time, you sure put up with some inconvenience. I know most young people have so much to do. I am really impressed you took the effort to get here today. Amazing, I am really amazed and I suppose you are one of those young people who have so many things to do. So, how do you spend your time?

C: I like sports, I will miss my aerobics class tonight because of this appointment.

Th: Aside from aerobics, what else are you interested in?

C: I like mountain climbing, but since I started my work-study, I can hardly find time to do it.

Th: Are you afraid of falling when you climb mountains?

C: No, why should I? I have nothing to lose.

Th: Any other things you are interested in?

C: I like to go to school and I like my job. I liked to meet with my girlfriends, but now they have no time for me anymore.

Th: You are really an interesting person. It seems you have many talents. Tell me, what needs to happen so that you can say to yourself today, or sometime later, that it's been worthwhile for you to come and see me today?

Comment. Cathy was already quite skinny and there was no missing the point that she looked anorexic. But I needed to learn her perspectives and her

language in order to engage with her correctly. With most adolescents, compli-
menting their successes and what they do well may be enough to shift the
conversation into more goal negotiation. But Cathy was not interested.

C: *I told you I have no problem. Well, of course I would like to see my girl*
      friends more often, but they all have boyfriends and I am not interesting
      to them anymore.
Th: *Oh, you seem like somebody who likes to socialize and you seem to have*
      difficulty doing that lately. That makes it really hard to put up with,
      especially for someone who has good social skills.
C: *Its, it makes me sad, I feel like I'm cast aside. I once had a boyfriend,*
      too, but I never forgot my girlfriends. Maybe they are right, I'm nothing
      special, maybe they are right that I think too much of myself.
Th: *Did I hear you right? You are one of those people who can be in love*
      with a boy and still can maintain friendships with girls? Where did you
      learn to do that? You are only 17!
C: *I never thought it was something special, I'm like that. I know how it*
      feels to be left behind and I don't want to make others feel like I did.
Th: *You may think it's nothing special, but let me tell you there are lots*
      of young people who are selfish and only think of themselves.
C: *You should tell that to my mother; she thinks I'm egotistical and she*
      says I'm terrorizing the whole family with my eating problem. She would
      never say anything like what you just told me.
Th: *So, what did you do to have more contact with other young people*
      again?
C: *I don't know, I tried to make new friends in school, but it's not easy.*

After we talked about her small success in having fun with other kids in
school, it seemed like a good time to ask the miracle question. Her answer: to
have more friends, have a boyfriend, to finish her school, become a medical
assistant, and work in a doctor's office, and have her parents give her more
privacy. The topic of having friends was the most important one: She called
a 3 for having confidence to have more girlfriends, and 2 on a boyfriend.

   Comment. Even though Cathy spontaneously mentioned the eating prob-
lem, it was too soon to focus on it, because the eating problem was important
to her mother and her boss, not to Cathy. She spent a lot of time talking about
her lack of social life.

   Her mother and her boss called after the first session. Her mother was
interested to find out whether Cathy told me how serious her eating problem
was, while the boss wanted to know what kind of treatment plan I had in
mind. I complimented the mother on how well she trained her daughter and
all the good values she taught her, such as how Cathy wanted to treat other
friends. This calmed down the mother, and she agreed that I could have a few

more sessions with Cathy alone, and I would be willing to have sessions with the mother or other family members.

With the boss, I obviously agreed with him that indeed Cathy had an eating disorder, but what was important to me was that he recognized the problem. I was impressed with how much interest he showed in the health issues of his staff, as it was very unusual for me to meet a boss who showed such interest in employees.

Second Session. As usual, the second session began with my asking, "What is different, even a little bit, since we met last time?"

C: I'm even more pissed at my so-called friend. I met her with her boyfriend and she didn't even say hello to me.

Th: That sounds terrible. What else is different?

C: Yesterday we had a really busy day at the office, even more hectic than usual, and in the evening my boss told me I had done a good job, said it was like I had been doing this job for a long time.

Th: That's great! How did you manage to do it?

C: I just used my observation skills and common sense, that's all.

Th: This sounds simple, but I'm sure it was not easy. Your observation skills and your common sense, is this something you often use?

C: Well, I'm a quick thinker, my classmates used to tease me because of that, they said I had no emotions. But sometimes it is better to keep a clear head and get on with what is going on.

Th: Yes, of course. What else is different, or just a little bit better than last time we met?

C: Nothing. I told you I have no problems except for my wish to get more friends, but I will not get friends by coming here.

Th: You are right, you won't meet friends here. Making friends is a rather complicated matter because you cannot buy friends in a shop. It is a difficult thing to do, even for adults. By the way, these good observation skills you have, do you use them when you are with other people?

C: What do you mean?

Th: Sometimes it is helpful to watch and observe carefully what is going on between young girls and boys. Listen to what they say and do, their gestures and looks, and so on. You can do this in subways, in restaurants, in schools. You can learn a lot by observing what they like and don't like, and decide what to use and what not to use. It's like swimming without getting wet.

C: (nodded her head but was silent)

Th: If there is nothing you want to talk about, then I would like to tell you about two phone calls I received, one from your mother and the other from your boss. They both tell me that they are very concerned about your eating problem, that you lost a considerable amount of weight during the last few *weeks, and they seem to think that you should talk about this problem with me. From the two meetings we had, I got to know you as a young girl with many skills, many interests, and some very good ideas.*

I don't know whether you have what we call an eating disorder. Whether or not you consider this a problem, I think it could be useful to talk about this because I am interested in how you look at this. Within a certain range it is OK, but when the weight loss is too much, it becomes dangerous. It seems your weight loss is considerable, and therefore it would be important that you check out how far away you are from the danger point. Have you heard of the body mass index? Well, this is a number that indicates the relationship between the length of your body and your weight. Not every-body has to have the same ratio, but from the medical point of view there is a limit that one should not go below, and I do not like to see you below this range. I would like to ask you to make an appointment with your family doctor to get your body mass index checked, and set up a plan for what will happen should it go below. This will give us the freedom to work on what is important to you, such as making friends. If there is anything about eating or food you want to discuss with me, I'm ready to talk about that with you, but unless you bring it up, I will not bring it up. I have been talking a long time now, which I usually do not do. Do you have a question or a comment?

Cathy was very surprised and confused about the way I brought up the eating problems. She said that nobody had talked to her in this way and that she did not know what to say. "I usually get told off and then I know exactly what to say," she said. She wanted to know what would happen once she went below the limit. I told her that this was the moment when the clients have to be hospitalized in order to be fed and monitored. She reacted very strongly to this and said, "I will never, ever let that happen to me." I told her that she was competent enough not to end up in a situation like that, and added that I once had a client who had to be hospitalized because she could not find another way to avoid being hospitalized, but she found it helpful. After the thinking break, I complimented Cathy on her success at her job, her clear thinking, her ability to observe and use it in a useful way, and her ability to listen carefully.

Comment. When the "eating problem" is handled in the manner described here, clients frequently bring up their concerns in the following session. Even though Cathy was anxious to avoid the topic, she also was eager to talk about it because she knew why she was seeing me. We believe an eating problem is usually related to a matter of balance: Like most adolescents, Cathy was caught up in seeing everything in life as an either/or battle—believing that life is made up of only two options: black/white, good/bad, right/wrong, and so on. It is not an eat or not eat issue, or being preoccupied with food and nothing else. *Cathy also had other concerns besides her weight—her job, and becoming competent in other areas as well.*

During the following several sessions, the topic of eating was very much the focus and Cathy described what starving meant to her. When her girlfriends started to date, she felt miserable, worthless, and as if her life was getting out of control. When she began starving, it gave her a wonderful feeling of "beating the nature" as she put it, along with the fantasy that a handsome young man would come and rescue her from starvation. Listening to this view of her meaning of starvation made it clear that what she really wanted was to be in control of her life, which she felt she was losing. Cathy wanted to be in control while feeling close to somebody, and at the same time maintain her ability to make independent decisions.

Throughout these sessions, I never brought up her anorexic behavior, but concentrated on how she could gain control of her life and feel independent in a more relaxed and easier-going manner, so that she could be more satisfied with her life. When I asked Cathy to describe her experience of feeling close to someone while feeling independent, she described her relationship with her mother. She felt close to her mother, whom she described in a tender, loving way, but also felt dominated and forced by her mother's repeated warnings about making mistakes. By starving, she found for the first time, something she could control which her mother could not influence, that her mother could not make her eat or stop her from vomiting. At the same time, she liked the fact that her mother was worried about her and this made her feel close to her mother. So, the emerging theme indicates that her eating disorder was related to her difficulty maintaining the balance between how much independence and dependence she wanted to maintain in relation to her mother. This provided a good opportunity to suggest to Cathy that she look for other relationships in her life. She could also renew her relationship with her mother when she felt that she could be close without losing her sense of independence.

In order to maintain balance in therapy, I used more activities, like hand puppets, scribble games to make up stories at the end, and even clay to create an object that represented her goals of achieving balance. During the hand puppet game, Cathy selected a dolphin as her symbol of what she wanted to become, and she eventually bought a little dolphin to keep in her pocket so that she could be reminded of her goals. Using scribble games and stories, Cathy expressed her anger and aggressive feelings. We ended sessions a few times during this phase with a dart game.

Between the 10th and 11th sessions, Cathy and I faced a crisis: Her weight dropped close to the limit at which we agreed that she would be hospitalized. When she was forced to face this agreement, she was outraged about how unfair it was to send her to the hospital when she was doing well in other areas of her life, and said that all the adults conspired to put pressure on her and make her do things against her wishes. She said she might as well kill herself. I knew it was a risk I had to take by not taking over the responsibility and not backing down from the agreement we had made. In one very difficult session, I kept reminding her that she was stuck in a very difficult situation and had to make a very tough choice for herself, like all grown-up people do. My position was that I was not going to back down from the agreement and that it was her choice to either end up in a hospital, which she detested, or start to eat and gain weight. When she threatened suicide again, I calmly kept asking her "How would it be helpful to you?" Her desperation turned into anger and she finally burst into tears. Without an effort to comfort, I sat beside her, thinking and hoping Cathy would learn that growing up is a very difficult job and that it was OK to experience all these mixed emotions.

I must say this session with Cathy was one of the most difficult sessions I had. I felt challenged about whether I truly believed in the SFBT assumption that the client is the expert, and that the client has everything necessary to find a solution and make good choices. I knew that we adults had to convince Cathy that she would not be allowed to starve herself to death. Whether she would end up being fed intravenously was now up to her.

To my and everybody else's great relief, Cathy had the strength to eat again. Much later she explained how angry she was at first at me, but then how proud she was when she later realized that I was not going to intervene and make decisions for her. I must say, however, that sometimes, some young girls do not have the strength to begin eating again, and certainly hospitalization is the appropriate intervention in such cases.

I need to make a few points about my contacts with Cathy's parents and her boss. I met with the parents three times. It was indeed clear that Cathy and her mother were very close and her mother had only good intentions and good will toward Cathy. She wanted to do her best by giving her daughter a lot of advice. Among many issues we discussed about being parents for such a strong-willed child as Cathy was the value of allowing adolescents to make mistakes and learn from the experience. During the third session with the couple, they came up with the idea that they could use the crisis with Cathy as a chance to closely examine the long-standing difficulties in their marriage, and asked for a referral to another therapist.

I could not have asked for better cooperation with Cathy's boss. He was indeed a caring person who was interested in empowering her in as many small ways as possible. Cathy chose to explain to him her desire to be more like a dolphin and the independence it symbolized for her. He was wise enough use this metaphor and often reminded Cathy whenever he recognized a dolphin showing up in his office.

Cathy is eating normally now, even though she still watches her weight and continues to be active in sports. She reached her initial goal of "independent thinking" ability about 85% of the time now, up from the 15% when we first met. She has had two boyfriends and at the time of this writing she is not "going" with any particular young man, because "I like to be free and enjoy knowing that several young men are interested in me." During the early phase of treatment, Cathy and I met weekly for about eight months, then we reduced the frequency gradually to every two and three weeks. After a year of therapy, Cathy decided recently that she would like to come and see me about once a month, and currently we are discussing what would tell her that she would no longer need to come to see me.

Chapter 9

Looking from the Therapist's Chair

WE WANT TO ADDRESS QUESTIONS THAT COME UP OFTEN, USUALLY IN hushed voices, on what to do with our nagging doubts that we may have failed with a client. It is a difficult question to ask and even more difficult to answer. Yet, we think we should be asking the question from time to time and in an open forum: Are we serving our clients as we should and want to? What is the best way to serve our clients? What does it mean for us to fail?

Of course all therapists want to be successful, and solution-focused therapists are no exception. We want to strive to be successful because we want our clients to lead more satisfying lives. However, we must be careful about using words like "failure," since the word is the opposite of "success" and realize that our version of "success"—in which all our clients would "live happily ever after" and we would feel good about our work—is often impossible and unrealistic. It is also a self-centered way of viewing our work, because such notions can override the client's idea of what success is for them. We have seen plenty of situations in which the therapist's desires and wishes to create a positive outcome supercede those of the client. Since all our sessions begin by asking clients what they want, we are guided by what the client's goals are—even a child's, so it only make sense to have our work judged by the client we serve. Yet, it is natural to wish for a "successful outcome" in every case. We frequently come across situations in supervision and consultations where a therapist's criteria for success are much higher than those of the client.

We prefer to substitute the word "helpful" or "useful" for "successful." The problems of living are far too complex to divide into such simple categories as success or failure, and we are aware that what one person would consider a success could easily be a failure for someone else.

Our experience tells us that asking for a client's sense of progress toward their desired goal (on a scale of 1 to 10, where 10 stands for the client's life is going OK, and 1 stands for how badly the client felt when he or she first called for this appointment) is a good reminder for us. It reminds us to not become overly ambitious for the client, nor behave like we know what the criteria for success or failure for our client ought to be. We discovered that the best way to know whether therapy has been successful or not, or useful or not, is to ask the client. The client is the consumer of our services and therefore the best judge of whether our services have in some way helped them to achieve their next goal.

If a therapy lasts longer than 20 sessions, for example, do we consider this a failure? If a teenager made a suicide gesture, is this a failure? If a child gets over the presenting problem and the parents end up getting divorced, did we fail? If a client becomes hospitalized, is it a failure? If a child repeats a grade or is expelled from a school, or had to go an institution, or even ends up in jail, do we consider this a failure? Our experience tells us that it all depends. Some clients believe that going to a hospital or an institution might be just what he or she needed at the time. In some cases children move from one school to another—whether because of expulsion or a voluntarily withdrawal—and we have no way of knowing whether it was ultimately good or bad for the child. We can only know whether a certain solution was a success or a failure by the outcome it generated. Perhaps getting away from the extreme tension between parents and a teenager may be the best solution for both. At times, it may take a crisis of suicide gestures or a suicide attempt to make such solutions happen. It is difficult to predict the outcome, even though we have a fairly good intuitive sense about what the outcome might be.

CASE EXAMPLE: I'M STILL ANGRY AT YOU!

An 11-year-old boy was forced to change schools because he had a serious learning problem that could be treated at a different school, since his current school district was not equipped to offer the child the services he needed. To this boy, I (TS) was the one who forced him to change schools against his wishes because I had to initiate the application for the transfer and sign the paper to make it happen. He told me years later, "I tried to be angry at you because I did not want to lose my friends at the old school, but somehow I couldn't stay angry and that made me even more angry." "Why couldn't you get angry at me?" I asked the boy. "You are right, you lost your friends when you were transferred to the different school and I would not be surprised if you were still angry at me about such big changes." The boy replied, "I can't because I visited the new school and it looked like I could get rid of my learning problems at the school and be as smart as you told me I was . . . but shit . . . I would still like to be angry at you from time to time."

We suggest that you always ask and listen carefully to the answers clients give you to find out what has been useful and helpful for them, rather than assuming you know what is best for the client. Even this 11-year-old boy knew what was good for him and useful to him, even though he did not like the answers.

We want to briefly list some steps to take when you have a hunch that the case may not be moving along in the desired direction, or when you feel you have reached an impasse.

Review the Goals

Clients' goals change over time. One client explained that "until I got up to 6 (on a scale of 1 to 10, where 10 stands for how you want your life to be, and 1 stands for the worst your life has been) I did not think that my life could ever get better. Now that I am doing much better, maybe my 6 looks more like 4 and I want to do better than a 4." As long as the new 6 is realistic, concrete, interactionally described, and meets other criteria we described in Chapter 4 for a good goal, we believe it makes sense.

Some year ago we had this nagging doubt about how successful we were with our clients and decided to review those cases that we felt were unsuccessful. In reviewing a number of these cases, we discovered one very important lesson: We found that the cases involving parents who wanted to terminate their legal and emotional ties with their own children, and who were trying to "give away" their children for various reasons, were all prematurely terminated. Often, the clients in these cases did not even return for second session. Parents were either overwhelmed with life and felt that raising children compounded their problems and strained their resources, or felt exhausted and "burned out." Some decided that raising children to adulthood was just too inconvenient and they were not interested or invested in such an endeavor. In reviewing these "failure" cases, we discovered that in such cases we felt a definite moral and ethical disagreement with the clients over their wishes. We came to the conclusion that we were so put off and shocked by the parents who wanted to "throw away" their own children, that we must have made it very obvious to the clients. I (IKB) remember vividly feeling shocked and dismayed at a mother who calmly described her decision that since her 16-year-old son would become a legal adult in two years, she felt that she had to reclaim her personal life. She did not want to allow her son to interfere with her ability to keep a boyfriend who could make her much happier in her middle age than her son could. Her solution was to chose her boyfriend, who clearly stated that he did not want to put up with her difficult teenager. She was asking me for help in placing him outside the home because she did not have any relatives who would take him. It was more than 30 years ago and I was pretty naïve and unsympathetic towards the mother's position, and was quite self-righteous about such parents. This case haunted me for many years because she was the first mother who taught me that a parent can decide to choose his or her own destiny and not necessarily be bound to the role. I will never forget my shock at this discovery, and I try to remember this and respect their right to want such things. Of course, the boy's wish to stay with his mother was just as important as the mother's wish to have him leave. Most of all, I learned that it is better not to agonize over each case, since we really don't know what is the best solution for everybody.

The change of treatment goal rarely occurs with children themselves, but mostly with their parents. Earlier in this book you met Sarah, whose mother was very harsh toward her and was extremely critical of her little girl (Chapter 4). Even though Sarah's behavior at home and school improved considerably, the mother rarely put her assessment of Sarah above 5 and she explained that Sarah had to be at 7 in order for her to think that her life was manageable. During the following three sessions Sarah was in a rather bad mood, her temper flared up again, and she finally stole some money from other children in her class.

In an outpouring of words, the mother began describing her own frustrations with her boyfriend, who did not treat her with respect and was physically abusive to her. Even though the mother was clearly aware of the difficulties she was having with her boyfriend from the beginning, it took some time for her to decide that her relationship with her boyfriends was not working out to her satisfaction. The mother and I had five sessions (without Sarah) during which she decided that the relationship was not working and eventually broke up with the boyfriend. Sarah's behavior improved dramatically and she eventually finished her grade with honors.

What to Do When Faced With an Impasse

I (IKB) once had an opportunity to consult with a wonderful child protection worker who regularly makes home visits. The visit to the client's home is not generally welcomed because it is a mandated (or statutory) relationship, that is, the visit is legally sanctioned to make sure that the children are safe and not neglected by their parents. The parents generally feel they are forced to talk to these workers against their wishes (Berg & Kelly, 2000). Frequently, just getting in the door is a major accomplishment because parents are afraid of being labeled as bad parents, and the worst fear is that the social worker will "snatch" the children from them.

One worker reported that she managed to get inside the door and started talking with the mother, but the conversation was not going very well because the mother was very defensive. She was having trouble connecting with the mother, who was very guarded and not revealing much. So, the worker decided to be very honest with the client and told her, "This talking between us is not going very well, certainly not the way I like to talk to mothers. What do you think?" The mother agreed that indeed it was not comfortable for her either. So, the worker suggested that they start over. Surprised by this proposal, the mother nodded her head and waited to see what the worker had in mind. The social worker got up and went outside and closed the front door. After catching her breath, she began knocking on the door again and when the mother opened the door, the worker explained the purpose of her visit and then asked for the mother's permission to come inside and talk. This second attempt went much smoother for both of them.

We believe this is a good metaphor for how we must take the professional responsibility to make sure that the relationship with the client is a collaborative one. The client does not have the sole responsibility to get along with us. We are often asked what to do when parents "sabotage" the child's therapy by refusing to bring the child to the therapy session, looking for another therapist, minimizing the child's improvement. Such complaints about clients are not very helpful because it is similar to blaming the client by labeling them as "resistant" when we really don't know how to cooperate with the client first. When we see parents who "sabotage" their child's therapy, it is most likely an indication that the therapist has not given the proper credit for the child's progress to the parent.

Most clinicians want to make sure that treatment moves forward toward what the client wants, and when there is no movement, that is, the client reports that nothing is changing, then it is indeed a time to reflect on what could be done to change the path so both sides feel that things are better. When such feelings occur in a case, there are several things a clinician can do to correct the situation. We suggest you ask the following questions:

1. What would the client say you have done that's been helpful, even a little?

2. What does the client (or parent) see as signs of a successful out-come?
3. Is this outcome realistic?
4. What do you or your program or funding source see as sign(s) of success?
5. If different, what needs to be done so that you are working on the same goal?
6. Where on the scale would the client say he or she is at (on a 1 to 10 scale)?
7. What needs to happen so that he or she can move one point closer to 10?

Frequent use of scaling questions with the client and other important persons in the client's life would give you a good gauge for how much progress and movement you and your client are making.

Giving Credit to the Caregiver (or Parent)

It is important to remember to always give others—the parents, teach-ers, other professionals who contribute to the child's well-being—the credit for how the child progresses in therapy with you. Indeed, our time with the child is so minuscule when compared with how much these other people devote their time and energy to them, and how much their influence is greater than ours could possibly be. Therefore, when you feel that you are facing an impasse, it is always a good idea to assess who else has contributed to the child's improvement. Listening to the client (and parents) means taking what they say seriously enough so that we do not presume to know what is and is not important to the client. If nothing else works, always ask the client.

CASE EXAMPLE: FROM THE BEGINNING TO THE END OF TREATMENT FOR A DEPRESSED CHILD

Written words open many doors to therapy techniques that are new to us, yet it is not the same as experiencing and observing an entire case unfold from the initial meeting to termination. We tried to describe many useful techniques of SFBT when applied to working with children. Written words leave so many gaps that need to be filled only with the reader's imagination; therefore, recognizing that we will never be able to present the missing pieces, we will now present a complete case from the beginning to the termination. Unless you observe six hours of interview conducted by Therese, it may still leave something missing. But given the limit of the medium of wiring and reading, this is the best we can do to describe how the useful techniques we listed so far may look, sound, and feel in live sessions. We recommend that if at all possible, you would benefit from observing videotaped sessions conducted by master therapists or, better yet, spend hours and hours behind a one-way glass. The tension, drama, the twists and turns of live sessions cannot be replicated here, but we want to describe how Therese worked with 9-year-old Jason and his parents in six sessions in six months.

Initial Meeting. Jason's mother, Mrs. Shuler, called because she was very worried that her son may be suffering from depression. The usual questionnaire (See Appendix) was sent to the mother and the first appointment was made in two week's time.

Nine-year-old Jason came with his mother. Her concern was that he seemed very depressed. Jason's father's side of the family had had two members who committed suicide, so she began reading a great deal about symptoms and treatment of depression. In addition, being a consultant to a program for foster children, she was very knowledgeable about childhood depression. When asked some specific concerns about Jason, the mother related that Jason stayed in his room a great deal, he seldom explained his concerns even when asked or when he looked very worried, had difficulty getting along with other children, and he had temper outbursts that seem to come from nowhere. Of course, this upset the family and Jason's mood permeated the household.

Even though she felt responsible for Jason's mood, Mrs. Shuler could not clearly explain in what ways she was responsible for his "depression," except to say that because the father's job-related travels took him out of town a great deal, she felt like a single parent raising the boy all alone. During the session I learned that Jason was very interested in reading, and was good at math, and at fixing things with his hands. He was particularly interested in learning about how things worked, and he had good observation skills. He was proud that he had already given his father some good suggestions about how to fix things.

His answers to the miracle question were that he would ask his friends to play with him, he would get up in the morning on his own, be better able to handle his temper outbursts, remember his dreams, and would still have lots of time to think about the world. His mother would realize that a miracle happened when Jason came out of his room more often and stood up for himself to those around him, such as his family and friends. She believed that when this happened, she would be calmer, more relaxed, and more direct and assertive with her husband, and have more time to read.

After a thinking break, I complimented Jason on his deep interest in the complexity of the world, and how he showed me how such a young boy could think about such complex issues of the world that only adults would think about. Although it was clear that Jason was a "deep thinker" (his words), I was glad to see that he realized the need to get up in time for school on his own, and take responsibility for controlling his bad temper. I complimented the mother on the way she made sure that Jason's life was better for him, yet she was able to see her own life could be better when Jason's problem was solved.

It became clear that there were verbal gaps between the mother and Jason, that is, the mother, who was very articulate and well-informed about psychological issues, needed a great deal of information from Jason, who was not able to articulate his own thoughts to his mother in an understandable manner. We often meet adults who confuse a child's intelligence with their ability to express themselves with words. Therefore, it was helpful to use techniques of visualization instead, so Jason could learn to communicate with his mother through more concrete steps. I explained to Jason that I heard him saying he wanted to make some changes and that he wanted to be more in charge of the changes he needed to make. I placed several pillows on Mrs. Shuler's lap and asked her to hand one pillow over to Jason while deciding which solution the pillow stood for. Both agreed that the pillow stood for Jason getting up in the morning on his own without his mother's help. During the second week the mother could hand over another pillow to Jason and again they needed to decide what kind of change the pillow stood for.

After a brief thinking break, I complimented the mother for her tireless effort to reach Jason and make sure that Jason grew up to be a well-rounded child, and for making sure that Jason got the kind of help he needed. I complimented Jason for his ability to think about big world problems while being able to think about things that he needed to learn like most 9-year-old boys. Mother and son were advised to look carefully at what differences the use of pillows made in Jason's life.

Session 2—1 month later. The mother stayed in the room the entire session. I asked Jason to build a "success tower" which involved stacking wooden blocks for each positive change he made since our last session. The mother helped Jason to remember many changes he had made and Jason was told to stack the wooden blocks for each change. After completing the list, I suggested Jason take an instant picture of the "success tower," and we discussed to whom he wanted to show his picture.

Through this exercise, I learned that Jason was getting up on his own in time and he called some of the kids in his class to organize a time to play together at his house. Some children turned down the invitation but Jason managed to play a game with some of them. The mother was very upset at learning that Jason had to endure rejection from some of the children. While Mrs. Shuler and I talked together about how she managed her own experiences of rejection and failure, I saw Jason listening very carefully, as if this was the first such intimate story he was hearing from his mother.

I complimented both on many small and big changes and told them to continue to pay attention to what other changes they would notice.

Session 3—1 month later. At the beginning of this session, Jason gave a very clear signal to his mother that he would like to spend the time with me alone. He suggested that his mother could go shopping while he talked with *me. The mother was very surprised and I asked if it would be all right if I spent some time with his mother and then she could leave the session. The mother agreed. This time I used the combination of scaling questions, wooden blocks, and a rope that measured his success. For every improvement the mother and Jason agreed that he succeeded in achieving, Jason placed a colored wooden block along a rope around the floor. Jason jumped the wooden blocks placed next to the rope, which indicated all the improvements he had made since he was first brought to see me. He had a big smile on his face. Recognizing that he liked to move around physically, I asked Jason to pretend that he was a horse or a frog, and to hop or jump around the blocks on the floor once more. In fact he did it twice.*

When I asked the mother to scale Jason's progress so far, Mrs. Shuler put it at 6, but it was clear that she was still worried about his not being happy and being too quiet. She thought that Jason should express his opinions more loudly and forcefully and stand up for himself. The atmosphere in the room changed dramatically and became much heavier when the mother brought up her concerns, and I realized that I had to do something a little bit differently. I asked them permission to show them a children's picture book. The story was about two monsters who have fights, they tell each other reasons for being angry with each other, and then they end up having fun together. After 25 minutes passed, I complimented Jason on making lots of improvement with friends and controlling his temper outbursts, and asked them to observe carefully what was helpful to Jason in order for him to stand up for himself like the two monsters in the story book. The mother left the session after agreeing to another session a month later.

Alone with Jason, I suggested that we play a scribble game because it seemed that Jason had gained some self-confidence and courage. The scribble game is a wonderful way to empower the child by showing signs of competence. One picture showed a snake. At the end of the session we took about 5 minutes to make up a story about the snake. Jason came up with a story of a snake and a mouse. He laughed a lot and had the snake eat the mouse. I had the impression that for the first time, Jason was feeling confident enough to show his powerful and strong side with some pleasure in dealing with conflicts.

Session 4—1 month later. The father came along with Jason. This was my first meeting with him and I decided to take advantage of this meeting and asked him what Jason was good at, and what kind of progress Jason was making. He reported how pleased he was that Jason was getting along better with his friends, but confessed that he was one of those fathers who was clumsy and awkward at dealing with boys as they got older. He thought he was fine when Jason was young, but he just didn't know how to accept and help Jason become more independent. He still liked having Jason on his lap and cuddling, but also recognized that Jason had to become more independent and needed courage to express his opinions and stand up for his ideas. Because he felt so clumsy at encouraging his son to become assertive, he said, he was pleased that we continued to work in this area. I asked Jason to build something with the wood blocks that stood for courage, like a symbol. Jason asked his father to leave the room and when left alone, he decided to build a "courage house" first and then he wanted to build a "hesitating house." He concentrated on this building project for about 15 minutes on his own. It seemed like he was coming out of a trance when he finished the project and said, "I want to show this to my dad when the meeting is over." I agreed and suggested that we play a little card game called "only courage." I decided to choose this game when I realized what Jason said, "at the end of the session." It occurred to me that by saying this he indicated that he was still in a trance, and he needed some more time.

At the end of the session, we asked his father to return to the room and Jason asked his father to guess which he thought was the "courage house" and which was the "hesitation house." After his father pointed at the right one, Jason suddenly knocked down the "hesitation house" with a great deal of power and obvious pleasure. At first, the father was surprised, but he joined his son in loud laughter.

When Jason was absorbed in building houses, I concentrated on what kind of compliments to offer this father and son. I recognized that Jason reached a milestone on his own because his parents and I were excluded from his concentration of building two houses. I complimented Jason on his finding a constructive way to use his power and finding something to laugh at with his father. I also complimented the father on his desire to help Jason become independent and his ability to laugh with his son, which I thought was a very good beginning.

Session 5—1 month later Jason returned with his mother. Many improvements were reported since our last session and Jason volunteered the information on his own without prompting. His voice was strong, his inflection and facial expressions were more spontaneous and natural. He had joined a soccer team and often played goalie. Although he missed catching the ball sometimes, it did not bother him because he said everybody had to learn first before they become good at something. He scaled his having friends at 8 out of 10. When he felt his bad temper coming, he would go outside and runs around the block twice. In his opinion, mom could put up much better with his aggressiveness, and it helped him that she was OK with it. The mother rated Jason's overall picture as 7 or 8, but she was not sure whether this would last, or if it was just a temporary improvement. I agreed with her that it was natural to be skeptical about such positive changes and then we further discussed what might be the sign of improvement that would tell her that Jason could maintain the changes. At this, Jason piped up and reassured his mother that his confidence was very high and that he would prove it to her.

It was obvious that the main goal of therapy had been accomplished, and it was a question of consolidating and integrating the positive changes Jason had accomplished. Apparently, before coming to the session, the mother and son had decided that he needed some time alone with me without his mother. After the mother left the room, I suggested that Jason do the color experiment of mixing and matching. This game gives the child a sense of accomplishment and empowerment through creativity, because whatever the child does, it cannot be wrong. Jason was given white, yellow, red, and blue paint. He was asked to mix these four colors in any way he wanted to create as many different colors as possible. He had to guess before he began how many colors he thought he could create out of these four, and he guessed 14. At the end of the session, he showed his mother 23 different colors with a big smile on his face!

Session 6—2 months later. Jason arrived with his mother. It did not take long to realize that both had achieved their goals. I again carefully asked them to list what had improved since our last session and what had helped to keep them going. The mother said that she had learned a lot and the most important lesson was that they both had to change. Mrs. Shuler was pleased that Jason's problem was gone now, and she thought differently about Jason's behavior from 8 months ago. "I don't think in terms of depression anymore, but it is more how Jason is and how he deals with the world. He still withdraws quite lot into his room and he still reflects more about the world than other children his age. But I began to think of this as a good quality rather than a defect, and that makes a big difference."

After taking a thinking break, I complimented both on the hard work they did, and I had Jason choose a stone out of about 50 polished semiprecious stones I keep in a jar. I pointed out how they had both turned what they thought was a problem, like a big stone, into a strength and a part of Jason that could stand on its own. Jason carefully chose the stone he liked best and told me that he would put the stone in a special place on his shelf in his room to remind himself that things can become different.

Postscript

WE BEGAN WITH THE PURPOSE OF DEMYSTIFYING THE MAGICALLY POWER-ful moments of working with children and thus making the "therapeutic process" more transparent. By doing so, we wanted to show the readers many different ways to nurture children's natural ways of learning, solving problems, and growing up to be competent and happy adults. Having devoted many years to the process of changing everyday, simple, spoken words into tools to transform people, we wanted to show that the same process could take place with children as well. While adults use grown-up words, children use a richer variety of mediums to learn, change themselves, and get along with others. They use their bodies, imaginations, creativity, and expressions to communicate what they cannot express through words.

In the process of writing this book together, we used e-mail, file sharing, telephone calls, and meetings in Switzerland and France, talking and talking about this book. But what is most important of all is that we both learned a great deal about the subject and about each other. We both have grown to be more creative, for example, to appreciate the art of transforming a small object like a balloon into a useful tool to communicate with a small child who is scared to walk into a therapist's office. Using a simple red balloon, we can transform the child's fear into a sense of control. That's sheer magic!

By constantly comparing our two individual styles to deal with children's problems, we both learned to appreciate the similarities and differences of our cultural heritage, language, values, and therapy methods. We have become wiser, and more thoughtful, and have come to appreciate what we have learned about ourselves and about each other. In the process, we have become good friends. For this, we are thankful.

Insoo Kim Berg and Therese Steiner

Appendix

SAMPLE QUESTIONNAIRE

NAME OF THE CHILD: _____

ADDRESS: _____

_____

PHONE: _____ PARENTS: _____

Please answer the following:

1. Please list what your child is able to do and the good qualities she
    or he shows:
    Example: tolerance, patience, persistence, abilities related to school,
    athletics, creativity, and others that come to mind.

2. Which of the skills listed above does your child show regularly?

3. Which of the following circumstances is easiest to change:

    Situations and circumstances your child can change:

    Situations and circumstances you can influence so as to change:

    Situations and circumstances that the teacher or school can change:

4.   When and how does your child ask for help in order to solve a problem?

5.   When, where, and with whom does your child feel at ease?

6.   How does your child express joy and happiness?

7.   What do you think bothers your child the most at the moment?

8.   Suppose you want to have a good conversation with your child. What seems to help the most?

9.   Please describe the situation in which your child's problem(s) shows less, even a little bit?

School/Work

1.   When and how does your child perform well in school?

2.   When and how does your child improve his or her performance in school?

3.   What kind of homework or chores does your child do independently?

4.   What seems to be most helpful to get your child to do what he/she needs to do?

Thank you for your cooperation.

References

Anderson, H., & Goolishan, H. (1992). The client is the expert: A not-knowing approach to therapy. In S. McNamee & K. J. Gergen (Eds.), *Therapy as social construction* (pp. 25–39). London: Sage.

Berg, I. K. (1994). *Family based services: A solution-focused approach*. New York: W. W. Norton.

Berg, I. K. & DeJong, P. (1996). Solution-building conversations: Co-constructing a sense of competence with clients. Families in society: *The Journal of Contemporary Human Services*. 77(6), 376–391.

Berg, I. K., & Dolan, Y. (2001). *Tales of solutions. A collection of hope inspiring stories*. New York: W. W. Norton.

Berg, I. K., & Kelly, S. (2000). *Building solutions in child protective services*. New York: W. W. Norton.

Berg, I. K. & Miller, S. (1992). *Working with the problem drinker*. New York: W. W. Norton.

Berg, I. K., & Reuss, N. (1997). *Solutions step-by-step: Substance abuse treatment manual*. New York: W. W. Norton

Cantwell, P., & Holmes, S., (1994). Social construction: A paradigm shift for systemic therapy and training. *The Australian and New Zealand Journal of Family Therapy*, 15, 17–26.

Crowley, R. J., & Mills, J. C. (1989). *Cartoon magic*. New York: Brunner/Mazel.

Davis, T. E. & Osborn, C. J. (2000). *The solution-focused school counselor*. Philadelphia: Accelerated Development

DeJong, P., & Berg, I. K. (2001a). Co-constructing cooperation with mandated clients. *Social Work*, 46(4), 361–374.

DeJong, P., & Berg, I. K. (2001b). *Interviewing for solutions* (2d ed). Pacific Grove: Brooks/Cole.

De Shazer, S. (1984). Death of Resistance, *Family Process*, 23, 11–21.

De Shazer, S. (1985). *Keys to solutions in brief therapy*. New York: W. W. Norton.

De Shazer, S. (1988). *Clues: Investigation of solutions in brief therapy*. New York: W. W. Norton

De Shazer, S. (1991). *Putting difference to work*. New York: W. W. Norton.

De Shazer, S. (1994). *Words were originally magic*. New York: W. W. Norton.

Erickson, M. & Rossi, E. (1979). *Hypnotherapy: An exploratory casebook*. New York: Irvington.

Gingerich, W. & Eisengart, S. (2000). Solution-focused brief therapy: A review of the outcome research, *Family Process*, 39(4), 477–498.

Haley, J. (1973). *Uncommon therapy: The psychiatric techniques of Milton H. Erickson, M. D.* New York: W. W. Norton.

Hoyt, M. & Berg, I. K. (1998). Solution-focused couple therapy: Helping clients to construct self-fulfilling realities in Dattlilio, F. M. (ed). *Case Studies in Couple and Family Therapy.* New York: Guilford Press.

Lee, M. Y., Sebold, J. & Uken, A. (in press). *Accountability for solutions: Treatment of domestic violence offenders.* Oxford University Press: New York.

Miller, G. & de Shazer, S. (2000). Emotions in solution-focused therapy: A re-examination. *Family Process,* 39(1), 5–23.

Watzlawick, P., Weakland, J. & Fisch, R. (1974). *Change: Principles of problem formation and problem resolution.* New York: W. W. Norton.

Winnicott, D. W. (1970). *Playing and reality.* London: Tavistock.

Winnicott, D. W. (1971). *Therapeutic consultation in child psychiatry.* New York: Basic Books.

Index

Letter | Share | Note

Cay Dia
Ron Vo - Mina + Alan
Ada Ag¹ - inattention

Tue - This week
MickMick Tan
Nao Lee Na

[Bay Cud